The International Debt Crisis in Historical Perspective

The International Debt Crisis in Historical Perspective

edited by Barry Eichengreen
and Peter H. Lindert

The MIT Press
Cambridge, Massachusetts
London, England

Second printing, 1991

This book was set in Palatino by Asco Trade Typesetting Ltd., Hong Kong and printed and bound in the United States of America.

Library of Congress Cataloging-in-Publication Data

The International debt crisis in historical perspective / edited by
  Barry Eichengreen and Peter H. Lindert.
    p.   cm.
  Includes index.
  ISBN 0-262-05041-2
  1. Debts, Public—History—20th century. 2. Debts, External—History—20th century.
  3. International economic relations—History—20th century. 4. Debts, External—
  Latin America—History—20th century. I. Eichengreen, Barry J. II. Lindert, Peter H.
  HJ8011.I63   1989
  336.3'435'09—dc20   89-8095
                                                                              CIP

Contents

List of Contributors

Vinod K. Aggarwal	University of California at Berkeley and Graduate Institute of International Studies Geneva
Eliana A. Cardoso	Tufts University
Rudiger Dornbusch	Massachusetts Institute of Technology
Barry Eichengreen	University of California at Berkeley
Albert Fishlow	University of California at Berkeley
Erika Jorgensen	Harvard University
Peter H. Lindert	University of California at Davis
Charles Lipson	University of Chicago
Richard Portes	Birkbeck College University of London and Centre for Economic Policy Research
Jeffrey Sachs	Harvard University

Preface

In assembling this volume, we have incurred debts that will difficult to repay. We thank Terry Vaughn of The MIT Press for his encouragement and support. For their financial support of the conference at which preliminary versions of these chapters were discussed, we thank the Institute of International Studies of the University of California at Berkeley and its director, Carl Rosberg; Berkeley's MacArthur Program in International Security (and especially Benjamin Ward); the Institute of Governmental Affairs of the University of California at Davis and its director, Alan L. Olmstead; and the Center for Economic and Monetary Affairs of Menlo Park, California (and especially Lu Cordova). The Federal Reserve Bank of San Francisco graciously provided a superb venue for the conference. The chapters were greatly improved by the penetrating comments of three anonymous reviewers and the conference discussants: Benjamin J. Cohen, Jeffrey Frankel, Jeffry Frieden, Thomas Huertas, Harold James, Miles Kahler, Ronald I. McKinnon, Kenneth Oye, Richard Portes, and Benjamin Ward. None of this would have been possible without the sterling assistance of Shelagh Eldon and Peggy Phillips of the Institute of International Studies.

The International Debt Crisis in Historical Perspective

1 Overview

Barry Eichengreen and
Peter H. Lindert

In retrospect, the three decades following World War II seem to have been a golden era of tranquility in international capital markets, a fulfillment of the benediction "May you live in dull times." Neither the bond markets nor the banks were leading agents in the process of lending to developing countries. Instead, governments gave and loaned to other governments, in the form of foreign aid or export credits and increasingly through the agency of multilateral institutions like the World Bank and International Monetary Fund. Sovereign defaults and liquidity crises were relatively rare.

In the wake of the 1973–74 oil crisis, the process took a revolutionary turn. Money center banks raced to lend to developing countries, bringing smaller regional banks as members of their syndicates in train. The volume of bank lending to foreign governments surged as OPEC surpluses and accommodating monetary policies made available an ample supply of credit. The denouement, previewed by the Polish debt crisis in 1981, came with the Mexican crisis in the summer of 1982. Voluntary lending stopped abruptly. One country after another fell into arrears, negotiated new debt settlements, or both. In the desperate effort to service its debts, Latin America compressed income and investment, suffering its worst recession of the twentieth century. The crisis in the African debtor nations has been, if anything, even more severe. Rather than flowing downstream from the developed to the developing countries, since 1982 capital has flowed upstream from the debtors to the creditors. Increasingly bankers and government officials, both foreign and domestic, have been forced to acknowledge that the prospects are dim that the debt incurred in the 1970s will ever be repaid in full.

This seemingly perverse outcome has directed suspicions at all participants in the lending process. Banks are accused of loan pushing and disaster myopia. Inexperienced in the business of sovereign lending, they are said to have underestimated or ignored entirely the possibility that foreign governments might default. Alternatively, a principal-agent problem, in which junior loan officers sought to maximize the value of loan commitments without regard to shareholders' interest in performance and profitability, is said to have led to the extension of dubious loans. The borrowers, for their part, are blamed for having squandered foreign funds on uneconomic projects and for adopting macroeconomic policies, such as overvalued exchange rates, that undermined their capacity to service external debts. Nor do the U.S. government and multilateral agencies emerge unscathed: critics charge that the United States, in league with the IMF, has pressured the borrowers to maintain debt service at all cost. While this policy may be consistent with the continued stability of the U.S. banking system, it is not consistent with income growth in developing countries or with a prosperous world economy. The debt crisis has proved so severe and so protracted that some observers have been led to wonder whether the world economy would not have been better off under the kind of institutional arrangements that prevailed before the 1960s.

1.1   Parallels and Contrasts

Answering their question requires serious consideration of earlier historical experience. History reveals both striking parallels and notable contrasts with the experience of the 1970s and 1980s.

The similarities include a sequence of decade-long surges in foreign lending, followed by revulsion and ultimately default. The surge in foreign lending in 1974–82 was not new. Similar lending waves had occurred at intervals throughout the nineteenth and twentieth centuries, with the 1820s, 1880s, 1900–14, and the 1920s serving as prominent examples. In each of these cases important loans quickly lapsed into default, occasioning the same complaints of reckless lending and misuse of borrowed funds heard in the 1980s. The striking range of parallels between present and past crises is a recurring theme in the chapters that follow, particularly Vinod Aggarwal's reading of Mexican debt history in chapter 6.

The contrasts include the lending mechanism and the ways in which defaults were settled. In earlier periods international loans were sold to a wide range of bondholders, rather than kept by the original lending banks as in the 1970s and 1980s. The change in lending mechanism brought a major change in the incidence of default risk. Even though international sovereign debt is a steadily declining share of creditor-country wealth, it has become so concentrated in the hands of the top money-center banks that their financial survival is a focal concern of creditor-country policy. Accordingly, creditor countries felt less pressure to intervene in the debt-settlement process in the bond era than they do today. Debtors and private creditors tended to confront each other directly, eventually working out compromises that called for partial repayment.

Both the similarities and the differences have prompted scholars to reassess the history of international debt and default. To cite but a few recent studies, Albert Fishlow (1985) and Barbara Stallings (1987) have studied the successive waves of lending to the developing world in the nineteenth and twentieth centuries. Arminio Fraga (1986), William McNeil (1986), Steven Schuker (1988), and Steven Webb (1988) have explored the analogy between German reparations in the 1920s and Latin American debt in the 1980s. Barry Eichengreen and Richard Portes (1986) and Peter Lindert and Peter Morton (1988) have analyzed the onset and aftermath of default. Charles Lipson (1985) and Jeffry Frieden (1987) have studied government responses to default and repudiation.

As the debt crisis drags on, the attention of policymakers and scholars alike has turned from its onset to its resolution. It was the observation that leading scholars from a number of disciplines—including economics, political science, and economic history—were studying the resolution of debt crises from an historical vantage point that led to this volume. Chapters 2 through 8 are largely devoted to offering historical perspectives on the resolution phase of international debt crises. They offer perspectives, however, on the behavior of the participants throughout the debt cycle. What they share is the conviction that history, both political and economic, has a comparative advantage in current debates about the causes and cures of debt crisis. Three of the chapters (2, 3, and 8) explore the rate-of-return legacy of past lending and crises in order to prompt questions about what financial markets and policymakers might learn from the past. Albert Fishlow's paper (chapter 4) opens the door to comparative-historical research on the social locus and political strength of pro-repayment forces in the debt-policy debate within debtor countries. Cardoso and Dornbusch (chapter 5) and Aggarwal (chapter 6) use history as a mirror, noting the remarkable recurrences and the parallels of past and present en route to analytical conclusions. The strength of the link of debt-crisis outcomes to political and military developments is tested by both Aggarwal and Lipson (chapters 6 and 7). Two chapters (2 and 8) use history not as a mirror, but as a contrast to the present, to spotlight the perils of official intervention in the 1980s.

1.2   What Do Private Creditors Remember?

A first question prompted by debt-crisis experience is what private creditors learn from the past. Not only is default recurrent, but the countries that
default tend to be the same ones, generation after generation. Economists'
models of international lending in the presence of potential repudiation
typically assume that countries that default pay a penalty in the form of
subsequent inability to borrow (otherwise there would be no reason for
debtors ever to pay, the theorists reason). Yet there is remarkably little
evidence that defaulting countries acquire a reputation for unwillingness
to pay, which in turn hinders their ability to borrow. The most striking
example is the sequel to the widespread defaults of the 1930s. A large
minority of developing-country debtors did repay their debts on schedule
in the 1930s. Caribbean nations in the shadow of Uncle Sam did so. So
did Argentina. Yet as Jorgensen and Sachs show for Argentina in chapter 3,
they did not get any preference in new lending from the 1930s through
1960s. Even in the 1970s, four decades later, there is little indication that
countries that had defaulted earlier paid a higher price for foreign funds, or
were meted a lower credit ration thereafter (chapter 8), though recent
results by Ozler (1988) argue that there may have been some long-delayed
effect of earlier default on creditworthiness.

Why this apparent failure on the part of the markets to learn from the
past? Chapters 2 through 8 suggest four explanations. A first is that
bankers have short memories. In the early 1970s it was not uncommon for
bankers to assert that sovereign default was inconceivable. The assertion is
easier to understand once one recalls that bankers in the 1970s were a
different generation from those who lent overseas in the 1930s. Second,
even if creditors had studied the past, it would not have taught them that
loans to sovereign debtors go sour on the average. On the contrary,
sufficient premia were earned on the good loans to cover the spectacular
losses on a few major defaults. A third explanation is that debtor governments have short life spans, complicating the task of inferring individual
"country risks" from history. The governments in power in the 1970s or
1980s often had entirely different complexions from those that had defaulted in the 1930s. (Indeed, foreign debts might themselves play a role in
the transformation, as in Argentina where the efforts of an orthodox
government to maintain debt service arguably contributed to a populist
reaction.) A fourth explanation, advanced by Albert Fishlow in chapter 4, is
that it is not so much past debt-service reputation as current macroeconomic policies that determine creditworthiness. Creditors are willing to

lend even to countries with a lurid history of default if their governments seem to have adopted fiscal and monetary policies consistent with sustained income and export growth. Perhaps as a result creditors hear no strong signal from the distant past, even though countries that have defaulted in the past are significantly more likely than others to become problem debtors again.

Although default thus brought no clear taint on later creditworthiness for the individual debtor country, it did bring a heavy collective cost to debtor countries as a group. The reason is that private creditors seem to have been as undiscriminating in the shutoff of credit after a crisis broke as they were in the previous lending boom. As Eichengreen (1988) has shown, the costs of defaults were largely external to the defaulting countries. Especially in the great crisis of the 1930s, the damage to creditworthiness, capital formation, and growth spread to all borrowing countries, engulfing the faithful repayers along with the defaulters. In a specific illustration of the general point, Eliana Cardoso and Rudiger Dornbusch show in chapter 5 that from the 1930s to the 1960s Brazil, the defaulter, had no more trouble borrowing than the faithful repayer Argentina. Erika Jorgensen and Jeffrey Sachs, as noted, also find Argentina unrewarded for its faithful repayments, this time in contrast to Bolivia, Chile, Colombia, and Peru. Albert Fishlow in chapter 4 makes a similar point about Argentina and Brazil in the late nineteenth century. Again, in the 1980s, the slowdown in capital formation and growth in the wake of debt crisis seems to have spread to all developing countries, at least in Latin America and Africa, not just to the conspicuous problem debtors.

1.3   When Do Debtors Repay?

If many debtor countries default during debt crises yet suffer little more from the crisis than those not defaulting, there is reason to wonder why any of them acquiesce in the transfer of resources back to their creditors. On this issue, as on others, the longer history has much to add to the brief lessons of the 1980s.

When lending has been gradual and there is no global macroeconomic crisis, debtor countries have shown little inclination to initiate default out of the blue. In such times the case for good repayment behavior has seemed strong enough, especially as long as fresh lending continues to make burdensome transfers unnecessary. Such normalcy has been of sufficient duration to give creditors a competitive return overall and to prevent default in most years for most countries. The exceptional countries that defaulted without a global crisis were treated harshly before World War I, as in the cases of Egypt and several Caribbean nations. By contrast, the problem debtors in the calm generation after World War II were treated far more gently.

A global macroeconomic crisis destroys the incentive to suffer significant transfers back to one's foreign creditors. In such a setting it is not hard to sense that credit will dry up in any case. So said the experience of the 1930s, both in the generality of debt repudiation and in the poor results for the minority of debtor nations who tried faithful repayment. To many observers, the debtors of the 1980s have seemed to behave differently, allowing net resource transfers to their creditors while continuing to negotiate in the hope of a revival of fresh private lending. Yet, as Lindert argues in chapter 8, the 1980s may not have differed from the 1930s in this respect after all. Behind official data seeming to show net transfers to creditors lie biases that, when corrected, seem to show that very few debtor nations—perhaps only three (Ecuador, Mexico, and Venezuela) out of 97 nations—have made major net repayments during the crisis, as in the global crisis of the 1930s. To explain why those few actually tightened their belts requires a careful look at their political conditions, both domestic and international.

1.4   Political Perspectives on Debt Conflict

As several chapters make clear, the decision of whether to suspend interest payments is rarely based on purely economic considerations. Transfers to foreign creditors have to be politically as well as economically viable. A number of papers, including Albert Fishlow's examination of Argentine and Brazilian experience in the 1890s (chapter 4) and Vinod Aggarwal's interpretation of the history of Mexico's external debt (chapter 6), cast doubt on the "unitary actor assumption" upon which most economic models of debt and default are based. Different domestic interest groups may attach very different priority to the mainenance of debt service. Domestic exporters and bankers prefer to avoid arrears and to settle defaults as soon as possible so as to avoid disrupting their trade credit lines and foreign business. Domestic industrialists and rentiers liable for the taxes needed to fund service payments and with a stake in domestic investment are likely to adopt a less sympathetic attitude toward foreign creditors. Understanding either the domestic politics of debt or the course of international negotiations requires disaggregating domestic interest groups.

What international political forces held back default? One, suggested by Eichengreen and Portes in chapter 2, is the possibility of retaliatory cutbacks in the provision of trade credits and access to export markets, although indirectly and to an extent that differed under alternative institutional arrangements. Another, implicit in a number of the chapters, is the linkage of international debts to creditor-country politics and foreign policy. Politics in the creditor countries were no more isolated from negotiations over international debts than were politics in the debtor countries. As Charles Lipson shows in chapter 7, international security and international financial relations have been closely connected with one another. In the nineteenth century the French and German governments encouraged investment in Russia, Eastern Europe, and the Middle East in an effort to cement strategic alliances. Although it was relatively rare, even in the nineteenth century, for a creditor-country government to intervene abroad solely to help citizens who had invested in overseas assets, default or nationalization often provided a convenient excuse for intervention already desired on security grounds.

Many of the chapters, including those by Lipson and by Eichengreen and Portes, argue that contrary to the contrast conventionally drawn between the 1980s and earlier periods, governments have always been intimately involved in the process of debt readjustment. Official involvement has been most apparent in cases in which governments themselves were creditors or when they at least had been responsible for encouraging private purchases of foreign bonds. But creditor-country involvement was by no means limited to such cases. In the nineteenth century governments often exerted subtle pressure for settlement. In the 1930s and 1940s it was even possible for governments to become directly involved in negotiations.

The accurate contrast in government's role between earlier episodes and the 1980s, as Lindert and Eichengreen and Portes conclude, lies not in the existence of government involvement but in its scope and direction. In the 1980s creditor-country governments, motivated by the desire to protect their banking systems, have exerted their greatest pressure on the debtor countries, urging full repayment and macroeconomic adjustment. The international agencies have adopted a similar stance. In earlier periods creditor-country pressure operated in more ambiguous directions. Sometimes governments viewed the obstinace of private creditors as an obstacle to the cultivation of harmonious international relations. Particularly with the approach of World War II, much of their pressure for concessions was applied to the private creditors. And whereas in the 1980s creditor government pressure has been applied disproportionately to the large debtor countries whose potential defaults pose a serious threat to the international banking system, in earlier periods pressure was applied more evenly, or even disproportionately to small countries which were easier to sway.

1.5 The Pattern of Settlement

Notwithstanding instances of government involvement, the settlement of bond defaults was predominantly a matter for negotiation between the debtors and bondholders' representatives. Global schemes like the Baker Plan and its more ambitious private counterparts were advanced also in the 1930s, but just as in the 1980s they bore little fruit (Eichengreen 1989). Rather, settlement was achieved on a case-by-case basis through bilateral negotiation. Some of the present authors have grappled with the daunting task of estimating the results of these settlements. In chapter 5 Erika Jorgensen and Jeffrey Sachs estimate the nominal cost of interwar borrowing for five Latin American debtors. They show that the cost of foreign funds differed significantly ex post between countries that lapsed into default and those that did not. Whereas Argentina's repayments exceeded the value of her borrowings by 25 percent in present value terms, Bolivia, Chile, and Peru repaid less than 60 percent of what they borrowed (again in present value terms), while Colombia repaid 85 percent. Jorgensen and Sachs infer that the costs of bad loans in the 1930s were borne by debtor and creditor alike. Eichengreen and Portes report estimates of the internal rate of nominal return on a larger sample of interwar loans floated in the 1920s in London and New York. Although they find that foreign lending paid better overall than did lending to the five Latin American countries studied by Jorgensen and Sachs in chapter 5, their results confirm that settlements of interwar defaults provided the creditors considerably less than full compensation for their losses. Peter Lindert's chapter (extending Lindert and Morton 1988) presents real rates of return on lending to the top debtor countries from 1850 through 1986. His results suggest that if anything interwar creditors received even more favorable treatment than their nineteenth-century predecessors. Luck mattered: the average real return on interwar loans was raised by high returns on loans to faithful repayers Argentina, Australia, Canada, and Japan, whereas a large share of the pre-1914 loans had gone to the three great revolutionary defaulters of the 1910s (Mexico, Russia, and Turkey).

These outcomes were achieved through the utilization of a number of mechanisms also contemplated in the 1980s. Debtor countries sometimes discriminated among different classes of creditors in an effort to make the limited resources available for debt service do as much work as possible. There is an analogy, as Eichengreen and Portes note, with proposals for debt subordination and exit bonds currently under consideration. Countries repeatedly engaged in the practice of buying back defaulted bonds on the market as a way of liquidating a debt overhang, as the chapters by Jorgensen and Sachs and by Eichengreen and Portes explain. Both sets of authors suggest that such practices may have contributed positively to the process of debt readjustment, Jorgensen and Sachs in stronger terms than Eichengreen and Portes.

1.6   Memory as a Predictor

Will the cycle of lending and default again repeat itself despite postwar attempts to introduce policy innovations? Will policy respond more successfully in later cycles? It is unwise, of course, to hazard a simple answer. We would only suggest, as much for constructive provocation as out of conviction, reasons to believe that the cycle will repeat itself.

In extrapolating from history, one must first take care to treat developing-country debt separately from the new international debt that dominates in the 1980s. The largest net debtor by far, the United States, is also a leading gross creditor and will not consider defaulting outright. It also differs from developing-country debtors in that it has borrowed almost exclusively in its own currency. Partial default depends on unexpected inflation and dollar depreciation. The new international lending may be as unstable as the old, but for very different reasons.

One prediction from the history of developing-country debt is that the current round of negotiations could drag on for a long time. As Eichengreen and Portes note in chapter 2, neither the 1930s or the 1980s offers a precedent for speedy resolution of global debt crisis. The only cases of speedy resolution are instances in which individual debtors won quick creditor acquiescence in a compromise, against a backdrop of a buoyant international economy.

It seems equally clear that soon after debt/GNP and debt/export ratios have finally been reduced, probably by significant write-downs, there will be a new round of enthusiastic lending to developing countries. As we have noted, private creditors do not see any clear signal in the past history of repayments crises, despite the emergence of a problem-debtor tradition in many countries. Starting from low initial debt ratios, the creditors will return, probably in a rush.

Each past lending wave has always combined with an economic or political shock to form a debt crisis, and nothing in the longer historical trend suggests any future immunity. To the contrary, macropolicy in many developing countries continues to worsen, to judge from the still-widening gap in inflation rates between developing and developed countries. This despite the heavy professed emphasis on policy reform in the 1980s. It is not hard to imagine which countries are most likely to repeat the crisis cycle. Several generations of history nominate Bolivia, Brazil, Chile, Peru, Romania, Turkey, Uruguay, and Yugoslavia. Their record since independence also nominates most African countries south of the Sahara. Scholars have yet to explain why there should be such consistency in countries' external credit histories, but consistency there has been.

Once the next crisis has hit, its festering will again bring considerable damage to the debtor economies, even if most of them are unwilling to pay out large transfers of resources to their creditors. Both in the 1930s and in the 1980s, just the uncertainty about the debt-service overhang was enough to depress capital formation and growth in debtor economies. Public agencies feared new budget cuts and private firms feared new taxes in the event of a future top-level decision to honor external debts. Investment was depressed by the fear as much as the actuality of outward transfers.

There will be another delayed compromise settlement involving a partial debt write-down. That is, creditors will share in the burden of the crisis, even if the whole chain of creditors makes competitive aggregate rates of return over the lending cycle. It has never been otherwise, and for a fundamental institutional reason: sovereignty itself. Unless debtors' sovereignty is violated by creditor hegemony and coercive enforcement of creditors' legal rights in foreign countries, collateral on international loans will always fall short. The present generation of economists and policymakers is to be congratulated for the care and imagination with which it has designed debt-crisis solutions that would be workable if they could be politically imposed and enforced. But the gains from official intervention appear to have been questionable in the 1930s and 1940s and negative in the 1980s. Neither official policies nor imaginative plans for debt settlement can eliminate the special risks of international lending.

References

Eichengreen, Barry. 1989. Resolving Debt Crises: An Historical Perspective. In Sebastian Edwards and Felippe Larrain (eds.), *The Latin American Debt Crisis*. Oxford: Blackwell.

Eichengreen, Barry, and Richard Portes. 1986. Debt and Default in the 1930s: Causes and Consequences. *European Economic Review* 30, 599–640.

Fishlow, Albert. 1985. Lessons from the Past: Capital Markets during the Nineteenth Century and the Interwar Period. *International Organization* 39, 3 (Summer): 383–439.

Fraga, Arminio. 1986. *German Reparations and Brazilian Debt: A Comparative Study*. Princeton: Princeton University, International Finance Section. Essays in International Finance, no. 163.

Frieden, Jeffry. 1987. *Banking on the World*. New York: Harper and Row.

Lindert, Peter H. and Peter J. Morton. 1988. How Sovereign Debt Has Worked. In Jeffrey D. Sachs (ed.) *Developing Country Debt and Economic Performance: The International Financial System*. Chicago: University of Chicago Press for the National Bureau of Economic Research.

Lipson, Charles. 1985. Bankers' Dilemmas: Private Cooperation in Rescheduling Sovereign Debts. In Kenneth Oye (ed.), *Cooperation under Anarchy*. Princeton: Princeton University Press.

McNeil, William C. 1986. *American Money and the Weimar Republic: Economics and Politics on the Eve of the Great Depression*. New York: Columbia University Press.

Ozler, Sule. 1988. Have Commercial Banks Ignored History? UCLA, Department of Economics, Working Paper no. 48 (August).

Stallings, Barbara. 1987. *Banker to the Third World: U.S. Portfolio Investment in Latin America, 1900–1986*. Berkeley: University of California Press.

Webb, Steven B. 1988. Comparing Latin American Debt Today with German Reparations after World War I. U.S. Department of State, Bureau of Economic and Business Affairs, PAS Working Paper no. 5. February.

2

After the Deluge: Default, Negotiation, and Readjustment during the Interwar Years

Barry Eichengreen and Richard Portes

2.1 Introduction

The ongoing debt crisis of developing countries bears a striking resemblance to previous episodes in which international capital markets were disrupted by outbreaks of sovereign default. The current crisis was preceded by rosy forecasts of the prospects for developing-country loans, followed by a pessimistic revision of expectations and an abrupt collapse of lending. In all these respects it recalls the debt crisis of the 1930s and its nineteenth-century predecessors. The onset of debt-servicing difficulties in the 1980s coincided with a worldwide recession, severe real interest rate shocks, a dramatic decline in primary commodity prices, and resurgent protectionism in the creditor countries, once again paralleling the situation in the 1930s. The alternative proposals for dealing with the crisis— ambitious global schemes for restructuring debtor-creditor relationships, either through some form of debt relief or through the establishment of an international entity to buy up outstanding debt, versus the "muddling through" approach of case-by-case negotiation—both have antecedents in proposals considered by interwar policymakers.[1]

Although the parallels between the current debt crisis and its predecessors are striking indeed, according to the received wisdom the crisis of the 1980s differs from those of the 1870s, 1890s, and 1930s in one fundamental respect: In prior instances, debt-servicing difficulties generally culminated in abrupt, unilateral, and complete suspension of interest and amortization payments. The 1930s, when sovereign default was widespread, provide the most dramatic illustration of this general point. In the 1980s, in contrast, unilateral suspensions have been at most temporary and isolated, extremely rare exceptions to the rule. Through repeated reschedulings, involuntary lending by the banks, and injections of supplemental funds by international organizations, the debtors so far have succeeded in warding off default.

The explanation for this unprecedented avoidance of default, according to the conventional wisdom, is the equally unprecedented involvement of creditor-country governments.[2] In earlier epochs governments maintained a decidedly ambivalent attitude toward intervention on behalf of investors. Admittedly, French and German government officials were less committed to a stance of neutrality than their British counterparts. Even British officials were not above exerting influence on behalf of bondholders, and the entanglements to which the interplay of economic and strategic interest could lead were epitomized by the establishment of a British protectorate in Egypt.[3] Washington, D.C., repeatedly dispatched the Marines when politics or policies in the Caribbean or Central America were seen as threatening American investments. But in most of these instances economics was little more than an excuse for intervention desired on other, usually military or strategic, grounds. Most observers concur that there was little systematic use of government influence on behalf of investors in the nineteenth century, and still less in the 1930s.[4]

This contrasts, the argument continues, with developments in the 1980s in which the governments of the leading creditor countries have been deeply involved. With the U.S. banking system more vulnerable to destabilization by default on foreign loans than at any time in the past, the United States has intervened aggressively to ensure the maintenance of debt service.[5] Washington has made clear the importance it attaches to continued debt service in bilateral negotiations, in Paris Club reschedulings, and in the form of proposals such as the Baker Plan. Its influence has been strengthened, the critics allege, by the support extended by the International Monetary Fund. In contrast to the passive role of the Bank for International Settlements in the 1930s, the Fund has been intimately if not always directly involved in debt negotiations. The banks typically require that countries reach an agreement with the Fund as a precondition for rescheduling. For its part, the Fund, before extending assistance, normally requires that countries come to terms with their commercial creditors to prevent the proceeds of the IMF loan from simply going to debt service. With a Fund loan hanging in the balance, the creditors have added leverage in their efforts to extract favorable rescheduling terms.

In this chapter we critically assess both strands of this conventional wisdom, that which draws a strong contrast between the 1930s and the 1980s in the extent of default and ease of settlement and that which attributes the difference to greater government involvement in the 1980s. In the end we do not reject outright either of these strands, though we argue that both must be strongly qualified. Contrary to the popular characterization of default in the 1930s as a sharp, dichotomous variable, we show that interruptions to debt service often were partial and intermittent. Settlement was far from straightforward, and the terms on which it was achieved were far from predictable. While it sometimes was possible to suspend debt service abruptly and to redirect resources toward uses conducive to domestic growth, it was not possible to do so with finality or certainty. Neither were creditor-country governments as disengaged from the settlement process as is sometimes suggested. Often they were intimately involved in the process of debt negotiation. The contrast between the extent of government involvement in the 1930s and the 1980s tends to be overdrawn.

We establish these points by analyzing the negotiations through which interwar defaults were settled. A complete account of the readjustment of interwar defaults must view the issue from both qualitative and quantitative perspectives. It must consider the political and institutional context in which negotiations took place and at the same time provide a quantitative assessment of the outcome. These are the dual goals of this chapter. The first half of the chapter analyzes political and institutional aspects of the process of debt renegotiation, emphasizing features with implications for the course of negotiations and the terms of settlement. We explore the extent of overlap between creditors extending long-term loans and those providing export credits, and suggest that conflicts of interest between the two categories of lenders gave rise to significant divisions within the creditor community. We consider alternative approaches to the problem of readjustment, ranging, on the one hand, from the organization of bilateral negotiations between borrowers and bondholders' representative committees to, on the other hand, unilateral initiatives such as repurchases of existing liabilities by debtors at market prices. We devote special attention to the role played by creditor-country governments and to the effectiveness of the instruments at their command. Finally, we appraise the influence of global commodity- and credit-market conditions on the process and terms of settlement.

Section 2.2 provides quantitative estimates of the outcome of these negotiations. We calculate realized internal rates of return on samples of over 200 dollar bonds and 125 sterling issues floated in New York and London in the 1920s. By contrasting realized rates of return on loans to national governments, municipalities, and corporations, we can compare the extent to which principal and interest were written down or recovered on various categories of loans. By contrasting realized rates of return on loans extended to different countries by different creditors, we can assess the effectiveness of the strategies adopted by the various parties to settlement negotiations.

The conclusion draws together evidence from the two sections with implications for current debt negotiations.

2.2   The Structure of Sovereign Debt Negotiations[6]

Defaults on foreign bonds generally were settled through negotiations between the foreign borrowers and committees representing the bondholders. One or more bondholders committees typically announced their intention to represent the interests of the creditors as soon as debt servicing difficulties arose. If and when they wished to initiate negotiations, foreign officials contacted a committee. The committee then dispatched a representative to the foreign country to negotiate with local officials. Upon the satisfactory conclusion of negotiations, the committee would announce its recommendation through the press, advising bondholders to indicate their acceptance of the offer by cashing coupons or submitting bonds for exchange. Bondholders dissatisfied by the terms could choose to hold out for better ones, as some continue to do to this day.[7]

By the 1930s the Corporation of Foreign Bondholders (CFBH) had emerged as the universally acknowledged representative of British investors. Founded in 1868, the CFBH originally was a creation of the loan houses and brokers. The Council, the Corporation's governing body, was at first dominated by representatives of banking firms and brokerage houses and included only some token bondholders. In 1898 the CFBH was reorganized by an act of Parliament: to prevent it being viewed as a creature of the bankers, the representatives of the issue houses were removed from its Council, which was expanded to embrace representatives of the British Bankers' Association and of the London Chamber of Commerce, along with some miscellaneous members at least six of whom were to be substantial bondholders. By the 1930s these miscellaneous members had come to include representatives of the Association of Investment Trusts, the British Insurance Association, the Bank of England, and the Stock Exchange.[8]

Much of the influence of the Council derived from its close working relations with the Stock Exchange. One of the rules of the Exchange, adopted in 1825, was to refuse quotation to new loans to governments who were in default on existing obligations and who had refused to negotiate in good faith with their creditors, and in extreme instances to strike from the list all loans of the offending government.[9] For information on the status of loans and readjustment negotiations, the Exchange relied upon the CFBH. Although some trading in London might take place outside the Stock Exchange and although new loans conceivably could be floated in other markets, lack of access to the London market was a serious sanction.

In the United States, where foreign flotations first reached significant levels during World War I, there existed no comparable organization until 1933. In America the practice in the event of default was to establish ad hoc committees to negotiate with each foreign government. Reliance on temporary committees had obvious disadvantages, including high administrative expenses, inability to speak credibly for the bondholders, and lack of contact with the U.S. government. Moreover there was no way to regularize ties with the Stock Exchange. In response to these problems and because dealings with bondholders were absorbing so much staff time, in 1932–33 the State Department sponsored the formation of a working party to draw up plans for a permanent organization. That new organization, the Foreign Bondholders Protective Council (FBPC), was founded in 1933 with finance from charitable foundations and the Stock Exchange to tide it over until commissions earned through the negotiation of debt readjustments rendered it self-sustaining.

Similar associations of bondholders existed in France and other creditor countries. The leading members of these associations appreciated the advantages of creditor solidarity, which they hoped to achieve through international cooperation. As the CFBH put it in 1937, there was "no question that in theory cooperation between all the Bondholders' organizations is most desirable and that such cooperation is more than ever necessary in view of the present attitude of the debtors."[10] Unfortunately from the creditors' standpoint, the practice was more problematic than the theory. In Europe, where the bondholders' representative committees had years of experience in dealing with both foreign governments and one another, cooperation was relatively advanced. Often, responsibility for the actual negotiations was delegated to the committee with the largest stake, which kept the other associations informed. Relations between the European and American committees were less harmonious. Sterling and dollar bond covenants could differ significantly in their interest rates and in the security offered by the borrower. As a result the British and American committees often disagreed on the appropriate treatment of different categories of bonds. The CFBH was critical of its U.S. counterpart for the latter's tendency to settle unilaterally, leaving the British no choice but to accept American terms. It complained that communication by telephone was expensive and unsatisfactory and that the president of the FBPC often failed to respond to letters in timely fashion.

The goal of the committees was, of course, to maximize the repayment of interest and principal. To this end they opposed writing down principal, forgiving interest arrears, and yielding concessions on future interest payments. Their position on principal and arrears was particularly unyielding. While acknowledging that there existed circumstances in which it might be acceptable to reduce future interest payments if bondholders endorsed the terms in advance, they argued that as a matter of principle it was inappropriate to write off capital or interest arrears since these obligations had been incurred prior to any renegotiation of the bond covenants. But even though characterizing this position as a matter of principle, in practice the CFBH exhibited considerable flexibility. It was willing to swap arrears of interest and amortization for more favorable future treatment. In 1940, for example, the CFBH agreed to inform the Ecuadorean negotiator that "the Council might be prepared to abandon the arrears if he would put forward a reasonable offer for the future service of the debt...." In 1943 the Council negotiated an agreement with Brazil under the terms of which bondholders could opt for writing off principal in return for a cash payment and a higher interest rate.[11]

In considering whether to endorse a readjustment offer, the bondholders' committees had to consider both economic and political conditions in the debtor country. A domestic polity united in opposition to the resumption of full debt service greatly undermined the creditors' bargaining power. In 1940, in a letter to the CFBH representative negotiating readjustment terms with Brazil, Sir Otto Neimeyer, the renowned financial expert and member of the Council, characterized the political considerations as preeminent. "There are two entirely different kinds of facts which we have to consider," he wrote.

The first one is the political facts and the second one is the economic facts or ... [rather] the economic probabilities. It is very necessary not to confuse the two sets. On the first set of facts [it is] not possible at the present moment to extract from the Brazilian Government an offer ... different from that which you have ... [obtained], and for this reason I am in favour of accepting that offer.... But I do not think the position is the same when one comes to the economic argument. When we are talking of a permanent settlement, we have to deal with a long period not subject to the passing phase of the moment.... People in Rio are always unduly impressed with the Brazilian exaggerations of momentary local conditions.[12]

The objective of the debtors was to minimize their financial obligation while at the same time limiting the damage to their creditworthiness. As the U.S. Securities and Exchange Commission, not one to mince words, ex-

plained in 1937, "The willingness of the issuer to negotiate with representatives of the bondholders and eventually to agree to readjust its default
generally has two motivations: a desire to restore the prestige and reputation of the nation, and a desire to borrow more money."[13] There was
considerable dispute over the extent to which terms of settlement in fact
were linked to credit-market access. Whatever the reality, it was in the
interest of the bondholders to emphasize the linkages not only between
acceptable settlement and capital-market access but also between market
access and economic growth. In negotiations with Brazil in 1939, the CFBH
"explained how impossible it would be for Brazil to recover and prosper
without the goodwill of foreign capitalists." The debtors' receptivity to
such arguments depended both on the state of the international capital
market—since damage to the nation's credit mattered little in periods
when creditors were in any case unwilling to lend—and on the value
attached to ability to borrow relative to other objectives. As Sir Henry
Lynch, Rothchild and Sons' representative in Brazil, explained to the CFBH
in 1936, "the Brazilians knew that they had no credit and ... they thought
therefore that they might as well cease payments on their External Debt.
There were many people who wished to devote sums now used to pay
interest to the internal needs of the Country and they were exerting strong
pressure on the President and the Finance Minister to cease payments."[14]

The role of governments in readjustment negotiations was more complex than formal statements of their hands-off position would suggest. At
a minimum governments played an informational role. The American State
and Commerce Departments regularly provided the FBPC with information on the situation in foreign countries, while local embassy staff and the
Foreign Office in London conveyed such information to the CFBH. Information might be supplemented with direct advice. In 1938 an official of the
South American Department of the British Foreign Office recommended
"that it would be helpful if somebody from the Council went out to Brazil.
He was naturally discreet, but it seemed clear that his view was that
both Sir Hugh Gurney [British ambassador to Brazil] and Sir Henry Lynch
[the CFBH's negotiator] had become unduly influenced by Brazilian opinion
and needed stiffening by personal contact with a representative of the
Bondholders."[15]

Government officials sometimes played a direct role in the initiation or
conduct of negotiations. British officials, in the course of unrelated discussions with the foreign government, might drop a veiled hint that the other
matters under discussion could be brought to a successful conclusion if debt
negotiations were reopened. Once those negotiations were underway,

embassy staff including the ambassador might act as go-between. If the ambassador took it upon himself to question the CFBH's negotiating position, for example, by criticizing a communique as too strongly worded, the CFBH did not hesitate to remind him that the Council and not the government was responsible to the bondholders. When in 1938 the British ambassador to Brazil hesitated to convey a sharply worded letter from the CFBH to the Brazilian government, the Council informed the Foreign Office that "the Memorandum should be delivered to the Brasilians without further delay ... we have no reason to modify its terms."[16] It is clear, nonetheless, that the involvement of the British Embassy was likely to raise questions in the minds of the debtor's representatives about the capacity in which British officials were acting.

Finally, governments could threaten to invoke other sanctions against uncooperative debtors. They could link the resumption of debt service to official credits, for example. Usually, however, the interests of bondholders took a back seat to other government objectives. As Sir John Simon of the British Foreign Office described the position in 1934, "my predecessor Lord Palmerston, who is not generally regarded as having been backward in the defence of British interests, laid down the doctrine that if investors choose to buy the bonds of a foreign country carrying a high rate of interest in preference to British Government Bonds carrying a low rate of interest, they cannot claim that the British government is bound to intervene in the event of default."[17] In practice, the British position was more ambiguous. In 1938 the British Treasury wrote to the CFBH for a list of countries in default and expressed a desire

to make it a rule that the Treasury does not consent to issues of loans or to guarantees by His Majesty's Government of Medium Term Credits to countries which are in default to British bondholders. He [the Treasury official] made it clear that he did not imply that the Treasury could make this an absolute rule and that, as at present, each case must continue to be considered on its own merits. He was, however, anxious to ensure that the Treasury should not give their consent without being fully aware of the defaults which exist.[18]

Intervention by the U.S. State Department generally was limited to cases in which foreign governments discriminated against American bondholders. When, for example, Germany suspended debt service, European governments retaliated with threats of clearing arrangements, and Germany restarted service on its European but not its American debts, the State Department at the request of the FBPC made "the appropriate representations."[19] The State Department protested discrepancies in the terms offered

dollar and nondollar bondholders by the Hungarian and Polish governments. It pressed for modifications in Brazil's 1934 readjustment plan on
these same grounds. Although it was not the practice of U.S. authorities to
make the extension of Export-Import Bank loans conditional on the resumption of debt service, U.S. officials made clear that the extension of
Ex-Im Bank loans was a political matter whose progress could be accelerated by indications of good faith on the debt front.

The exchange of views and influence between the bondholders and
their governments operated in both directions, of course. The influence of
government over the bondholders' committees is clearest in the American
case. The FBPC had been created on State Department impetus, and the
extent of its independence was never entirely clear. As one author puts it,
the "semi-official character of the FBPC led the institution to much more
readily adapt its claims to American foreign policy."[20] There was less
question about the independence of the CFBH. Notwithstanding this traditional independence, the British government's attempts to enlist the committee in its alliance-building efforts intensified with the approach of World
War II. In 1938, for example, the CFBH was engaged in negotiations with
Egypt. The Foreign Office pressed the CFBH to soften its position on the
grounds that "friendship with Egypt is of vital importance to the Country."
In July 1939, with the British government anxious to conclude a treaty
with Greece, the chancellor of the exchequer and the foreign secretary
impressed upon the president of the CFBH the "political importance of a
settlement of the Greek default." The president's interpretation was that
the chancellor "in so many words ... advised us to take whatever was
available."[21]

In contrast to the standard characterization, then, creditor-country governments were intimately involved in interwar debt readjustments, much
like their successors in the 1980s. The difference between the 1930s and
1980s lies not in the extent of government involvement but in its direction and in its systematic nature. Whereas intervention in the 1930s was
sporadic, in the 1980s it has been systematic. Whereas creditor-government
intervention in the 1980s has not accelerated the process of readjustment,
on this earlier occasion official intervention had more ambiguous effects, in
some instances having a positive and in others a negative effect on ease of
settlement.

If the creditors could not rely on their governments for sanctions, they
still could attempt to impose sanctions on their own. They might attempt
to refuse commercial credits to debtors in default. Members of the CFBH
were divided over the advisability of using this lever. On the one hand,

they recognized that trade credit embargoes might be a powerful nego-tiating device. On the other, they acknowledged that exports were the source of the foreign exchange that might make the resumption of debt service possible.

Different segments of the creditor community had very different inter-ests when it came to the question of suspending export credits. The extension of trade credits remained profitable business for the banks in the aftermath of default. In contrast to long-term bonds, which had only been underwritten by investment bankers before being resold to the public, short-term credits were retained by the original lender or sold to other financial specialists. Those engaged in a profitable import-export trade hesitated to allow their business to suffer in the interest of the bondholders. Repeatedly the representatives of the bankers reaffirmed that they were "unable to associate themselves with any attempt of the Council to oppose export credits to a defaulting country or to put the bondholders in a better position than the traders."[22]

For their part, the indebted countries attached considerable value to trade credits. Even while service on foreign bonds was in suspension, many debtor nations continued to service their commercial debts.[23] Doing so was in their self-interest: although the bond market had closed down, the market for commercial credits was still active, providing an incentive for borrowers to stay current on their commercial debts. The CFBH implicitly endorsed these priorities, as in 1938, for example, when it recommended that "the sums at present being paid by Brazil as a result of agreements with England, France and the USA for commercial arrears, should be allo-cated to the service of the external debt as *and when* the commercial arrears are paid off."[24]

The creditors' most potent threat was to enlist their government in the imposition of a clearing arrangement. This mechanism was available to any country running a trade deficit with a debtor country and hence with an excess of outlays on foreign goods which it could sequester. The 1934 Act of Parliament creating a clearing office to regulate British trade with Ger-many illustrates its operation. The clearing office was to recover, out of the proceeds of German trade with Britain, a sufficient sum in sterling to pay interest on British tranches of the 1924 Dawes Loan and the 1930 Young Loan.[25] The effectiveness of the threat is revealed by the speed with which a German financial delegation was dispatched to London, where it ne-gotiated an agreement under which Britain would impose no sanctions against Germany, while Germany would continue to service the Dawes and Young Plan bonds held by British citizens. No clearing arrangement was threatened by the United States, and from June 1934 only partial interest was received by investors in dollar bonds.[26]

Having made extensive use of bilateral clearing as well (Ellis 1941), Germany could hardly invoke free trade principles in objection. Nonetheless, clearing arrangements tended to be the exception rather than the rule. The readiness with which other European governments utilized them against Germany reflected their direct involvement in the flotation of the Dawes and Young Plan Loans. For governments that had urged their citizens to invest in German bonds, it was hard to continue to insist that default was a private matter. But the "German case was deemed to be exceptional." "The support given the Young and Dawes loan bondholders ran contrary to the general policy of the British government ...."[27] In the case of loans whose flotation creditor-country governments had not actively encouraged, the authorities were reticent to intervene. The position of the British Treasury, stated, for example, in connection with Greece in 1937, was that it was undesirable "to link together any question of purchase of Greek goods with negotiations for a settlement of the Greek External Debt." In the case of British trade negotiations with Colombia in 1938, the head of the British delegation, Sir Thomas Hohler, informed the CFBH that "he would not discuss the debt problem with Colombia but ... would take any suitable opportunity to impress upon the Colombians the importance from the point of view of their own credit of coming to an agreement over their external debts."[28]

The U.S. State Department similarly opposed explicit linkage of trade and debt. The bondholders did their best to disguise this fact. In 1934 the FBPC attempted to convince Colombia that "increasing pressure is being brought both upon the Council and upon Washington by bondholders who are insisting that some sort of coercive measure shall be adopted against Colombia along the model set up by European countries or by levying a special tariff against Colombian coffee...."[29] True, representatives of investors in Colombian bonds appeared before the Tariff Commission in the course of hearings over a reciprocal trade treaty with Colombia. But Sumner Welles, the assistant secretary of state, summarized the official position as follows:

The position of the Department is that the primary purpose of the trade agreements negotiated under the Act of June 12, 1934 is the revival of international trade, and the agreement with Colombia does not, therefore, contain provisions specifically relating to the resumption of service of Colombia dollar obligations. However, inasmuch as the decline in international trade was one of the principal causes of financial difficulties in many countries, it is to be expected that the revival of international trade which the trade agreement program seeks to foster will aid in remedying conditions which have led to defaults.[30]

Promises and threats related to trade became increasingly commonplace with the outbreak of World War II. Early in 1940 a Greek mission meeting in London to confer with British officials over trade arrangements was told that "the Chancellor of the Exchequer was anxious to help the Greek to establish a market for their tobacco, but he could not defend such a course unless a settlement on the debt were reached...." When Peru failed to remit interest for the first half of 1940, the British Treasury informed the Peruvian Minister of Finance that if the June coupon was not met, the British government would be "obliged to reconsider their purchasing policy towards Peru." In general, the U.S. government remained less interventionist than its British counterpart. In 1943 the president of the CFBH complained that although the United States was Brazil's largest export market and leading source of credit, "the U.S. Government has not shown much regard for even its own Bondholders. In the interest of trade and of the Good Neighbour policy, it is lending money to Brasil regardless of Brasil's attitude toward its external bonded debt...."[31]

Debtors were, if anything, more inclined than creditors to link trade and debt. Governments in default repeatedly offered commodities in lieu of financial transfers in negotiations with the CFBH. In 1937 the Greek government proposed "that if Great Britain could take more currants, tobacco and iron ore it would enable them to make a better proposal for a permanent settlement." The 1940 dispute over tobacco had been initiated by Greece itself, which in 1939 had proposed British purchases in exchange for debt concessions. The scope for such transactions widened with the approach of World War II and the growing involvement of governments in trade. When in September 1939 the British government purchased sunflower seeds from Bulgaria (in part to deprive Germany of them), Bulgaria agreed to allocate more than a third of the proceeds to service on sterling bonds.[32]

The alternative to protracted negotiations was for countries to buy out their creditors through bond purchases on the secondary market. The practice was understandably controversial. Bondholders complained that creditors engaging in this practice violated not just the letter but the spirit of the bond covenants by diverting foreign exchange from debt service to capital repurchase.[33] Repurchases revealed that foreign exchange was available; bondholders argued that it should be properly devoted to debt service until interest was up to date and only then to debt retirement. Permitting countries to repurchase defaulted bonds at market prices allegedly strengthened the incentive to default, for suspending debt service both depressed bond prices, making repurchase more attractive, and relaxed the foreign exchange constraint that limited the scope for bond market operations. Most important, from the investor's standpoint the low prices at which repurchases were attractive to the debtor implied disappointing rates of return compared to those offered ex ante. As the FBPC summarized its position in its annual report for 1935:

If the bonds have service, according to their contracts, the debtor governments of course are well within their rights in availing themselves of the opportunity of purchasing the bonds on the market even if they are selling substantially below par but to do so when the bonds are depreciated abnormally on account of default ... is a practice which the Council most strongly condemns; against which it has repeatedly protested.[34]

If small bondholders universally objected to the practice of repurchasing defaulted bonds, financial specialists were more ambivalent. They noted that by entering the market and bidding for bonds, the foreign government put upward pressure on bond prices, ceteris paribus. Repurchases of defaulted debts were a way to eliminate costly lending mistakes. By removing the residue of nonperforming loans from the market, it would be possible to list new issues on the Stock Exchange and to restart the lending process. Since repurchases were also resales—that is, voluntary transactions on the part of the bondholders—they represented a market solution to the problem of how to share the losses associated with an unsatisfactory loan.

Officially the CFBH opposed repurchases of defaulted bonds. When in 1938, with its defaulted debt trading at £29, the Guatemalan government broached this issue with the Council, the latter advised that "if the Government now have funds available for the repurchase of bonds, the proper course would be that they should offer to resume the Sinking Funds, in whole if possible, or if not, in part ... haphazard purchases of Bonds by the Government, at the time when the Sinking Fund is suspended on the ground of lack of funds would naturally be considered irregular and would do damage to their credit." The CFBH also noted the practical difficulties of completing large purchases in a thin market. Yet the Council may have revealed its true attitude when it went on to suggest that "if a firm order were given at a price not exceeding, say 33, for the purchase of up to say—£5000 Bonds ... it might be possible to complete the order in the course of a few weeks." Indeed, the CFBH accepted repurchase provisions of components of interim settlements. In the four-year settlement with

Brazil recommended by the Council in 1940, for example, in addition to restarting partial interest payments the Brazilian authorities undertook to "devote at least $400,000 in each of four years ... in the English market."[35]

2.3 The Outcome: A Quantitative Assessment

It is difficult to summarize concisely the outcome of a large number of complex debtor–creditor negotiations. One useful summary statistic is the rate of return realized by foreign investors, which can be compared with the returns offered ex ante and with the yields on otherwise comparable domestic investments. In the calculations to follow we compute the internal rates of return realized by the creditors on two large samples of foreign bonds issued in New York and London in the 1920s. We track interest and principal repayments on these bonds and any successor issues into which they were converted subsequently until the debt is extinguished.[36] We include national, municipal, and corporate bonds in an effort to replicate the foreign bond portfolios held by investors in the lending countries. This approach is complementary to that of Jorgensen and Sachs (chapter 3), who focus on sovereign loans to a select group of Latin American countries in an effort to analyze the repayment records of different governments. Where Jorgensen and Sachs view the problem from the debtor government's perspective, we adopt the perspective of the typical foreign investor.

In Eichengreen and Portes (1986) we reported the results of a pilot study of realized rates of return on foreign loans floated during the interwar years. We computed realized rates of return on samples of dollar and sterling bonds floated in the 1920s on behalf of not just foreign governments but states, provinces, municipalities, and corporations. Our estimates revealed that the performance of loans to sovereign governments differed significantly from that of loans to other foreign borrowers. The nominal own-currency internal rate of return on dollar loans to sovereigns exceeded 5 percent; dollar loans to state and local governments yielded three percentage points less, and loans to foreign corporations less still. While average returns on sterling loans were considerably higher, the variation across loans to different entities was strikingly similar; on average, loans to sovereigns significantly outperformed loans to other foreign borrowers from the creditors' standpoint. We conjectured that the superior performance of loans to sovereigns reflected the tendency of debtors and creditors alike to regard the status of such loans as a particularly important indicator of creditworthiness, in conjunction with the greater scope for negotiating directly with sovereigns. We argued that the superior performance of sterling loans was due to a combination of factors: the direction of British lending (oriented disproportionately toward the Empire and Commonwealth, in contrast to U.S. lending to Germany and South America), more active intervention on behalf of the bondholders by British officials and more effective representation of their interests by British officials and the Corporation of Foreign Bondholders.

Our previous estimates were subject to three limitations. First, they extrapolated from a relatively small sample of 50 dollar and 31 sterling issues. However representative of average experience, that sample was too small to shed much light on variations across borrowing countries. Second, they were limited to the years 1923–30 (1924–30 in the case of dollar bonds). Our sampling strategy was to span the period of large-scale foreign lending, which reached a peak in 1927. But there is reason to suspect that rates of return were somewhat higher in the immediately preceding years (see Mintz 1951). Third, our calculations did not incorporate repurchases at depressed market prices of defaulted foreign bonds. Creditors who sold back their bonds at market prices typically received only partial repayment of loan principal; for this reason our previous calculations may have overstated the realized rate of return.

Here we revise and extend our previous analysis of rates of return on foreign loans in an effort to surmount these limitations. We analyze a larger sample of 250 dollar bonds and 125 sterling issues, covering the years 1920–29.[37] We adopt the same strategy for calculating realized rates of return on sterling as on dollar bonds, although differences in the materials available on the operation of the two national capital markets dictate some differences in implementation. For Britain, we construct estimates for all 125 overseas bonds offered for subscription in London between 1920 and 1929 and listed by the *Stock Exchange Yearbook*. No corporate issues were listed. For the United States, we drew a stratified sample of 250 dollar foreign bonds issued in the 1920s from the list of 1,468 such bonds compiled by the U.S. Department of Commerce and published in its *Handbook on American Underwriting of Foreign Securities* (see Young 1931). That sample was stratified along three dimensions: year of issue, destination of capital (Europe, North America, Latin America, Far East), and type of borrower (government versus corporate). Combining tranches of single loans listed separately and eliminating stocks mislabeled as bonds left us with 207 dollar issues.

We tracked interest payments and repayment of principal, computing own-currency nominal realized internal rates of return. Principal sources of information on interest, amortization, and conversions were the annual reports of the FBPC and the CFBH.[38] When bonds were converted or replaced by successor issues in the course of negotiations over defaulted loans, those successor bonds were treated as parts of the initial issue in the rate of return calculation. When domestic currency, blocked balances, or scrip was issued in lieu of foreign exchange (as in the case of German bonds outstanding in the 1930s), we incorporated these restricted payments only at the point when they could be converted into foreign currency.[39]

An important extension of our earlier estimates was the incorporation of repurchases of bonds by the borrower at market prices. Our procedures for dollar and sterling bonds differed. For dollar loans, we first assumed that any bonds extinguished during the period of default were repurchased at market prices. Information on the value of bonds still outstanding is reasonably complete for most issues, although occasionally we were forced to interpolate due to the absence of information for some years. For dollar loans not in default, we assumed that repurchases took placed at either market price or par as specified in the bond covenant, at whichever was lower when the choice was the borrower's. For sterling loans, the necessary information was not readily available; hence we constructed two rate of return estimates under the alternative assumptions of capital repayments at market price and par.

Table 2.1 summarizes the results. The nominal internal rate of return (weighted by the value of the loan) is almost exactly 4 percent for dollar issues, roughly 5 percent for sterling bonds (4.98 percent when repurchases are assumed to have taken place at market price, 5.18 percent when they are assumed to occur at par). The positive internal rates of return indicate that, overall, both British and American bondholders succeeded in recovering their principal. At the same time, the realized returns were significantly lower than those offered ex ante, which were generally in the range of 7 to 8 percent.[40] On average, bondholders settled for slightly less than half of contractual interest. British bondholders did better than their American counterparts: for British investors, overseas lending paid better than contemporaneous domestic investments, while for Americans, the opposite was true.[41]

The gap between the returns on sterling and dollar bonds is somewhat smaller than in our previous study, due principally to our upward revision of the estimated return on dollar loans floated in the 1920s. Although the larger and more reliable sample utilized here may contribute to the difference, the revision is due mainly to two other factors: first, the extension backward of the period encompassed by the sample from 1924 to the beginning of the decade (when loans bore higher interest rates) and, second, greater success in tracking the returns on loans to foreign corpora-

Table 2.1
Summary of realized rates of return (%)

	Dollar bonds	Sterling bonds par repurchases	Sterling bonds market price repurchases
Overall IRR	3.99	5.18	4.98
Europe	3.24	4.15	3.64
North America	5.13	5.18	5.18
Latin America	3.06	3.00	1.44
Far East	5.96	5.75	5.59
Government	4.64	—	—
Private	2.54	—	—
Dominion/colonial	—	5.41	5.39

tions (German corporations in particular) through World War II and the postwar period.

The difference caused by moving from nominal to real internal rates of return is small. In the case of the dollar bonds, for instance, the return rises from 4.0 to 4.8 percent (when the GNP deflator is used). The average real return exceeds the average nominal return because as late as 1941 the price level remains lower than in the 1920s. But the overall difference between real and nominal returns is minimized by the rise in prices thereafter. Similarly, converting sterling investments and returns into dollars as they accrue to derive dollar-denominated rates of return to investors in bonds floated in London makes little difference to the results. An important factor contributing to the higher average return on sterling bonds is the lower incidence of default. Only 18 percent of the value of the sterling bonds considered in this paper lapsed into default, compared to 46 percent of the dollar bonds. But differences in the incidence of default cannot by themselves account for differences in the internal rates of return realized by investors in dollar and sterling issues. This is contrary to a frequently expressed view, for example, by Schuker (1988), that the tendency of the London capital market to direct funds to the Dominions and colonies rather than to Central Europe or Latin America was wholly responsible for British investors' relatively happy experience. Table 2.2, where the rate of return is regressed on a constant term and a dummy variable for default, shows that the average default on dollar bonds was considerably more costly than that on sterling issues. (As in every regression we report, all variables are weighted by the value of the issue.) The constant terms can be interpreted

Table 2.2
The impact of default on realized returns

	Number of observations	Standard error
Dollar bonds		
IRR = 5.97 − 4.33 default		
(0.25) (0.45)	207	5.06
Sterling bonds		
Par repurchases		
IRR = 5.47 − 1.71 default		
(0.14) (0.33)	125	1.40
Market price repurchases		
IRR = 5.44 − 2.70 default		
(0.16) (0.39)	125	1.66

Note: Regressions are estimated by weighted least squares. Standard errors are in parentheses.

as the average return on bonds on which interest payments were never suspended, the slope coefficient as the average loss in the event of default. The cost of the average default in terms of the realized internal rate of return is considerably greater on dollar than on sterling loans (4.3 percent versus 1.7 to 2.7 percent).

To what extent were these realized rates of return affected by the practice of repurchasing defaulted bonds at depressed market prices? To shed light on this question, we recalculated the internal rates of return on dollar bonds under the counterfactual that all repurchases took place at par. In a small number of cases, the change in the internal rate of return was substantial. A dramatic illustration is the case of Hungary: the internal rate of return on Hungarian Land Mortgage Institution bonds rises from − 7.7 to 2.5 percent; when it is assumed that all repurchases took place at par. For the British and Hungarian Bank, it rises from − 13.6 to 1.5 percent; for the City Savings Bank, from − 12.8 to 1.0 percent; and for the European Mortgage and Investment Bank, from − 14.4 to 1.4 percent. But the impact on the overall rate of return on bonds in the sample is relatively small. Assuming no repurchases below par, the internal rate of return on the entire sample of dollar bonds rises only from 4.00 to 4.96 percent, and the internal rate of return on those bonds that lapsed into default rises from 1.64 to 3.58 percent. While the practice of repurchasing bonds in default at a discount naturally reduced the returns realized by the bondholders relative to what they would have received had those repurchases taken place at par, these calculations suggest that overall the impact on creditors' returns was not large.

Table 2.1 also disaggregates our estimated internal rates of return by region and type of borrower, revealing considerable variation in the performance and settlement terms on different categories of loans. A first distinction is between dollar loans to governments and to corporations. From the bondholders' perspective the former performed almost twice as well as measured by the internal rate of return. These results reinforce the findings reported in Eichengreen and Portes (1986), although the differential between government and corporate issues was even larger there.

A second important distinction is between loans to different regions. In the case of dollar bonds, the best performing loans were those extended to countries in the Far East (principally Australia and Japan), followed closely by loans to Canada. These were followed at a distance by loans to European borrowers, with Latin America bringing up the rear. Results are similar for sterling bonds. The best-performing sterling loans are those granted to Japan and Dominion governments. These are followed by loans to European borrowers, with loans to Latin America again bringing up the rear. In table 2.3 we disaggregate further by region and test for the significance of the differentials, regressing the internal rate of return on a vector of dummy variables for location of the borrower. The internal rate of return on loans to the omitted alternative, Germany, is picked up by the constant term. Consider first the dollar bonds. The average return on dollar loans to Germany, 1.4 percent, is low relative to the alternatives. Only loans to Central America yielded less (but insignificantly so). The internal rates of return on loans to the countries of South America and Eastern Europe were only slightly higher (1.7 and 2.5 percentage points, respectively). Investors in bonds issued on behalf of borrowers in other regions did significantly better. Investors in loans to Western Europe did best of all, followed closely by Australia and at a distance by Japan.

The results for the sterling bonds are basically consistent. Absent any British loans to Central America, the three worst performing regions are Germany, South America, and Eastern Europe, just as in the case of dollar bonds. But where dollar loans to Eastern Europe and South America did slightly better than dollar loans to Germany, in the case of sterling loans they did slightly worse. Most of the difference is due to the superior performance of sterling bonds issued on behalf of German borrowers relative to dollar bonds for Germany (with internal rates of return of 3.6 to 4.4 and 1.1 percent, respectively). This contrast points to the importance of

Table 2.3
Rates of return by region of borrower

Dependent variable	Dollar bonds, IRR	Sterling bonds, par repurchases	Sterling bonds, market price repurchases
Weighted constant	1.12	4.38	3.61
	(1.03)	(0.68)	(0.79)
Central America	0.34	—	—
	(3.01)		
South America	2.38	−1.03	−2.17
	(1.26)	(0.85)	(0.99)
Australia	4.85	0.89	1.65
	(1.46)	(0.70)	(0.82)
Japan	5.08	1.23	1.69
	(1.37)	(0.91)	(1.06)
Western Europe	3.71	0.53	1.20
	(1.11)	(0.87)	(1.02)
Eastern Europe	0.92	−2.12	−2.16
	(2.06)	(1.07)	(1.25)
North America	3.96	0.80	1.57
	(1.11)	(2.33)	(2.72)
Africa	—	1.27	2.01
		(0.76)	(0.89)
Southeast Asia	—	1.61	2.31
		(0.79)	(0.92)
R^2	0.61	0.22	0.34
Standard error of regression	5.87	2.06	1.63

Note: Standard errors are in parentheses. Omitted variable is Germany.

differences in the ability of British and American creditors to recover from defaulting German borrowers.

To shed further light on bondholders' ability to recover, in table 2.4 we disaggregate the sample of dollar bonds by borrowing country and rank the countries by the size of the gap between ex ante and ex post returns. (The number of bonds issued on behalf of each country in the sample is indicated in parentheses. Given the relatively small size of the sample of sterling bonds, it proved difficult to construct a comparable table for Britain that was readily interpretable.) For Norway and Canada, the two countries that head the list, the realized returns exceed those contracted ex ante because of early debt retirement at favorable prices. For Hungary, which brings up the rear, the realized internal rate of return was nearly 15 percentage points less than the internal rate of return specified ex ante in the bond covenants. In between there is evidence that the kinds of economic and political factors described in the previous section had a decided impact on terms of settlement. Of countries that lapsed into significant default, U.S. bondholders much more successfully recovered from those who relied heavily on trade and financial relations with the United States (e.g., Panama and Cuba) than from those whose dependence on trade was more dispersed (Brazil and Bolivia).

In addition ability to recover varied significantly depending on whether the creditor was a national government, a municipality, or a corporation. Table 2.5 again ranks countries by the gap between realized and contractual internal rates of return, but for government bonds only. The difference is significant. France and Sweden, for example, which ranked surprisingly low in table 2.4 due to the dismal performance of loans to corporations, now move to the head of the class. The differential ability of American creditors to recover in the event of default is still evident; the contrasting performance of Panamanian and Cuban loans, on the one hand, and Bolivian and Brazilian loans, on the other, continues to come through clearly.

These results in table 2.5 are broadly consistent with those of Jorgensen and Sachs in chapter 3. With the exception of Peru, their ranking of five Latin American countries by the ratio of the present value of repayments to the present value of borrowings (table 5.8) coincides with our ranking of the five countries by the gap between ex ante and ex post internal rates of return.[42] The correspondence is striking given that Jorgensen and Sachs focus exclusively on loans to national governments, while we broaden the coverage to include also state and municipal bonds.

Table 2.4
Ranking of countries by gap between ex-ante and ex-post returns: all dollar bonds

Country	Gap (%)	Number of bonds
1. Norway	+0.62	4
2. Canada	+0.12	78
3. Switzerland	−0.12	1
4. Belgium	−0.24	3
5. Denmark	−0.38	7
6. Dutch East Indies	−0.50	2
7. Japan	−0.83	4
8. Argentina	−1.17	10
9. Austria	−1.19	2
10. Australia	−1.27	1
11. Panama	−1.51	2
12. Italy	−1.83	6
13. Peru	−1.95	2
14. Germany	−1.99	38
15. France	−2.86	5
16. Uruguay	−3.16	2
17. Cuba	−4.30	6
18. Colombia	−4.49	9
19. Chile	−4.71	4
20. Estonia	−4.87	1
21. Sweden	−5.09	2
22. Yugoslavia	−5.21	1
23. Costa Rica	−5.76	1
24. Poland	−6.70	2
25. Brazil	−7.40	5
26. Bolivia	−9.78	2
27. Hungary	−14.76	7

Table 2.5
Ranking of countries by gap between ex-ante and ex-post returns: government bonds only

Country		Gap (%)	Number of bonds
1.	France	0.39	3
2.	Belgium	−0.02	2
3.	Canada	−0.12	45
4.	Switzerland	−0.12	1
5.	Norway	−0.14	3
6.	Sweden	−0.32	1
7.	Denmark	−0.33	5
8.	Dutch East Indies	−0.50	2
9.	Italy	−0.87	1
10.	Argentina	−1.17	10
11.	Austria	−1.19	2
12.	Australia	−1.27	1
13.	Panama	−1.51	2
14.	Japan	−1.68	1
15.	Peru	−1.95	2
16.	Uruguay	−3.16	2
17.	Cuba	−4.30	6
18.	Colombia	−4.38	5
19.	Chile	−4.71	4
20.	Estonia	−4.87	1
21.	Yugoslavia	−5.21	1
22.	Costa Rica	−5.76	1
23.	Germany	−6.03	21
24.	Hungary	−6.90	6
25.	Poland	−7.70	2
26.	Brazil	−8.24	4
27.	Bolivia	−9.78	2

Tables 2.6 and 2.7 use regression analysis to analyze the differential performances of loans to different types of borrowers, where loans to national governments are the omitted alternative picked up by the constant term. In the case of dollar bonds, loans to national governments do better than loans to all alternatives, significantly so in every case at the 90 percent confidence level. The lowest rates of return are those on loans to foreign banking institutions, followed by loans to municipalities. The results for sterling bonds are similar. Loans to national governments outperform loans to foreign municipalities. They are outperformed in turn by two categories of loans with no American counterpart, British-guaranteed loans (British Funds) and loans to the dominions and colonies.

Table 2.8 disaggregates loans by year of issue. The earliest year is the omitted alternative picked up by the constant term. In the case of dollar bonds, realized returns decline significantly from their immediate post-World War I highs, reaching their nadir in 1927. This was also the finding in Eichengreen and Portes (1986) using the pilot sample of 50 dollar bonds. A number of authors, such as Mintz (1951), have argued that the quality of foreign bonds issued in the United States deteriorated over the course of the 1920s, a larger proportion of the loans issued in the second half of the decade being of questionable quality and lapsing into default once the Great Depression struck. Our results qualify this interpretation, implying that loan quality recovered in 1928–29 as the volume of U.S. foreign lending fell. If there had been no changes in loan quality over the decade, one would expect negative coefficients on later years on the grounds that loans issued relatively late had fewer years to receive interest before interruptions to debt service set in starting in 1931. Viewed in this light, the rise in the internal rate of return on dollar bonds issued after 1927 is striking. The coefficients on years for the sample of sterling loans accord more closely with the received characterization of loan quality. Sterling returns achieve their largest negative values in 1928–29.[43]

These results paint a more nuanced picture of interwar default and debt readjustment than those that have come before. We have noted that British overseas investors fared considerably better than their American counterparts. More strikingly still, even American investors ultimately reaped an adequate overall return on loans to foreign governments. Despite widespread sovereign default, U.S. investors who purchased a representative portfolio of foreign national bonds and held on until readjustments were complete generally did better than if they had invested in U.S. Treasury bonds. The realized internal rate of return on dollar loans to foreign

Table 2.6
Rates of return on dollar loans by type of borrower

Weighted constant	5.81
	(0.27)
State government	−2.27
	(0.86)
Municipality	−2.45
	(1.82)
National bank	−5.44
	(2.03)
Other banks	−9.04
	(2.08)
Corporation	−3.21
	(0.52)
R^2	0.66
Standard error of regression for 207 observations	5.41

Note: Dependent variable is weighted IRR; omitted variable is national government. Standard errors are in parentheses.

Table 2.7
Realized rates of return on sterling loans by type of borrower

	Par repurchases	Market price repurchases
Weighted constant	4.48	3.73
	(0.29)	(0.36)
British funds	0.44	1.18
	(1.10)	(1.34)
Dominion, provincial, or colonial central governments	0.94	1.67
	(0.33)	(0.41)
Dominion, provincial, or colonial local governments	0.98	1.70
	(0.80)	(0.97)
Foreign governments	−0.74	−1.08
	(0.92)	(1.12)
R^2	0.08	0.15
Standard error of regression	2.20	1.82

Note: Omitted variable is foreign stocks and bonds. Standard errors are in parentheses.

Table 2.8
Rates of return by year of issue

Dependent variable	Dollar bonds	Sterling bonds, par repurchases	Sterling bonds, market price repurchases
Weight	8.11	6.38	6.31
	(0.47)	(0.54)	(0.68)
1921	−0.91	—	—
	(1.13)		
1922	−2.88	−0.48	−0.65
	(0.59)	(0.79)	(1.00)
1923	−1.79	−0.69	−0.67
	(1.44)	(0.65)	(0.82)
1924	−2.81	−1.23	−1.24
	(0.81)	(0.62)	(0.78)
1925	−3.15	−1.24	−1.22
	(1.08)	(0.66)	(0.83)
1926	−2.73	−1.40	−2.05
	(0.65)	(0.76)	(0.97)
1927	−10.07	−1.16	−1.23
	(0.72)	(0.61)	(0.77)
1928	−3.76	−2.18	−2.79
	(0.59)	(0.69)	(0.87)
1929	−8.50	−2.50	−2.64
	(0.90)	(0.77)	(0.98)
R^2	0.80	0.14	0.14
Standard error of regression	4.23	1.47	1.87

Note: Standard errors are in parentheses. Omitted variable is 1920.

governments (4.6 percent) exceeded the average nominal yield on U.S. Treasury bonds for the decade of the 1920s (4.1 percent). Admittedly 4.6 percent was significantly less than the ex ante return on foreign government loans. But if Treasury bonds are an appropriate basis for comparison, the risk premia charged ex ante were on average more than sufficient to compensate American investors for the additional risk of sovereign default. In contrast, American investors in foreign municipal and corporate securities failed to recover a sufficient fraction of their principal and future interest sufficient to leave them as well off as if they had invested in Treasury bonds.

The superior performance of sterling versus dollar bonds and of loans to central governments versus loans to other foreign borrowers is amenable to two interpretations: differing degrees of investor sophistication at the lending stage, and different institutional and political arrangements at the settlement stage. That British investors recovered a significantly larger share of potential losses of interest and principal in the wake of default confirms that differences in the position and approach of British and American creditors to readjustment negotiations contributed to their very different experience. But there remains scope for different degrees of investor sophistication at the lending stage. The greater prevalence of default on dollar than on sterling bonds is consistent with the notion that the London market more successfully discriminated between good and bad credit risks. American investors took up the lion's share of the German and South American bonds that experienced the most serious defaults. While American issue houses also floated loans on behalf of Australia and Canada, in the British case loans to Empire governments formed fully 75 percent of overseas government issues, and not one of those loans lapsed into default. It is tempting to link this behavior to political factors but also differences in the experience of institutional investors in the two markets. By the 1920s London had accumulated more than half a century of experience with large-scale foreign lending. For New York, in contrast, foreign borrowing rather than foreign lending had been the norm prior to 1913. The transformation of the United States from a net foreign debtor to a net creditor and the emergence of New York as an international financial center was telescoped into the five short years spanned by World War I. British investment houses with reputations to protect might well hesitate to put their stamp of approval on risky overseas loans, while their American counterparts, as new entrants to this market who had not yet invested in the same industry-specific sunk costs, had less to lose if risky loans turned out badly but much to gain from generous commissions.[44]

In addition the British and U.S. governments intervened at the lending stage to very different extents. U.S. intervention was tightly circumscribed. Banks originating foreign loans were asked only to consult the State Department prior to floating an issue. Following consultations, the State Department then announced whether or not it had an objection. In the 1920s it objected primarily to loans to foreign governments that had not yet negotiated terms for repayment of war debts owed the United States. Even these objections did little to more than temporarily influence the lending process.[45]

British government efforts to channel foreign lending were more systematic and comprehensive.[46] The three successive Colonial Stock Acts adopted between 1877 and 1900, which accorded favorable terms to overseas issues on behalf of British colonies, remained in force throughout the 1920s. Under their provisions managers of trusts were empowered to invest in colonial stocks but not in the bonds of foreign governments. In addition in the l920s the government intermittently embargoed overseas loans, generally with an eye toward buttressing a weak British balance of payments position and perhaps also diverting funds toward domestic investment. During two short periods before November 1925 and for two after mid-1929, the Bank of England exercised veto power over various foreign issues (primarily on behalf of governments). Again, it accorded preferential treatment to loans to the Empire. The embargo could be evaded in a variety of ways: foreign borrowers could arrange a bankers' overdraft in London to be funded once the embargo was removed, for example. But the available evidence suggests that Bank of England regulation had some impact on the composition of British overseas lending and therefore on the return. The tendency of realized returns on sterling loans to decline by year of issue (table 2.8) may reflect in part the progressive relaxation of Bank of England regulations discouraging loans to the non-Commonwealth countries.[47]

Once their different degrees of involvement in the lending process during the 1920s is recalled, the differing tendency of the British and American governments to become involved in the readjustment process should come as no surprise. The British government had always been more heavily involved in directing the flow of foreign lending, in ways that could be seen as benefiting British investors once the disasters of the 1930s struck. Having heavily influenced the lending process, they could hardly continue to claim, as in the nineteenth century, that default was an entirely private matter.

2.4   Conclusion

Our review of the readjustment negotiations of the 1930s suggests a number of conclusions relevant to the debate over the ongoing LDC debt crisis. First, even prior to the era of interlocking official export credits, Paris Club reschedulings, IMF stabilization loans, and World Bank development assistance, the process of settlement tended to be protracted. Negotiations could suffer serious setbacks owing to changes in political and economic conditions at home and abroad, and decades could be required to conclude a negotiated settlement successfully. Debtors may have found it easier to suspend debt service unilaterally in the era of bond finance, but they still found it difficult to achieve the kind of permanent settlement needed to put behind them the uncertainty created by default. This is not to dispute that by choosing unilateral suspension debtors were able to redirect resources toward investment and thereby to stimulate growth, but rather to point out that this strategy created residual uncertainty that continued to complicate foreign investment, trade, and diplomatic relations for a period of years.

Second, the readjustment of defaulted interwar loans universally involved some burden sharing among debtors and creditors. Although the pronounced heterogeneity in returns that is the most prominent feature of our calculations makes any generalization problematic, this fact seems to have been uniformly the case. In no instance in our sample did bondholders succeed in recovering the total of the interest arrears incurred between suspension and readjustment. How much they recovered depended on the attitude of the country to which they had lent and the effectiveness of the leverage exercised by their representative committee and government. While U.S. investors lost on average 75 percent of interest due in the event of default, British investors lost only 30 to 50 percent. The contrast frequently drawn between an authoritative CFBH and an active British government, on the one hand, and a more tentative FBPC and passive U.S. State Department, on the other, though subject to exaggeration, seems to be supported by the quantitative evidence.

Third, as is implicit in the preceding discussion, the contrast often drawn between the degree of creditor government involvement today and in the past is all too easily exaggerated. It may be true that in the era of bond finance governments were less inclined to press for favorable settlements on behalf of private creditors because their banking systems were not at risk, but it would be misleading to conclude from this that governments were uninvolved. If governments were disinclined to intervene systematically on behalf of bondholders or to subordinate trade policy and political objectives to the interests of the bondholders, their presence was continually felt nonetheless in readjustment negotiations. The suggestion that defaults were easier to settle in the past because creditor-country governments were not involved must be carefully tempered.

But did this creditor-country government involvement encourage or impede settlement? Where a strong case can be made for the 1980s that creditor-government involvement has contributed to the protracted nature of the crisis, for the 1930s the evidence does not point in any one direction. On a significant number of occasions, U.S. or U.K. officials made clear that export credits and market access were tied, however obliquely, to the resumption of debt service. On other occasions they applied pressure not to the debtors but to the creditors. Since default did not pose the same risk to creditor-country banking systems as in the 1980s, the interests of private creditors and their governments did not possess the same natural complementarity. And with the approach of World War II creditor governments were more inclined to press for concessions from investors to keep debtors out of enemy camp. The strong contrast between the 1930s and the 1980s lies not in the extent of government involvement but in the extent to which such involvement worked in a single direction.

Several other factors worked to increase ease of settlement. In the 1930s, in contrast to today, the provision of long-term finance and of trade credits was basically in the hands of different sets of lenders with divergent interests. The links between those arms of government concerned with debt and trade were even more remote than in the 1980s. Only buybacks of defaulted bonds had an ambiguous impact on ease of settlement. Although this helped to remove the debt overhang, it did so at the expense of ill will on the part of small bondholders who objected to the practice.

With all these factors increasing the ease of settlement, why could debt adjustments still require 25 years or more to conclude? The answer is that macroeconomic conditions exercised a powerful influence over settlement. As developing-country export markets recovered with the outbreak of World War II and with the continued strength of commodity prices thereafter, the costs of settlement declined. As it once again began to appear that the United States would be willing to lend, the benefits of settlement rose. This suggests that an important contribution by the creditor countries to the resolution of the current crisis lies in the adoption of macroeconomic policies conducive to the maintenance of steady growth, open markets, and financial stability.

Notes

1. A review of global plans for resolving the interwar debt crisis is Eichengreen (1989a).

2. We find two other explanations for the contrast unconvincing. One emphasizes the relative magnitude of the macroeconomic shocks of the 1930s and 1980s and suggests that the greater severity of the interwar depression accounts for the greater incidence of default in the 1930s. But if from a global perspective the macroeconomic shock of the 1930s remains unmatched, from the perspective of Latin America's debt-servicing difficulties the disturbances of the early 1980s were of comparable magnitide (Díaz-Alejandro, 1983; Maddison, 1985; Eichengreen and Portes, 1987). The one dramatic macroeconomic difference, the very different behavior of export volumes, which fell dramatically in the 1930s but have continued to rise in the 1980s, is attributable as much to the response of the debtors, who have made great efforts to expand exports precisely in order to maintain debt service, as to differences in global economic conditions. Similarly, the greater scope for new money in the era of bank finance does not suffice to explain the contrast. Although new money has been forthcoming, it has been insufficient in quantity to relieve the need for net resource transfers to the creditors (by Latin America, $130 billion between 1982 and 1986, according to the World Bank).

3. See Fishlow and Lipson (chapters 4 and 7 in this volume).

4. For discussion, see Royal Institute of International Affairs (1937).

5. For a forceful statement of this position, see Sachs (1986).

6. Many of the points in this section are elaborated in Eichengreen and Portes (1989).

7. Typically, the market for unassented bonds would shrink as the deadline for acceptance (usually five years) approached and the bonds' option value expired. But these deadlines have not been a universal feature of settlement offers. In some cases there is still a market in their unassented bonds. Peru's 6 percent sterling bonds of 1928 illustrate the point. As of August 1987, the amounts outstanding included £51,600 in assented and £11,000 in unassented bonds. The assented bonds were last traded on the London market on 12 June 1987, the unassented bonds in 1976.

8. Securities and Exchange Commission (1937), pp.39–53.

9. See Jenks (1927) and Feis (1930), pp.114–115.

10. Minutes of the Council of the Corporation of Foreign Bondholders (hereinafter "Minutes"), Cooperation, 25/11/37. The document went on, "the debtor not infrequently managed to pay in all, less than he would have been willing to do had there been no difference of opinion among the Bondholders' Organizations."

11. Minutes, Ecuador, 14/3/40. Details on the provisions of the Brazilian settlement are provided in Eichengreen and Portes (1989).

12. Correspondence files of the Council of the Corporation of Foreign Bond-holders, Letter from Sir O.E. Niemeyer, 2/40, 241/1228.

13. Securities and Exchange Commission (1937), p. 31.

14. Minutes, Brazil, 27/10/36; Minutes, Brazil, 9/12/37.

15. Minutes, Brazil, 23/6/38.

16. Minutes, Brazil, 14/7/38.

17. Cited in Abreu (1978), p. 118.

18. Minutes, Foreign Loans, 24/2/38.

19. Securities and Exchange Commission (1938), p. 390.

20. Abreu (1978), p. 131.

21. Minutes, Egypt, 17/2/36; Minutes, Greece, 17/1/40. In both instances the Council successfully resisted the government's attempt to pressure it into immediate settlement. Still, official pressure in 1938–39 may have had something to do with the fact that both defaults were settled in 1940.

22. Minutes, Egypt, 16/3/37.

23. For example, between 1931 and 1934, when Chile was in total default on its long-term external debt, it negotiated with its principal short-term foreign creditor, National City Bank, a considerable reduction of the outstanding short-term debt. Securities and Exchange Commission (1937), p. 542.

24. Emphasis added. Minutes, Brazil, 7/11/38.

25. British purchasers would be required to pay for German goods by depositing the relevant amount of sterling in the clearing office. Exporters of goods to Germany would then be paid in sterling from the funds that accumulated in the clearing office. Any surplus that accumulated would be devoted to debt service. For further details, see Einzig (1935).

26. In 1934 partial interest was paid out of the accumulated funds in the hands of the trustees. Thereafter bondholders were paid in blocked Reichsmarks, and from October 1935 they were given the option of selling their coupons for up to 70 percent of their face value in cash. Meanwhile European investors in these loans received full service. See Foreign Bondholders Protective Council (1935), pp. 217–218 and subsequent volumes.

27. Atkin (1977), p. 264.

28. Minutes, Greece, 18/3/37; Minutes, Columbia, 14/7/38. Similarly, in response to CFBH efforts to link the discussions of a British trade mission to Colombia to negotiations over debt, the Board of Trade responded that "if we now pressed the Colombians to settle their foreign debt, they would insist on linking this question with the trade discussions and ... neither we nor the Trade Mission make any

headway." The Board urged the Council to wait for trade discussions to end before pursuing the debt question. Minutes, Colombia, 17/11/38.

29. Foreign Bondholders Protective Council (1934), p. 95.

30. Securities and Exchange Commission (1937), pp. 445–446.

31. Minutes, Greece, 17/1/40; Minutes, Peru, 13/6/40; Minutes, Brazil, 24/8/43.

32. Minutes, Greece, 18/3/37; Minutes, Bulgaria, 7/11/39.

33. The State Department protested German purchases of defaulted bonds in 1934 on these grounds. Securities and Exchange Commission (1937), pp. 312–13, 496.

34. Foreign Bondholders Protective Council (1935), p. 12.

35. Minutes, Guatemala, 22/9/38; Correspondence, Letter from Aranha to CFBH, 9/30/40, 241/1299; Minutes, Brazil, 14/3/40.

36. We make no attempt to distinguish the rate of return received by the original purchaser of the bond from the rate received by a subsequent investor to whom the bond might have been resold between issue and retirement. We adopt the collective perspective of the sequence of bondholders.

37. Detailed descriptions of the construction of these estimates are available in a pair of working papers: for the dollar bonds, Eichengreen and Werley (1988); for the sterling bonds, Portes (1987). Eichengreen and Portes (1988) contains a listing of each bond in the sample along with its ex ante and ex post internal rates of return.

38. Other sources included various issues of publications of A. Iselin and Co. (*Foreign Bonds Issued in the United States*), White, Weld, & Co. (*Foreign Dollar Bonds*), Moodys, Standard and Poors, and *Fitch's Bond Book*.

39. The assumption that domestic currency or scrip had a shadow value of zero is strong. In the case of Germany, such balances could be used for domestic travel or purchase of consumer goods but not to acquire real estate. It is hard to know the appropriate shadow exchange rate to impute to these balances. Fortunately, the impact on estimated rates of return is not pronounced. Eichengreen and Werley (1988) re-estimate the returns on dollar loans to Germany, imputing a shadow value of 0.5 to blocked balances, and find that the difference is minor.

40. Information on ex ante returns on dollar loans can be found in Eichengreen (1988).

41. Table 5, p. 627 of Eichengreen and Portes (1986) reports yields on alternative domestic investments. For example, U.S. yields ranged from over 4 percent on high grade domestic municipals to nearly 6 percent on Baa corporate bonds, while yields on British public debt ranged from 4 to $4\frac{1}{2}$ percent.

42. The difference is a function of the fact that our sample of dollar bonds contains only one Peruvian national issue.

43. Relaxation of earlier Bank of England regulation of the market designed to influence the direction of foreign lending may have played a role in the development of this pattern, as we suggest below.

44. For a parallel discussion, see Kuczynski (1932).

45. Feis (1950), p. 13.

46. For discussion, see Atkin (1977), ch. 2, and Moggridge (1974).

47. It is revealing that floation of poorly performing sterling loans that depressed the realized returns on British lending to Latin America were concentrated in the late l920s, in a period when the Bank of England was not intervening directly in the market.

References

Abreu, M. 1978. "Brazilian Public Foreign Debt Policy, 1931–1943." *Brazilian Economic Studies* 4, pp. 105–140.

Atkin, John Michael. 1977. *British Overseas Investment, 1918–1931.* New York: Arno Press.

Corporation of Foreign Bondholders. Various years. *Annual Report of the Council of the Corporation of Foreign Bondholders.* London: Corporation of Foreign Bondholders.

Díaz-Alejandro, Carlos. 1983. "Stories of the 1930s for the 1980s." In P. Aspe Armella, R. Dornbusch and M. Obstfeld (eds.), *Financial Policies and the World Capital Market: The Problem of the Latin American Countries.* Chicago: University of Chicago Press, pp. 5–40.

Eichengreen, Barry. 1988. "The U.S. Capital Market and Foreign Lending, 1920–1955." In Jeffrey Sachs (ed.), *Developing Country Debt and Economic Performance.* Chicago: University of Chicago Press.

Eichengreen, Barry. 1989. "Resolving Debt Crises: An Historical Perspective." In Sebastian Edwards and Felippe Larrain (eds.), *The Latin American Debt Crisis: Perspectives and Solution.* Oxford: Blackwell.

Eichengreen, Barry, and Richard Portes. 1986. "Debt and Default in the 1930s: Causes and Consequences." *European Economic Review* 30, pp. 599–640.

Eichengreen, Barry, and Richard Portes. 1987. "The Anatomy of Financial Crises," in Richard Portes and Alexander Swoboda (eds.), *Threats to International Financial Stability.* Cambridge: Cambridge University Press, pp. 10–58.

Eichengreen, Barry, and Richard Portes. 1988. "Foreign Lending in the Interwar Years: The Bondholders' Perspective." Institute of Business and Economic Research Working Paper no. 8856. University of California at Berkeley.

Eichengreen, Barry, and Richard Portes. 1989. "Settling Defaults in the Era of Bond Finance." *World Bank Economic Review* (forthcoming).

Eichengreen, Barry, and Carolyn Werley. 1988. "How the Bondholders Fared: Realized Rates of Return on Foreign Dollar Bonds Floated in the 1920s." Institute of Business and Economic Research Paper no. 8869. University of California at Berkeley.

Einzig, Paul. 1935. *The Exchange Clearing System*. London: Macmillan.

Ellis, Howard S. 1941. *Exchange Control in Central Europe*. Cambridge: Harvard University Press.

Feis, Herbert. 1930. *Europe, the World's Banker, 1870–1914*, New Haven: Yale University Press.

Feis, Herbert. 1950. *The Diplomacy of the Dollar: First Era, 1919–1932*. Baltimore: Johns Hopkins University Press.

Fishlow, Albert. 1985. "Lessons From the Past: Capital Markets during the 19th Century and the Interwar Period." In Miles Kahler (ed.), *The Politics of International Debt*. Ithaca: Cornell University Press, pp. 37–94.

Foreign Bondholders Protective Council. Various years. *Annual Report*. New York: Foreign Bondholders Protective Council.

Jenks, Leland H. 1927. *The Migration of British Capital to 1875*. Cambridge: Harvard University Press.

Kuczynski, Robert R. 1932. *Bankers' Profits from German Loans*. Washington, D.C.: The Brookings Insitution.

Maddison, Angus. 1985. *Two Crises: Latin America and Asia, 1929–38 and 1973–83*. Paris: OECD.

Mintz, Ilse. 1951. *Deterioration in the Quality of Foreign Bonds Issued in the United States, 1920–1930*. New York: National Bureau of Economic Research.

Moggridge, Donald. 1974. "British Controls on Long Term Capital Movements, 1924–1931." In Donald McCloskey (ed.), *Essays on a Mature Economy: Britain Since 1840*. Princeton: Princeton University Press, pp. 113–138.

Portes, Richard. 1987. "Rates of Return on Sterling Bonds Floated in 1921–1930." Unpublished manuscript. Birkbeck College, University of London.

Royal Institute of International Affairs. 1937. *The Problem of International Investment*. London: Oxford University Press.

Sachs, Jeffrey. 1986. "Managing the Debt Crisis." *Brookings Papers on Economic Activity* 2, pp. 397–431.

Schuker, Stephen A. 1988. "American "Reparations" to Germany, 1919–33: Implications for the Third-World Debt Crisis." *Princeton Studies in International Finance*, no, 61 (July).

Securities and Exchange Commission 1937. *Report on the Study and Investigation of the Work, Activities, Personnel and Functions of Protective and Reorganization Committees, Part V: Protective Committees and Agencies for Holders of Defaulted Foreign Bonds*. Washington, D.C.: GPO.

Young, Ralph A. 1931. *Handbook on American Underwriting of Foreign Securities*. Washington, D.C.: GPO.

3

Default and Renegotiation of Latin American Foreign Bonds in the Interwar Period

Erika Jorgensen and Jeffrey Sachs

A national bankruptcy is by no means illegal, and whether it is immoral or unwise depends altogether upon circumstances. One can hardly ask of the present generation that it alone shall suffer for the folly and waste of its predecessors, for otherwise in the end a country could hardly be inhabited because of the mass of its public debts.

Hugo, *Lehrbuch des Naturrechts*, Berlin, 1819).[1]

3.1. Introduction

The Latin American debt crisis of the 1980s has regenerated academic interest in the widespread bond defaults of the 1930s, an experience that seems to parallel recent events. The decade preceding each crisis witnessed a significant increase in lending to developing countries and to Latin America, in particular. Repayment difficulties were widespread and triggered mainly by external shocks, including sudden shifts in commodity prices and real interest rates and slump-induced reductions in demand by industrialized countries for developing countries' exports. There were ex post accusations of myopic behavior by international bankers, notably of a relaxation in credit standards, characterized by overly aggressive bond marketing in the 1920s or loan-pushing in the 1970s. When sovereign borrowers reneged on their loan contracts, creditors faced the expensive and time-consuming process of renegotiation.

The differences between these two eras are just as striking. The institutional arrangements of today's capital markets are far more sophisticated than in the 1920s as are the macroeconomic policy tools utilized by governments in the pursuit of stability. The existence of the International Monetary Fund as a referee for the extension of new credit is especially important in creating a cooperative environment for avoiding outright default. In addition the legal consequences of sovereign default have become more harsh since the 1930s.[2] Furthermore private-sector lending to sovereign entities today consists almost exclusively of syndicated bank loans instead of publicly floated bonds. For bondholders, debt moratorium simply means a capital loss. For the money-center banks, default on sovereign debt could mean failure, with unpredictable consequences on the international economy. Such default, however, may well be less likely than a bond default since potential defaults are more easily rescheduled with fewer creditors at the negotiating table. The difficulty in resolving interwar defaults was a reflection of the myriad of bondholders whose consent was required. Nevertheless, it was this very same dispersion that allowed final settlements to include partial debt forgiveness. Therefore, as an illustration of the process and consequences of negotiation and settlement, albeit in different institutional and legal environments, the interwar defaults of Latin America remain of great interest.

Historical parallels reach back much further than the 1930s. As one of us has written earlier, before the current debt crisis broke out:

The history of international capital movements since at least the early nineteenth century is characterized by large-scale borrowing of developing regions, and large-scale defaults. Many of the same debates over prudential standards, government guarantees of foreign loans, rescheduling of debt, and so forth, have been pursued for one-hundred-fifty years. And even many of the actors remain the same. A number of Latin American countries that are still among the most problematic for foreign loans first entered the London bond market upon independence in 1822–1825, and defaulted soon after, setting in train a hundred years of alternating solvency and default.[3]

Intermittent bond defaults were a normal cyclical occurrence for Latin America by the late nineteenth century. As a rule they were rapidly followed by settlement so that parties on both sides could get back to the business of shifting capital from Europe, especially Britain, to the periphery.[4] Because these default settlements involved the forced rewriting of loan contracts, some modern observers have suggested that they are directly comparable to today's multilateral reschedulings.[5] However, such a characterization obscures an essential component of the nineteenth-century bond settlements—substantial debt forgiveness.

In contrast to the nineteenth-century pattern, the defaults and subsequent negotiations of the interwar period were greatly disruptive to capital inflows to Latin America, with some bonds evading permanent settlement for decades. The general impression is that penalties for choosing to default in the 1930s were severe. Access to credit was, indeed, limited for decades following the numerous defaults, and capital flows of equivalent magnitude to those of the 1920s did not reappear until the 1970s. However, the aftermath of these bond defaults is not well understood. One question is whether exclusion from international borrowing was a consciously imposed penalty of default or whether the general breakdown of international capital markets accompanying (and somewhat preceding) the defaults of the Depression era, followed by the turmoil of World War II and the emergence of new international financial institutions, created this international capital immobility without discrimination. In an attempt to discover the existence and harshness of penalty imposed on interwar borrowers in Latin America, it seems sensible to start by comparing outcomes for defaulters to those for nondefaulters.

This chapter adds to recent investigations of the realized cost of foreign capital to individual sovereign borrowers[6] in Latin America and assesses the impact on that cost of choosing to default or not to default in the 1930s. A central emphasis of this analysis is the calculation of the extent of debt forgiveness implicit in the sequence of debt moratorium, anonymous buy-back of debt at deep discounts, and eventual renegotiation of the bond contracts. Argentina, Bolivia, Chile, Colombia, and Peru were selected as illustrative examples of borrowing behavior. Argentina was one of the few Latin American countries in the 1930s that maintained full servicing on its national debt; the other four countries mentioned joined the burgeoning ranks of sovereign defaulters.

By calculating the net present value of the stream of income and repayments on the dollar-denominated external government bonds of these countries, we show that defaulters and nondefaulters in Latin America had very different rates of loan repayment in present value terms. Argentina, the sole nondefaulter in our study, made substantially larger loan repayments in present value terms but was not rewarded by easier credit access in the postwar period. Furthermore it appears that interwar defaults, like those of the nineteenth century, resulted in eventual settlements of a *concessionary* nature, which we would characterize as new contracts written to share the burden of the unforeseen contingency that led to default.

Debt relief in present value terms came in three forms: first, the debtors anonymously repurchased bonds at deep discounts during default; second, the final settlements extended maturities and lowered interest rates; and, third, unpaid interest was *never capitalized*. However, principal was not canceled for any of the countries of this study. This kind of relief may well be mutually beneficial to creditors and debtors.[7] Default did not mean that the countries paid nothing. Many offered partial payments even during default, and after settlement, the countries resumed payment on a substantial scale. The defaulting countries repaid far less than full present value on their loans but far more than zero.

Section 3.2 provides some descriptive background on interwar lending to Latin America. Section 3.3 discusses the subsequent defaults of the 1930s, the extent of buy-backs of debt on the open market at deep discounts, and the terms under which final settlements were reached in the following decades. Section 3.4 presents results on the actual payments made by four Latin American defaulters and one nondefaulter over the lifetime of the relevant loans. The present value of receipts and payments by the country on its national and nationally guaranteed dollar bonds and the ratio of the present values of payments to principal provide alternative measures of the effective cost of lending from the creditor's point of view and indicate the ex post borrowing terms available to the Latin American states. Section 3.5 explores the longer-term repercussions of default, examining the flows of external finance to these countries in the 1950s and early 1960s when penalties of restricted credit access against defaulters might have been enforced. Finally, section 3.6 provides a summary of results and conclusions of relevance to the Latin American debt crisis of the 1980s.

3.2 Lending in the Interwar Period

Foreign lending to Latin America has a long history as predominantly private funds have been repeatedly channeled into the region in the forms of loans to governments or private enterprise, as well as equity capital. Each episode of substantial capital inflow has displayed a distinctive character but all have included some signs of failure of capital markets, the details of which bear lessons for present experience. The wave of lending through the nineteenth century to the newly independent Latin American states, mostly by Britain, exhibited a recurring pattern of lending, default, and settlement, with only moderate financial repercussions on the defaulters and, for the latter part of the period, no extended exclusion from international capital flows.[8]

The far shorter and more dramatic period of lending between the world wars witnessed the rise of New York as the dominant financial center and an acceleration of loans to governments in Latin America. Although the value of Latin America's gross external obligations never matched that of North America, Asia, or Continental Europe, its debt was highly concentrated in a few countries, especially Argentina and Brazil. Furthermore Latin America accounted for up to one quarter of new capital issues floated in the United States by foreign entities in the 1920s, borrowing over $2 billion in bonds on the New York market as well as accounting for almost half of American direct investment.[9] When the general speculative surge in financial markets collapsed in 1929, Latin American borrowers were pushed into widespread default as the world economy tumbled into depression. However, it should be remembered that in contrast to Latin American repayment difficulties of the 1980s, Latin American defaults in the interwar period were but a footnote to defaults by larger European borrowers and the breakdown of international markets.

World War I marks a significant break from the previous pattern of international finance. The United States emerged as a net creditor, while Britain's lending subsided in response to its declining savings rate. The overall level of international capital flows, however, never recovered to that of its heyday in the period 1870 to 1914; flows of real private investment between 1914 and 1930 were only two-thirds as great as between 1900 and 1913.[10] Furthermore, during the interwar period, developmental finance for the periphery was overshadowed by lending between the industrialized countries for reconstruction and servicing of war debts.

The lending of the interwar period, primarily in the 1920s, created a new pattern of large capital flows going to sovereign debtors (rather than to the private foreign debtors more important in nineteenth-century lending). The new central actor, the United States, responding to the relatively long and defaultless boom period of the 1920s, provided rapidly rising flows to Latin America, peaking in 1927 and 1928, then dropping off in 1929 as U.S. domestic asset returns peaked, declining sharply as a result of the 1929 stock market crash and trailing off to zero by 1931.

After the end of World War I, the United States had stepped up its investment flows to Latin America in response to improved economic opportunities. Some Latin American countries had used wartime semi-autarky as a chance to expand industrialization. As export prices rose after the war, the borrowers' debt-servicing capacity improved. Both the Latin American governments and U.S. investors were eager for foreign investment. Between 1914 and 1919 U.S. investment in Latin America increased by half, and over the next decade, 1919 to 1929, it doubled from its 1919 level.[11] Between 1925 and 1929 net long-run capital flow from the United States was $200 million per year on average. In real terms, this flow to Latin America probably exceeded the previous levels reached by British capital in the decade preceding World War I, although it should be noted that American lending was a far smaller share of the U.S.'s current account surplus[12] and of its income[13] than Britain's in the half century before World War I.[14]

The principal borrowers in the early 1920s were the national governments of the stronger countries such as Argentina, Brazil, Chile, and Cuba. As the boom in public borrowing in the New York bond market grew over the course of the decade, riskier countries and numerous political subdivisions—provinces, departments, and municipalities—also found it possible to sell their bonds to American investors.[15] Between 1920 and 1929 foreign dollar bonds issued by Latin American countries totaled $2.2 billion of which $1.3 billion was owed by national governments.[16] However, flotation of securities remained primarily a South American phenomenon (with the exception of Cuba). Venezuela bucked the trend and chose instead to retire all external debt with the aid of petroleum royalties, while Mexico and Ecuador were unable to float bonds, suffering from impaired credit standings arising from recent and unsettled defaults. Fourteen Latin American countries did issue dollar bonds by the end of the decade.

These capital flows were equally significant from the perspective of the foreign lending operations of the New York market.[17] Between 1924 and 1928 Latin American security issues constituted 24 percent of all new foreign bonds in the U.S. market. In addition 44 percent of all direct investment between 1925 and 1929 went to Latin America. Meanwhile other lenders had shifted away from the region. Britain continued to accept new flotations in London, mainly to finance railroads, in the amount of £132 million ($650 million) between 1924 and 1930, but this gross flow was offset by large amortizations of old bonds and the sale of assets to Latin American nationals.[18] By the end of the decade Britain and the United States, the two major foreign investors, had together accumulated a stock of investment claims of all types equivalent to four times the value of exports for Latin America as a whole while the ratio of long-term external public debt to exports stood at 1.49. The ratio of the stock of all British and U.S. investments to annual merchandise exports in the late 1920s was[19]

Argentina: 2.8

Bolivia: 3.3

Chile: 3.9

Colombia: 2.4

Peru: 2.7

This level of debt burden was not to be reached again until the 1970s, but in recent years it has been far surpassed. The changing pattern of debt burdens from 1920 to 1945 can be observed in the debt ratios of Table 3.1.

Table 3.1
Foreign debt stocks and debt burdens, 1920–45 (millions of U.S. $)

	Exports	Total public debt stock	Debt ratio (%)	Dollar bond stock	Bond ratio (%)	Dollar bond interest	Interest ratio (%)
1920							
Argentina	1,013	247	24	0	0	0	0
Bolivia	50	4	8	2	4	0	0
Chile	289	137	48	0	0	0	0
Colombia	69	24	35	0	0	0	0
Peru	172	14	8	0	0	0	0
1925							
Argentina	793	382	48	144	18	6	1
Bolivia	41	32	79	29	70	2	6
Chile	229	152	66	38	17	3	1
Colombia	83	17	21	0	0	0	0
Peru	87	30	34	0	0	0	0
1930							
Argentina	875	402	46	273	31	17	2
Bolivia	26	62	237	59	226	4	17
Chile	277	334	121	264	95	16	6
Colombia	172	75	44	72	42	4	3
Peru	139	106	76	90	65	6	4
1935							
Argentina	501	420	84	237	47	15	3
Bolivia	36	62	172	59	166	4	12
Chile	96	329	343	243	254	15	16
Colombia	70	81	116	65	93	4	6
Peru	75	99	131	83	110	5	7
1940							
Argentina	428	354	83	147	34	6	1
Bolivia	49	61	123	59	120	4	9
Chile	140	288	206	157	112	10	7
Colombia	71	75	106	53	74	3	4
Peru	65	97	150	83	127	5	8

Table 3.1 (continued)

	Exports	Total public debt stock	Debt ratio (%)	Dollar bond stock	Bond ratio (%)	Dollar bond interest	Interest ratio (%)
1945							
Argentina	682	159	23	124	18	3	0
Bolivia	80	61	75	59	74	4	5
Chile	205	320	156	140	68	9	4
Colombia	141	87	61	53	37	2	1
Peru	104	96	93	83	80	5	5

Sources: Exports for 1920–25 from Wilkie (1974), 1930–45 from Wilkie (1980). Total debt stock from United Nations (1948).

Notes: Exports are current value of goods and services, including gold for Bolivia and Chile. Ratios are of debt or interest to exports. Total public debt stock is generally all foreign obligations of the national government, sometimes including short-term debts:

1920 value for Colombia is actually 1922.

1935 values are actually 1936 value for Bolivia and 1937 for Colombia and Peru.

1945 values for Bolivia and Colombia are actually 1944.

Colombia 1935, 1940, and 1945 include interest certificates issued in lieu of interest payments for some obligations; 1945 includes some nonguaranteed corporate bank bonds taken over by the government in 1942. Argentina 1940 reflects the redemption of $81 million of dollar debt in 1936–37, matched by an $87 million increase in domestic debt; also in 1945–46, $140 million of dollar debt was redeemed, financed out of reserves and new domestic debt.

Conversion of debt from NCU to $ using exchange rates in UNPD:

Argentina: end-of-year rates

Bolivia: actual conversion rate

Colombia: for 1920–35, parity rates; for 1940–45, parity rates for bearer bonds, and end-of-year rates for other obligations

Chile: parity rates

Peru: parity rates

Dollar bond stock is nationally guaranteed issues only. Dollar bond interest is contractual interest owned on outstanding dollar bonds.

What is most striking is the relatively modest size by today's standards of both debt stock and debt servicing to exports throughout the period.

During this decade capital markets became increasingly accessible and generous to Latin American borrowers as the United States, and Britain to a lesser extent, provided substantial long-term funds. As overseas issues crowded the New York market, the issuing houses set up extensive branch networks that successfully marketed the bonds to individual investors, eager for the large premia they offered over domestic returns. The investment climate seemed much improved over the past, claimed Madden, Nadler, and Sauvain in their 1937 review of America's overseas lending. During previous lending episodes, foreign bond defaults had been numerous, and direct investment often generated tension. In the 1920s virtually no defaults occurred on the over 800 foreign bonds issued in the United States nor on non-American lending.

As long as the capital markets of the world were willing to absorb new foreign issues and debtors could continue to borrow, there was no transfer problem, and hence no occasion for suspending external debt service.[20]

After the fact of widespread default on these loans, the U.S. Senate inquiry committee of 1932, as well as many contemporary observers, blamed excessive enthusiasm by the American investment houses and accused them of violating the principles of business ethics, utilizing such selling methods as permanently stationed overseas representatives, deceptive prospectuses, and bribery of foreign government officials. Fishlow (1985, p. 423) believes the real blame lies with a combination of the speculative surge occurring in all U.S. asset markets and the strong competition for overseas loans that New York faced from London, reflected in falling commissions and risk premia as the 1920s progressed. Mintz (1951) adds that bond quality deteriorated over the three successively higher waves of financial activity of 1921 to 1929 (as measured ex post by rates of default), but investor confidence grew. The long absence of default encouraged an illusion of safety and ever more optimistic projections by bankers whose techniques of risk analysis were understandably unable to predict a crash.

The average nominal yield to maturity on Latin America's dollar bond issues ranged from 8 percent in 1921 to 6.3 percent in 1928, consistently above the yield on U.S. high-grade corporate bonds. In addition the borrowers paid an average of 4 percent bankers' commission on top of an average initial sale discount of 3 percent.[21] For the five countries of this study, the average yield at time of issue on national and nationally guaranteed bonds during the 1920s ranged from 6.2 percent for Argentina to 7.6 percent for Bolivia (see table 3.6). The annual average for the five countries together varied from 8 to 99 basis points above the U.S. low-grade (Baa) corporate rate (except for in 1923 and 1924 when only Argentina issued bonds and at rates 99 and 47 points below the Baa rate). It is interesting to note that risk premia paid by these borrowers did not fall significantly through the decade. In fact, premia over the U.S. Baa rate of yields at date of issue rose up to 1927 and then fell slightly from 1927 to 1930 as lending slackened. This pattern is most dramatic for Argentina whose premium rose from 99 basis points below the Baa rate in 1923 to 60 points above in 1927. Only Colombia, borrowing in 1926 to 1928, maintained decreasing premia over all years (from 172 to 116 to 91 extra points).

The rising amounts of sovereign debt claims, a higher proportion of which were short term and all of which were issued at higher interest rates than pre-war loans, left the borrowing countries heavily dependent on revolving credit and the continuous rollover of debt. The international capital market improved over the course of the 1920s in its ability to funnel investment funds from creditor countries to debtors, but even at the time, there were signs of the precariousness of existing international financial arrangements as compared to those pre-war. The high average rates charged on overseas loans required equivalent returns on actual use of the funds and eventual higher export growth to enable repayment.

3.3   Default Experience and the Terms of Final Agreements

The business recession beginning in 1929 severely undercut the ability of foreign debtors to provide funds for debt service in their own currency and to transfer those funds into the currencies of their creditors. Both budget and balance-of-payments difficulties arose as export prices, as well as volumes, began to fall and as the joint effects of protection, depression, and the closing of international capital markets devastated both trade and government revenues (most of which were trade-related taxes such as import duties). The 25 percent fall in the U.S. price level between 1928 and 1932 was accompanied by a fall in world commodity prices that pushed up the cost of debt servicing in real terms. The 30 to 40 percent fall in the prices of coffee, petroleum, wheat, and tin created serious difficulties for Colombia, Peru, Argentina, and Bolivia.[22] Ratios of public debt service to exports rose dramatically for all of these countries in the first few years of the 1930s. Avramovic (1964, p. 46) provides data on these ratios of public debt service, actual or scheduled (if default occurred), as a proportion of exports:

Year	Argentina	Bolivia	Chile	Colombia	Peru
1926	10.0	7.3	5.5	2.7	2.6
1927	7.9	6.1	8.7	4.4	3.2
1928	8.9	8.5	9.5	8.1	6.0
1929	10.4	7.8	9.2	11.9	7.4
1930	18.2	13.5	18.0	14.0	9.5
1931	22.5	24.5	32.9	15.6	16.3
1932	27.6	50.0	102.6	21.8	21.4
1933	30.2	38.5	81.9	29.6	21.7

Also see table 3.1 for other debt burden ratios 1920 to 1945.

More important, the collapse of international financial markets eliminated the normal rollover of debt so that debt service obligations exceeded the value of new lending and net capital began to flow out of the region. In addition, during the active lending of the 1920s, many debtor countries came to rely on new external loans to provide foreign exchange to enable them to meet their foreign currency interest payments, supplementing that acquired through export trade.[23] The "crossover point" of annual payment obligations surpassing new investment flows was reached before defaults occurred and so cannot be interpreted simply as a reaction by creditors to unanticipated defaults.[24] See figures 3.1 through 3.5 for the crossover points for dollar borrowings. Instead, the cutoff of new lending may have encouraged debtor countries to consider defaulting since a crucial part of the penalty of default is the refusal of further credit.[25] These countries were left with greatly increased burdens of debt but severely reduced means of payment and no available instrument for international settlement through negotiation to substitute for default.

The first default was by Bolivia in January 1931, after its failure to meet sinking fund payments in December 1930. See tables 3.2 through 3.5 for summaries of the debt histories of the defaulting countries of this study. When payments stopped, the U.S. fiscal agent for the issue (who cashed the bond's coupons as they came due with funds provided by the debtor) then declared it to be in default and the bond contracts to be broken. Peru followed suit soon after in April as did Peruvian provincial and municipal

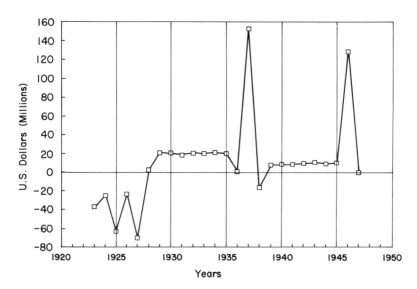

Figure 3.1
Argentina: nominal net payments on dollar bonds

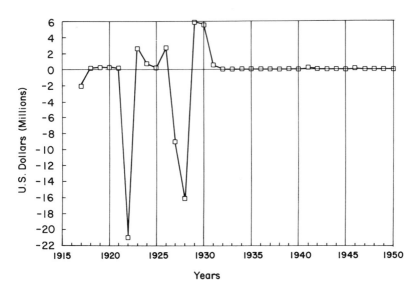

Figure 3.2
Bolivia: nominal net payments on dollar bonds

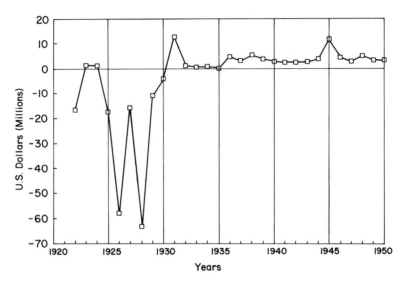

Figure 3.3
Chile: nominal net payments on dollar bonds

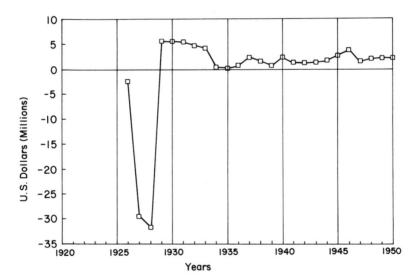

Figure 3.4
Colombia: nominal net payments on dollar bonds

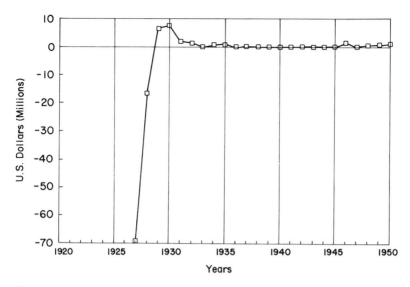

Figure 3.5
Peru: nominal net payments on dollar bonds

governments. Chile succumbed to the combined pressures of revolution
and a severe slump in the nitrate and copper industries in August, breaking
its long record of compliance with external obligations. The government
imposed exchange restrictions preventing the transfer of funds abroad,
forcing the default of Chilean nonnational debt as well. All three of these
countries defaulted following political upheaval and the institution of revolutionary governments who tended to place a low priority on the maintenance of a good credit standing. Once the ice was broken, however,
defaults by other Latin American countries (and by European borrowers)
followed in rapid succession. By 1934 only Argentina, Haiti, and the
Dominican Republic, out of all the Latin American states, had not suspended normal debt servicing.[26]

Default was made easier by its very commonness. The failure of the entire system
went far beyond the capacity of individual bankers to ameliorate, and none tried
.... Capital markets were essentially closed to long-term movements and only
functioned to sustain short-term flight to the United States, providing little incentive for conformity with the rules.[27]

The loan contracts of the defaulted bond issues technically guaranteed
against loss of principal or interest, usually by pledging the "good faith and
credit" of the government as well as by the common inclusion of a security

Table 3.2
Bolivia's history of borrowing, default, and settlement

1917	Republic bond issue of $2.4 million at 6% due 1940	1958	Publication of 1958 plan with interest at 1%, rising to 3% by 1963. Maturity extended to 1993, and 5% of interest arrears to be capitalized by increasing par value of each $1,000 by $100. Starting in 1962, to be exchanged for new bonds with sinking fund provisions. FBPC recommends approval. Full interest of 1.5% on all 4 issues
1922	Republic bond issue of $29 million at 8% due 1947		
1927	Republic bond issue of $14 million at 7% due 1958		
1928	Republic bond issue of $23 million at 7% due 1969		
1930	Default on sinking fund in December		
1931	Default on interest in January; partial interest of 2% paid on 1922 s8	1959	Full interest payments of 1%
		1960	Remittances under 1958 plan cease in July. Full interest of 1.5% paid on 1927 s7. Partial interest of 0.75% paid on other issues
1940	Default on principal of 1917 s6 issue		
1941	Partial interest of 1% paid on 1922 s8		
1946	Partial interest of 0.5% paid on 1922 s8	1961	July announcement of reduced coupon payments in 1962–63 but assurances of speedy return to compliance. Over 70% of bonds outstanding stamped (accepting 1958 plan)
1947	Default on principal of 1922 s8 issue		
1948	Presidential proposal of reduced interest payments at 1%, rising to 3% by 1955. $100 of interest arrears per $1,000 bond to be capitalized in new bonds. FBPC gives provisional recommendation of approval. Partial interest of 0.2% paid on 1922 s8	1962–64	Fail to deliver new bonds. Promise to issue in 1965. Partial interest paid of 0.75% in 1962 and 1963 and of 1.75% in 1964
		1966	Proposal for delivery of new bonds
1950	Bolivian Congress approves 1948 debt plan, scheduled to commence in 1951 but never carried out by executive	1969	Begin exchange for new issue and resume adjusted service at 3% but with no provision for any arrears. $62 million outstanding
1955	Token interest payment of 0.5% paid on 1922 s8	1970	Partial interest of 1.1% paid on stamped bonds of all four original issues
1957	June announcement of new plan of service following prolonged negotiations with FBPC	1985	$47 million outstanding

Table 3.3
Chile's history of borrowing, default, and settlement

1922	Republic bond issue of $18 million at 7%		industries into Amortization Institute to service foreign debt. Reduced coupon payments to be announced each January, available only to bonds stamped in agreement with the law. FBPC recommends refusal.
1925	Guaranteed Mortgage Bank issue of $20 million at 6.5%		
1926	Republic bond issue of $42.5 million at 6%; guaranteed Mortgage Bank issue of $20 million at 6.75%; guaranteed Mortgage Bank issue of $10 million at 6%	1935	Law 5580 enacted
1927	Republic bond issue of $27.5 million at 6%	1936–39	Partial interest payments, averaging 1.25% per annum paid on stamped bonds
1928	Republic January bond issue of $45.9 million at 6%; Republic March bond issue of $16 million at 6%; Guaranteed Mortgage Bank issue of $20 million at 6%	1940	By January over 80% of national and guaranteed issues are stamped. December decree transfers $6 million away from debt payment but promises Chile will return to provisions of Law 5580.
1929	Republic bond issue of $10 million at 6%; guaranteed Mortgage Bank issue of $20 million at 6%	1942	Law 7160 passed, setting extra tax on copper companies, depleting funds available for debt servicing
1930	Republic bond issue of $25 million at 6%		
1931	Default begins in August with failure to pay on interest and sinking fund for Republic 1927 6s issue; other issues follow in turn	1948	Law 8962 replaces Law 5580, providing an issue of 1948 New Bonds with 46-year maturity to consolidate all dollar bond issues by exchange at par. Interest to be at 1.5% in 1948, rising to 3% by 1954. All payments under Law 5580 to be available as 10-year scrip. FBPC recommends acceptance.
1932	Nonguaranteed municipal dollar bonds default		
1934	Resumption of service on trade obligations. In October, Law 5580 passed setting aside all government revenues from copper and nitrate		

Table 3.4
Colombia's history of borrowing, default, and settlement

Year	Event	Year	Event
1926	Agricultural Mortgage Bank issues nationally guaranteed $3 million at 7%	1941	Decree 1388 offers settlement plan for Republic issues. Old issues to be exchanged at par for new 3% bonds due 1970 with convertible certificates for half of interest arrears from 1935–59. FBPC recommended refusal.
1927	Republic issues $25 million at 6%; Mortgage Bank issues $3 million at 7% and $5 million at 6%		
1928	Republic issues $35 million at 6%; Mortgage Bank issues $5 million. at 6%	1942	Redeemed new bonds offered out in exchange for Mortgage Bank issues under same conditions except only 20% of arrears covered and for nonguaranteed mortgage bond issues for 75% of face value and no allowance for interest arrears. Government reports that half of all mortgage bonds were repurchased during default.
1931	Some nonguaranteed municipal and departmental issues default		
1932	More municipal and departmental issues default; Mortgage Bank issues default on sinking fund		
1933	Mortgage Bank issues default on interest; Republic issues default on both		
1934	Two coupons on 1927 6s and one on 1928 6s paid $\frac{1}{3}$ cash (giving 2% and 1% payments) and $\frac{2}{3}$ scrip (redeemed for cash in 1937)	1944	Same offer extended to a municipal issue, again using redeemed new bonds and with all past interest canceled. Government reports 60% of issue had been repurchased. Another municipal issue reaches independent settlement.
1936	Payments of full annual interest on Republic issues in 4% scrip (redeemed in 1946)	1945	Only 10% of Republic issues remain unexchanged
1940	Payments of half of annual interest on Republic issues upon surrender of both coupons; government turned in $6 million in bonds purchased in the market since 1933	1949	Departmental and other municipal issues settled by exchange at 120% of face value for a new nationally guaranteed 3% issue. Government reports almost 50% of these issues had been repurchased.

Table 3.5
Peru's history of borrowing, default, and settlement

1927 Republic issues $15 million at 7% and $50 million at 6%; province of Callao issues nationally guaranteed $1.5 million at 7.5%	1945 Bill introduced to Congress but never passed, proposing settlement with interest at 1%, rising to 3% by 1950, sinking fund payments at 0.5% per annum, and all arrears to be canceled
1928 Republic issues $25 million at 6%; city of Lima issues nonguaranteed $3 million at 6.5%	
1931 Republic issues default on both interest and sinking fund payments	1947 Law 10832 authorizes government to resume payment on dollar and sterling bonds by issuing Series Exchange Bonds due 1997, one series for each of the Republic and Callao issues and one for two sterling issues, paying interest of 1% for 1947–48, 2.5% thereafter. All arrears to be cancelled. FBPC recommends refusal
1932 Provincial and municipal issues default	
1936 Government includes budget item for debt service at 0.5% but funds not transferred to fiscal agent	
1937 Payment of partial interest on Republic issues of 0.5%	
1940 Settlement reached on short-term dollar credits with payment of all arrears and interest reduced from 6% to 2%	1951 New plan announced. As of 1953, a new set of exchange bonds due 1997 to replace 1947 series for Republic and Callao and providing new series for Lima issue, all paying 3% interest and with noninterest-bearing scrip for 10% of arrears of 1931–46
1941 FBPC takes over negotiations (upon disbandment of rival bondholders' committee); Peru offers settlement on "Mexican basis" of one Peruvian sol per dollar	1954 1951 offer extended to 1947 series for sterling bonds

clause assigning specific government revenues or properties to the fulfill-ment of the stipulated servicing.[28] However, when defaults occurred, it turned out that these guarantees were meaningless. The relevant assets were rarely within reach of the creditors. Bondholders were faced with the difficult problem of a sovereign debtor, with the rights and powers of a state, unable to be sued without its consent and over whom foreign creditors had negligible legal influence. The U.S. government refused to employ economic sanctions or to claim redress on behalf of its nationals, leaving bondholders with only negotiation through privately formed com-mittees as a means of arranging resumption of payments.[29]

Furthermore, defaulting countries gained the advantages of being able to write off part of their debt through favorable readjustment plans in the future as well as the possibility of substantial buy-backs of debt at a con-siderable discount since the uncertainty of default depressed bond prices by

75 percent or more.[30] The debtor would repurchase its own bonds in the open market at a price less than 100, a procedure sometimes allowed under the original bond contract. For example, of the 36 bonds considered in this study, 23 of the contracts allowed such redemptions at market prices. After default, with those contracts broken, countries engaged in this practice whether previously allowed or not.

Table 3.6 summarizes the experience of the five debtors during default, presenting estimates of buy-backs at deeply discounted prices in the period between the original abrogation of the bond contracts and the date of final and binding settlement. Peru was most active in this process, purchasing 31 percent of the principal outstanding at default at an average price of 21 cents on the dollar. About one-fourth of these buy-backs occurred in the early years of default, but most took place in the late 1940s during the period of its unilateral offer to bondholders (at an average price of 22 cents). Colombia repurchased a smaller percentage, but over a shorter period, and is the only country directly accused by the Foreign Bondholders Protective Council, the negotiating body representing American bondholders, of encouraging a low market price for its debt for the purpose of discounted redemption.[31] Chile too bought back a significant amount of its debt, with about one-third occurring in the first few years of default. The Chilean government's sense of timing must have been less keen than that of Peru or Colombia because the effective discount was only 41 percent. The same might be said of Bolivia's government who failed to take advantage of the shockingly low prices to which their debt sank in the 1930s, repurchasing almost none. The net effect of this generally unobserved and uncontrollable activity on the part of debtors was to lighten the burden of debt before or during negotiations on adjusted service.[32]

Argentina stands out as the only major Latin American debtor to abide by its original bond agreements and continue full service on its national debt. Díaz-Alejandro (1983) argues that Argentina chose not to default on its bonds because of the overriding importance of its export dependency on Britain whose financial institutions used their considerable political clout to force an agreement upon Argentina. The notorious Roca-Runciman Treaty of 1933 provided limited guarantees for Argentine exports in return for onerous concessions, including continued debt service payments. The government must have believed that any tampering with debt service was sure to be commercially and politically costly. But it seems that continued servicing also had high political costs. The external economic pressures on Argentina were "additional causes of xenophobic antagonisms toward the very visible control that foreigners held over vital segments of the national

Table 3.6
National and nationally guaranteed dollar bonds issued in the 1920s: buybacks during default

Country	Value of bonds issued (principal received)	Years issued (interest rate; Baa pemium)	Amount outstanding at default (year of default; of final settlement)	Amount bought during default (average price)	As percent of outstanding at default
Argentina 10 issues	$290 M All nat'l. ($269 M)	1923–28 (6.16%; −4)			
Bolivia 4 issues	$68 M All nat'l. ($63 M)	1917–28 (7.55%; +304)	$59 M (1931; 1969)	$3 M (16)	5%
Chile 12 issues	$275 M 185 nat'l. 90 guar. ($255 M)	1922–30 (6.58%; +159)	$261 M (1931; 1948)	$46 M (59)	18%
Colombia 6 issues	$76 M 60 nat'l. 16 guar. ($69 M)	1926–28 (6.55%; +94)	$64 M (1932; 1941)	$14 M (22) $8 M nat'l (18) $7 M guar. (27)	22% 15% of nat'l. 53% of guar.

Table 3.6 (continued)

Country	Value of bonds issued (principal received)	Years issued (interest rate; Baa premium)	Amount outstanding at default (year of default; of final settlement)	Amount bought during default (average price)	As percent of outstanding at default
Peru	$92 M	1927–28	$88 M	$27 M	31%
4 issues	90 nat'l.	(6.77%; + 129)	(1931; 1953)	(21)	
	2 guar.			of which $12 M from original issues	of which 14% from original issues repurchased 1931–46
	($79 M)			(19);	
				$15 M from 1947 Exchange bonds	17% from 1947 exchange bonds repurchased 1947–52
				(22)	

Sources: Foreign Bondholders Protective Council, various vols.; authors' estimates.

Notes: Nat'l = bonds issued by the national government; guar. = bonds guaranteed by the national government. Interest rate = average of yields to maturity at issue dates weighted by principal issued. Baa premium = average premium over the U.S. Baa corporate rate in basis points in years of issue. Bolivia had buybacks in 1957 only. Colombia defaulted on sinking fund payments of its guaranteed issues in 1932, on interest payments of these issues in 1933, and on sinking fund and interest payments of its national issues in 1933. Final settlement was reached on its national issues in 1941 and on the guaranteed issues in 1942. As a result its buy-backs include 1933–40 for its national issues (with the addition of $14,500 retired in 1941) and 1932–41 for its guaranteed issues.

economy"[33] According to Mallon and Sourrouille, such antagonisms were crucial in the subsequent rise of Peron.

By the late 1930s many countries' ability to service their debt had markedly improved. Many governments had made unilateral offers of readjusted service which, depending on their terms, a number of bond-holders had accepted. Such acceptance gained the creditor some immediate coupon payments but at the risk of nullifying the original legal commitment and lessening pressure on the borrower. For example, Colombia's unilateral offer of 1941, rejected by the Council, was never superceded by another agreement. Insufficient pressure by the bondholders, most of whom accepted the offer from the start, or anyone else, left the Republic with no incentive to increase servicing. Bondholders indicated their approval of the new contract for repayment and the dissolution of the old by having their bonds stamped appropriately by the fiscal agent who would mark them as assenting or by exchanging the old bond certificates for new ones with the amended servicing obligations. Payments on coupons would then begin according to the new contract. Most of these offers were adhered to by the debtors (who had, after all, dictated their terms). However, even unilateral offers could break down. In 1940, Chile regretfully admitted that it had reneged on the terms of its 1935 offer by diverting funds away from promised payments but continued to do so at an increasing rate, adding to the pressure for it to make a new offer of servicing.

With the added advantage of having bought back some portion of their outstanding debt at well below par in foreign markets, the Latin American defaulters became disposed to negotiate a formal settlement (to replace the often confusing series of unilateral offers) with Britain's Corporation of Foreign Bondholders (established in 1868) or the new U.S. Foreign Bond-holders Protective Council (established in 1933), both private bondholders' committees. Readjustments were not negotiated by the issuing houses involved because of potential conflict of interest. Instead, the two private committees emerged. Britain's Corporation was an experienced and respected institution by the interwar period, whereas the U.S. Council served to replace a long series of ad hoc and sometimes competing bondholders' negotiating committees.[34] However, "in the absence of the lure of future capital flows (and the threat of their blockage) the power of the U.S. Bondholders Protective Council was nil," claims Fishlow (1985, p, 429). Perhaps as a result of this limited bargaining power, discussions with debtors tended to revolve around the debtor's "capacity to pay," a phrase signifying the appropriate degree of debt forgiveness since the result was generally the consolidation and extension of existing debt with significant reductions in interest and extensions of maturities, with some modicum of recognition paid to interest arrears. After a readjustment plan was agreed upon by both debtor government and bondholders' committee, bondholders were individually free to accept or reject the settlement, but once the committee accepted a plan and ceased negotiating, further concessions from the debtor became unlikely.

In some cases outside inducements assisted the negotiating process. In the post-1945 period the new International Bank for Reconstruction and Development would not lend to countries technically in default, a policy that in the immediate postwar years hit Latin America hardest. Chile had made a unilateral and ungenerous offer to holders of its defaulted issues in 1935 but then failed to uphold even its undemanding terms, to the continuing dismay of the U.S. Council. It was not until Chile made an application for a $40 million loan from the IBRD in 1946 that it saw fit to renegotiate a more lasting debt readjustment plan. The Bank's policy on outstanding default was to take the country's attitude into consideration but not to play an intermediary role nor to disqualify the borrower as long as some sort of settlement had been reached.[35] Nevertheless, its pressure on Chile to offer a plan acceptable to its bondholders was sufficient to elicit a new plan in 1948 that the U.S. Council could see fit to recommend. The day after Chile announced its settlement, the IBRD announced its approval of a $16 million loan to Chile. The Chilean settlement provided new 46-year bonds in exchange for national, Mortgage Bank, and municipal external bonds. Interest arrears were to be compensated as arranged under the earlier plan that had provided variable annual payments averaging 20 percent of the past interest due since 1935 (with no capitalization). Current and future interest, originally contracted at 6 to 7 percent, would be paid at a rate of 1.5 percent in 1948, rising to 3 percent in 1954. By comparison, the yield on U.S. Baa corporate bonds in 1948 was 3.47 percent. Most of the old bonds had been due in the early 1960s so the adjustment of maturity to 1993 represented a 30-year extension.

The terms of individual agreements varied. But, in general, the ones that lasted were the result of negotiations with the bondholder organizations, and they provided interest rate reductions ranging from 50 to 70 percent of the original rate (leaving a new rate of 3 percent in most cases) and extensions of maturities by 20 to 30 years. In general, a partial payment for unpaid interest was offered, summed without capitalization, often in the form of extra bonds. Chile, Colombia, and Peru achieved settlements of this type in 1948, 1941, and 1953, respectively. The maturity of Peru's debt was stretched out to 50 years, whereas Colombia's was only 30 years. Chile's settlement included payment of about 12 percent of its unpaid interest since default, Colombia's included about 20 percent, and Peru's included about 15 percent. In 1958, after many failed attempts, Bolivia reached a more forgiving arrangement, involving a 35-year extension of maturity, a 3 percent interest rate, and provisions to pay less than 8 percent of accumulated unpaid interest.

It is interesting to note that the longer a debtor held out, the better it fared in the conditions of settlement. Colombia settled unilaterally, but early and so paid more. Overall, the level of debt forgiveness involved in these settlements was clearly substantial. The yield on U.S. Baa corporate bonds ranged from 4.3 percent in 1941 to 3.5 percent in 1948 to 3.7 percent in 1953 and 4.7 percent in 1958.[36] Thus the new contracts for the defaulting countries provided finance at less than the U.S. Baa market yield, whereas the original contracts yielded consistently more than these rates.

The final settlements achieved by these interwar defaulting debtors, after long and tangled negotiations and many false starts, can be characterized as containing a realistic element of debt forgiveness. With an acceptable agreement in hand, countries could return to paths of growth and development unhindered by an excessive overhang of debt. By 1945 the ratio of the stock of public external debt to yearly exports for Latin America as a whole had declined substantially to 0.77,[37] benefiting from the combined effects of the recovery of international trade and the widespread practice of repurchasing bonds below par.

3.4   Estimating the Extent of Default and Debt Forgiveness

In this section we estimate the extent to which the debtor countries reduced the burden of debt servicing via suspension of debt payments, repurchases, and renegotiation of debt contracts. To measure the extent to which debtors escaped the burden of debt servicing, we calculate the nominal present value of the borrowing and net repayments of bonds issued in the 1920s and 1930s for several Latin American countries. This measure is calculated using all of the long-term nationally guaranteed bond debt issued in dollars and outstanding through the 1930s for five Latin American countries: Argentina, Bolivia, Chile, Colombia, and Peru. A comparison of these measures for defaulters and nondefaulters will indicate the effective level of debt forgiveness inherent in the process of default and settlement, as well as the direct ex post benefits of choosing default.[38]

All nationally guaranteed dollar bonds issued after 1920 were included,[39] each issue being tracked from the date of issue until redemption (or 1980). Dollar debt in the form of bonds constitutes the majority of public debt for all of these countries, and the debt of the central or national governments is usually the dominant component of total foreign debt.

Dominick and Dominick, a New York investment house, published a compilation of all foreign loans issued in the United States and still outstanding in 1936. These listings provided information on principal amount, issue price, and contract provisions for the sinking fund. The bonds were then followed from year to year, using a variety of sources[40] to obtain data on prices, amount of the principal outstanding at year's end, interruptions of contractual payments on interest or principal, and the conditions of subsequent resumption of servicing. In all, the bonds followed consisted of 14 Argentine bonds on which no default occurred and 4 Bolivian, 12 Chilean, 6 Colombian, and 4 Peruvian issues, all of which experienced default, as well as the exchange bonds offered by each defaulting country as part of its default settlement.

For each bond, information on market prices, on contractual interest obligations, and on amounts outstanding for each year was combined to generate estimates of annual payments of interest and principal. We assume that principal payments were made at market prices when sinking funds allowed repurchase at prices below par or when unrecorded buy-backs occurred. Information on the extent and terms of debt buy-backs is problematic only for the first few years after the onset of default. Almost all of the original contracts allowed repurchases at market value, and prior to default, all repurchases were reported in a timely fashion to the fiscal agents. Buy-backs *during* the period of default did not get reported at all to either the Council or the agent until settlement negotiations began and then only intermittently until a final settlement was reached and relations normalized. All of these countries initiated negotiations soon after default, at which time total repurchases during the preceding period were confessed. The gap in reporting rarely exceeds three or four years. Equal repurchasings during each year were assumed if no other indication was available. Adjustments were also made when there were service provisions for stamped (indicating acceptance of revised contractual obligations) as well as unstamped bonds, using reported information on acceptances.

The payments for all bonds in each year were summed so that national totals could be calculated. The patterns of receipts and payments for each country are displayed in figures 3.1 through 3.5. Present values of the payments were calculated using a risk-free discount rate, the yield to maturity on U.S. government bonds of comparable length.[41] This discounting evaluates the yield on issues from the investor's point of view, assuming that investors chose Latin American government bonds as long-term holdings. Finally, the resulting present values of borrowings, payments, and net payments and the ratio of payments to principal were calculated as summary measures. The ratio of repayments to debt flotations can exceed 1.0 if the debt is mostly repaid and at coupon rates in excess of the U.S. government rate. The ratio will be less than 1.0 if the risk premium on coupon rates was insufficient to compensate for the nonpayments of interest and principal and for the buy-backs at discounted prices.

As can be seen from table 3.7, Argentina paid an enormous sum in present value terms for the monies it borrowed abroad. Its stream of payments on interest and principal turned positive in 1928 and remained so, except for 1937 when a new credit influx pushed it negative again (see figure 3.1). The present value ratio of payments to principal reveals that when adjusted to present values, Argentina paid out 1.25 times what it received. The other debtors appear to have done very well in their dealings with international capital markets. The net present values of their dollar bonds to investors are definitively negative, and their present value ratios are well below unity. By borrowing heavily in the 1920s and then defaulting, these countries spread out their repayments over a much longer period of time than Argentina who repaid promptly (see figures 3.2 through 3.5). Chile, the biggest borrower after Argentina, achieved effective debt forgiveness of almost 50 percent. Peru, the most successful defaulter as measured by present value ratios, repaid just over half of principal in present value terms, although on substantially smaller total borrowings than Chile. Bolivia, essentially reneging on its debt obligations for over 30 years, gained forgiveness equivalent to Chile's for the moderate sums it managed to borrow in the 1920s. Colombia, on the other hand, defaulted completely on its obligations for a very short time (actually paying no interest for only three years) and quickly made a unilateral offer to settle, giving its debt a small negative net present value and leaving its present value ratio substantially higher than the other three defaulters although still well below unity. These levels of debt forgiveness were indeed an outcome of post-default behavior, as is made clear in the lower half of table 3.7.

Naturally, the defaulting countries display present value ratios substantially lower for the stream of payments after default than those over the entire lives of the bonds. Consequently, although principal was never forgiven for any of these countries, cancellation of unpaid interest and buy-backs at less than par had an equivalent effect. But it is also important to note that the present value ratios are substantially above zero, indicating that much of the debt was indeed repaid despite lengthy periods of default.

Table 3.7
Present values and present value ratios of dollar bond lending in the interwar period, 1920 and 1931

1920	Total borrowings (millions $)	Total repayments (millions $)	Net present value (millions $)	Present value ratio
Argentina	258.59	323.12	64.53	1.25
Bolivia	49.13	26.32	−22.81	0.54
Chile	178.12	99.25	−78.87	0.56
Colombia	46.59	39.74	−6.85	0.85
Peru	54.45	28.08	−26.37	0.52

1931	Principal outstanding at default (millions $)	Repayment after default (millions $)	Present value ratio postdefault
Bolivia	59.42	4.63	0.08
Chile	260.73	80.39	0.31
Colombia	65.53	41.19	0.63
Peru	88.36	34.38	0.39

Sources: Authors' estimates; see text for data sources.
Notes: Results are based on national and nationally guaranteed bonds. The base years for present value calculations are 1920 year-end for totals and 1931 year-end for postdefault amounts. The discount rate used is the yield to maturity on U.S. long government bonds. Borrowings are actual principal received. Repayments are actual payments on interest and principal received by the bond trustees. The present value ratio is the ratio of repayments to borrowings, both discounted to 1920 year-end. Default occurred in 1932 for Colombia and in 1931 for other defaultors. The present value ratio postdefault is the ratio of repayments after default to principal outstanding at default, both discounted to 1931 year-end.

Thus default resulted in substantial debt relief in the longer run, ranging from 15 to 48 percent. This relief was not completely intended but was the joint product of unobservable debtor activity (in redeeming bonds at below par) and the limited negotiating power of the Foreign Bondholders' Protective Council. It was not that the Council was oblivious to behavior such as debt buy-backs but rather that it had no choice but to accept the inevitable. These countries had defaulted and reasonable settlements according to capacity to pay needed to be arranged.

3.5 The Repercussions of Default in the 1940s and 1950s

Argentina paid dramatically more for the foreign capital it had borrowed in the 1920s than did the four defaulters. Were there offsetting advantages that accrued to Argentina in future decades? One legacy of the 1930s defaults was sharply restricted access by *all* developing countries to international capital markets until the late 1960s. However, Argentina managed to secure credit for refunding purposes, and one new loan through the issuance of dollar bonds in the late 1930s. The government retired all $246 million of its national bonds in 1937 with the issuance of $129 million of 35-year external conversion bonds and substantial domestic debt. In 1938 an additional $25 million 10-year bond was floated.[42] The risk premium was slightly lower than for its earlier loans, but a conversion loan is inherently less risky. The new issues yielded an average 4.7 percent when the U.S. rate on Baa corporate bonds hovered around 5.2 percent. (Earlier borrowing had yielded 6.2 percent, approximately equal to the Baa rate over that period.) Thus Argentina's good behavior did seem to earn it some return in easier credit access during the 1930s when capital markets were closed to most Latin American countries. However, such credit access was short-lived and was ostensibly provided merely to ensure repayment of earlier bonds. Argentina, as will be seen shortly, received no special treatment after this episode in the late 1930s (see tables 3.8 and 3.9).

In the period 1930 to 1945, a number of Latin American governments were repatriating, and thereby significantly reducing, both foreign debt and equity claims. By 1945 a large portion of the external debt of Latin American countries had been repurchased in the open market, often at prices dramatically below par. Meanwhile Argentina was repurchasing at close to par, and redeeming at par a good part of its external debt causing its stock of public external debt to drop by 55 percent between 1940 and 1945.[43] In addition the Chilean and Colombian governments took over some of the bonds of nonnational entities as part of default settlement plans in the early 1940s, causing their stocks of public external debt to rise (see table 3.1). For dollar bonds specifically, between 1930 and 1945 the value of all Latin American issues outstanding dropped by almost 40 percent: from $2.1 billion in 1930 to $1.3 billion in 1945.[44]

In the late 1940s and the 1950s, net flows of external finance switched direction and became positive again. In these years private capital flows to Latin America were much higher than official government flows and predominantly took the form of direct investment. International financial and money markets had not yet recovered from the 1930s, so the only indirect investment was a modest and erratic flow of suppliers' credits. As late as 1960 Latin America owed half of its total stock of debt to suppliers.[45] Direct investment, on the other hand, was somewhat larger, undertaken mostly by U.S. enterprises through the reinvestment of earnings, starting

Table 3.8
Fifteen-year averages of ratios to exports of various categories of recipients of external finance, 1950−64

	Government	Private	Official transfers	Total (including direct investment)
Argentina	−0.473	5.0085	0.0431	9.1614
Bolivia	1.6654	2.8509	22.046	36.502
Chile	4.0817	2.7391	1.8566	13.792
Colombia	2.4770	3.7858	0.5367	8.0554
Peru	1.4958	5.9489	1.0589	15.685

Sources: Wilkie (1980, 1981, 1985); International Monetary Fund (various years).
Notes: Exports are of goods and services. Government external finance includes local and central government nonmonetary assets and liabilities. Private external finance includes long and short term assets and liabilities. Total external finance is the sum of government and private external finance, official transfers and net direct investment.

Table 3.9
Ratios of five-year averages of various categories of recipients of external finance to five-year average of exports, 1950−64

	Government			Private		
	1950−54	1955−59	1960−64	1950−54	1955−59	1960−64
Argentina	−0.477	−4.727	3.5105	1.3695	6.0492	6.6369
Bolivia	1.9406	−3.777	11.145	−0.446	1.6698	7.3441
Chile	1.0719	0.0706	10.895	−1.435	−0.232	9.5820
Colombia	2.6878	−0.204	4.9753	3.6588	−2.537	11.367
Peru	1.0223	3.3736	0.3252	1.0677	9.8948	6.7967

	Official transfers			Total (including direct investment)		
	1950−54	1955−59	1960−64	1950−54	1955−59	1960−64
Argentina	0	0.0107	0.1227	1.2279	7.5454	17.235
Bolivia	4.2605	32.028	26.945	5.9781	43.662	57.150
Chile	0.1818	2.8681	2.2941	4.0053	10.624	25.478
Colombia	0.0492	0.2256	1.3258	6.8498	−2.067	21.015
Peru	1.0677	9.8948	6.7967	13.570	25.932	8.3252

Sources: Wilkie (1980, 1981, 1985); International Monetary Fund (various years).
Notes: Exports are of goods and services. Government external finance includes local and central government nonmonetary assets and liabilities. Private external finance includes long and short term assets and liabilities. Total external finance is the sum of government and private external finance, official transfers and net direct investment.

off in the petroleum industry, then increasingly spreading to manufacturing and the extraction of other minerals. The net inflow of private capital, direct and indirect, averaged $740 million per annum for 1950 to 1956. However, for 1954 to 1956, prompted by economic and political instability in the region, private long-term capital flowed out at an estimated rate of $40 million per annum. In 1957 sufficient change had occurred to draw this speculative flow inward again and at a level twice that for the early 1950s.[46]

Official flows from the U.S. Export-Import Bank and IBRD provided some additional capital through the 1950s. Of the five countries of this study, Chile and Argentina benefited most from Ex-Im credits, granted for the purposes of financing commercial arrears on imports from the United States, as well as for infrastructure projects, while Chile and Colombia received the bulk of IBRD funds to this group, the funds being directed toward the expansion of electric power and transportation facilities.[47] However, both private and official external finance remained at relatively low levels and varied substantially from year to year in response to political as much as economic events.

The flows of external finance to each of the five countries over the whole period of 1950 to 1964 are summarized in table 3.8. External finance is defined broadly as the sum of noncompensatory financing to government, net external financing to the private sector, official transfers, and net direct investment. These trends of this measure and its subcategories are of direct relevance to the analysis of the cost of default to the borrowing countries because it was not until the 1950s that the world had recovered from depression and a second world war. Although flows of international capital are modest in this decade, the supposed penalty for defaulting must have been paid then, if at all.[48] Therefore it is of interest to note that as a percentage of exports, the defaulters managed to obtain equivalent or larger capital flows than Argentina.

Over the period of 1950 to 1964, all five countries experienced rising flows of external finance, as shown in table 3.9 (broken down into categories of government sector, private sector, official transfers, and a composite including the previous categories and direct investment). Argentina does compare favorably with the other four countries in its ratio of *private* finance to exports. It achieved reschedulings that consolidated short-term obligations into longer-term debt both in 1956 after the overthrow of the Peron regime and again in 1959–60, the latter assistance package constituting its first significant postwar inflow of capital. Chile received slightly more government finance over the period than the others because of higher inflows in the early 1960s (partly bilateral refinancing and partly loans for earthquake reconstruction). It is rather amusing that Bolivia, the worst behaved of the five in terms of timely settlement of default, not reaching a lasting agreement until 1958, displays the highest ratio of external finance to exports (although only because of official transfers).

It is difficult to argue that any particular trend inevitably emerges from perusal of this data.[49] Not only must the accuracy of capital flow information for this period be somewhat suspect, especially given the existence of conflicting estimates from different sources, but the modest size of the flows and their high variability preclude any strong conclusions. As different categories of external finance waxed and waned over the period, switching the total flow from negative to positive and back again, trends are possible to identify only through the use of multiyear averaging. These switches can in many instances be explained by particular political events, such as a new American foreign policy or the overthrow of a regime unfriendly to foreign capital. Nevertheless, it can be said that Argentina, having conscientiously retained its creditworthiness by honoring its debt service obligations, did not receive noticeably better treatment in the 1950s in return for its admirable behavior in the previous two decades. Any lasting effect of reputation formed on the basis of behavior in the 1930s was an incidental factor in determining access to foreign capital in the 1950s.

3.6   Conclusions

The defaults of the 1930s present lessons for contemporary experience because these countries actually ceased payment on their foreign debts and these defaults were acknowledged, accepted, and eventually negotiated on favorable terms to the debtors. Examining the consequences of defaults that emanated from an era with so many similarities to the present provides, at the least, some interesting commentary on policies being advocated today for Latin American debtors.

From the borrower's perspective the costs of default involve both a direct component of actual payments made on existing debts and an indirect component of reputational effects on future access to credit. On the basis of the five countries studied here, it seems that both of these costs were low, so low as to be negative. The empirical results on actual payments over the life of all of each country's dollar bonds indicate the level of debt forgiveness that occurred. That relief was substantial, if the basis for comparison is the experience of Argentina, the single country that did not default. The debt burden of the defaulting countries was lightened not only by liberal final agreements with bondholders but also by the debtors' practice of secretly entering the bond market and buying their debt at deep discounts during default. It also seems that the costs of default in terms of future external financial flows were negligible. When the countries returned to international capital markets in the 1950s, no apparent systematic difference between the defaulters and the nondefaulter emerges, the patterns being dominated by other factors. This result is consistent with findings in Eichengreen (1987) and Lindert and Morton (1987).

The terms of the final agreements settling the defaults of the 1930s were highly favorable to debtors and, contrary to current rescheduling practices, involved a sharing of losses. The unpaid interest during the period of default was summed without capitalization and added to the total stock of principal due. The resulting total was consolidated into a new bond issue with a maturity of 30 to 50 years. Full present values were not demanded, and there was little fastidiousness about interest arrears. Maturities were extended to concessionary lengths, while interest rates were reduced below yields available on comparably risky assets. These deals were struck with realism, as fair compromises between creditors and debtors coping with the aftermath of severe unforeseen external shocks that rendered the debtors' abrogation of contracts excusable.[50]

Fishlow (1985) describes nineteenth-century lending to Latin America as a process of default-induced disruption of capital flows followed by timely settlements that allow the resumption of lending for development purposes. By comparison, it seems then that the trouble with the interwar period was not default per se but the general breakdown of trading and capital flows that removed incentives for rapid adjustment of servicing. Henry Wallich (1943) observed that debt forgiveness was both desirable and necessary to relieve the overhang of Latin American debt and improve the prospects of a return of international capital flows to the region. Thus a possible lesson of the tumultuous interwar experience is the desirability of negotiating reasonable default settlements and the debtor's reentry into the international system *more* quickly with potential gains to creditor and debtor.

Changes in the regulatory, legal, and political environment have led to a different outcome so far in the 1980s. No debt forgiveness has yet been granted, partly because the United States serves as the contract enforcer that was lacking in the 1930s. As a result it is quite possible that today's process of settlement through temporary reschedulings has been to the detriment of debtors and creditors and that the failure to reach realistic settlements in the timely manner of the nineteenth century may, instead, recreate much of the pain of the interwar period.

Notes

1. Quoted from Edwin Borchard, *State Insolvency and Foreign Bondholders* 1951. New Haven: Yale University Press, p. 5.

2. The sanctions that private creditors can impose on defaulting countries have increased significantly through changes in international law since 1945. Although these legal remedies have not been called upon in the current crisis, they may well serve as another incentive for sovereign borrowers to avoid outright default (see Alexander 1987).

3. Sachs (1982), p. 219.

4. See Fishlow (1985) for an excellent history of nineteenth-century lending.

5. Nordhaus (1986, p. 564) referred to rescheduling as "partial default under another name."

6. See Eichengreen and Portes (1986), Eichengreen (1987), and Lindert and Morton (1987) for independent investigations of many of these questions, using different samples of countries but generally reaching the same conclusions.

7. See Sachs and Huizinga (1987) for the argument that relief can be mutually beneficial in today's setting.

8. See Fishlow (1985).

9. Madden, Nadler, and Sauvain (1937), pp. 73–74.

10. Fishlow (1985), p. 390.

11. United Nations (1955), p. 14.

12. Ashworth (1952), p. 196.

13. Fishlow (1985), p. 384.

14. United Nations (1985), p. 15.

15. Madden, Nadler, and Sauvain (1937), p. 74.

16. From United Nations (1955), p. 15, and Foreign Bondholders Protective Council (1934), pp. 102–8, 145–51. For the five Latin American states in this study, see table 3.1 for debt stocks over time and tables 3.2 to 3.5 for debt histories of the defaulters. For detailed debt histories of all five countries, see Jorgensen and Sachs (1988), app. B.

17. It should be noted that overseas investment was never as large a share of the capital market in the United States as in Britain. In the 1920s foreign security issues averaged just 14 percent of all issues in the United States, hitting a maximum of 18 percent in 1927 and then falling to 7 percent in 1929 (Fishlow 1985, p. 424).

18. United Nations (1985), pp. 14, 18. Fishlow (1985), p. 419, quoted a conflicting figure of only £51 million in new capital issues in London for the entire 1920 to 1931 period.

19. Díaz-Alejandro (1983), pp. 26–27.

20. Madden, Nadler, and Sauvain (1937), p. 108.

21. United Nations (1955), p. 16.

22. Lewis (1938), p. 389.

23. Madden, Nadler, and Sauvain (1937), p. 110.

24. Eichengreen and Portes (1985), p. 6.

25. See Sachs (1982).

26. And even in Argentina some nonnational dollar bonds went into default for a brief period. It is sometimes argued that the readjustment of inter-ally debts and reparations payments in the 1920s for the former creditors to the world—Britain, France, and Germany—set a tempting example for the periphery and, in combination with the derogation of the gold clause by Britain in 1931 and the United States in 1933, succeeded in undermining Latin American belief in the sanctity of contracts (Wallich 1943, p. 322).

27. Fishlow (1985), p. 429.

28. Revenues from natural resources or domestic monopolies, such as railroads or the tobacco industry, and properties, such as bullion or commodities, were popular backing assets. For example, Peru's nineteenth-century loans were secured on its valuable guano deposits, whereas a 1922 British loan to Brazil was backed by coffee (Borchard 1951, pp. 83–89).

29. Borchard (1951), pp. 3–15, 93–96.

30. The market price on Bolivian bonds dropped to 3 cents on the dollar in 1939.

31. The Council denounced a published statement of Colombia's minister of finance in which he "enunciates the policy of Colombia to be to lower the interest rate as much as possible in order to depress the value of the bonds and take advantage of the necessities of the bondholders who are obliged to sell their bonds at the low prices forced upon them by the Colombian Government itself" (Foreign Bondholders Protective Council 1940, p. 33). For more details, see Jorgensen and Sachs (1988), app. B.

32. Argentina's bond contracts allowed repurchases through the sinking fund at market price. Between 1931 and 1936 it purchased a modest 15 percent, all

through normal sinking fund payments, at an average price of 73 cents on the dollar.

33. Mallon and Sourrouille (1977), p. 7.

34. Eichengreen and Portes (1985), pp. 27—29.

35. Mason and Asher (1973), pp. 155—58.

36. *Banking and Monetary Statistics* (1943).

37. Díaz-Alejandro (1983), pp. 27—28. More specifically, from table 3.1, the ratio of the stock of publich external debt to exports in 1945 was

Argentina: 23%

Bolivia: 75%

Chile: 156%

Colombia: 61%

Peru: 93%

38. Other authors have calculated similar measures for other samples of bonds. Eichengreen and Portes (1986) use a basket of 33 dollar bonds issued in the 1920s by foreign governments, or with government guarantees, and estimate the realized rate of nominal return to lenders to be 3.25 percent. They do not consider the impact of discounted buybacks. Lindert and Morton (1987) track all bonds issued by ten governments from 1850 to 1970, including Argentina and Chile. They calculate a number of summary measures in both real and nominal terms, finding that bondholders received a positive real return premium of 0.42 percent overall and of 1.21 percent for bonds issued from 1915 to 1945.

39. A Bolivian issue of 1917 with 25-year maturity was included because it marks the first of Bolivia's small borrowings in the New York market.

40. The main sources used were the annual *Report of the Foreign Bondholders Protective Council* and the monthly *Bank and Quotations Record*. For more details on sources and methodology, see Jorgensen and Sachs (1988), app. C.

41. Generally, the rate used was the average yield on all U.S. government bonds due or callable after 8 to 15 years.

42. See Jorgensen and Sachs (1988), app. B for details of Argentina's debt history.

43. The prices of Argentine issues never fell much below 75 cents on the dollar after 1935, leaving the government unable to reduce its debt at the hefty discount available to defaulters and seemingly unwilling to take advantage of what discount there was. Perhaps such behavior, although technically allowed under the bond contracts, would have threatened the conversion bonds.

44. United Nations (1955), p. 52; Foreign Bondholders Protective Council (1945).

45. Griffith-Jones (1984), pp. 26—29.

46. Pan-American Union (1958), pp. 85–90.

47. See Jorgensen and Sachs (1988), app. A, for amounts.

48. See Eichengreen (1987) for some econometric tests of this hypothesis.

49. In a similar vein Eichengreen (1987) fails to find evidence that default in the interwar years affected the ability to borrow in the period 1945 to 1955 from cross-sectional regressions of all external debts of governments for 32 countries in 1955 and regressions of private portfolio lending for 18 Latin American countries for 1946 to 1955.

50. See Grossman and Van Huyck (1985) for a formal model of excusable default.

References

Alexander, Lewis. 1987. "Three Essays on Sovereign Default and International Lending." Unpublished Ph.D. dissertation. Yale University.

Ashworth, William. 1952. *A Short History of the International Economy.* London: Longmans, Green, & Co.

Avramovic, Dragoslav. 1964. *Economic Growth and External Debt.* Baltimore: International Bank for Reconstruction and Development, John Hopkins Press.

Bank and Quotations Record. Monthly vols. for 1928–81.

Bernstein, Martin. 1966. *Foreign Investment in Latin America.* New York: Alfred A. Knopf.

Bitterman, Henry. 1973. *The Refunding of International Debt.* Durham, North Carolina: Duke University Press.

Borchard, Edwin. 1951. *State Insolvency and Foreign Bondholders.* New Haven: Yale University Press.

Díaz-Alejandro, Carlos. 1983. "Stories of the 1930's for the 1980's." In P. Armella, R. Dornbusch, and M. Obtsfeld, eds., *Financial Policies and the World Capital Market.* Chicago: University of Chicago Press.

Dominick and Dominick. Annual vols. for 1924–37. *Foreign Bonds Issued in the United States.* New York: A. Iselin and Company.

Eichengreen, Barry. 1987. "Til Debt Do Us Part: The U.S. Capital Market and Foreign Lending, 1920–1955." NBER Working Paper no. 2394. October.

Eichengreen, Barry, and Richard Portes. 1986. "Debt and Default in the 1930's: Causes and Consequences." Harvard Institute of Economic Research Discussion Paper no. 1186.

Fishlow, Albert. 1985. "Lessons from the Past: Capital Markets during the 19th Century and the Interwar Period." *International Organization* 39:3, pp. 383–439.

Foreign Bondholders Protective Council. Various years. *Annual Report*. New York: Foreign Bondholders Protective Council.

Griffith-Jones, Stephany. 1984. *International Finance and Latin America*. New York: St. Martins Press.

Grossman, Herschel, and John Van Huyck. 1985. "Sovereign Debt as a Contingent Claim: Excusable Default, Repudiation, and Reputation." NBER Working Paper no. 1673.

International Monetary Fund. Various years. *Balance of Payments Yearbook*. Washington, D.C.: International Monetary Fund. Vols. 5, 8–10, 12, 14, 17, 18.

Jorgensen, Erika, and Jeffrey Sachs. 1988. "Default and Renegotiation of Latin American Foreign Bonds in the Interwar Period." NBER Working Paper no. 2636. June 1988.

Lewis, Cleona. 1938. *America's Stake in International Investments*. Washington, D.C.: The Brookings Institution.

Lindert, Peter, and Peter Morton. 1989. "How Sovereign Debt Has Worked." In Jeffrey Sachs, ed., *The International Financial System*. Vol. 1: *Developing Country Debt and Economic Performance*. Chicago: University of Chicago Press.

Madden, John, M. Nadler, and H. Sauvain. 1937. *America's Experience as a Creditor Nation*. Englewood Cliffs, NS: Prentice-Hall.

Mallon, Richard, and J. V. Sourrouille. 1975. *Economic Policymaking in a Conflict Society*. Cambridge: Harvard University Press.

Mason, Edward, and Robert Asher. 1973. *The World Bank Since Bretton Woods*. Washington, D.C.: The Brookings Institution.

Mintz, Ilse. 1951. *Deterioration in the Quality of Foreign Bonds Issued in the United States, 1920–1930*. New York: National Bureau of Economic Research.

Nordhaus, William. 1986. "Comments on Cohen and Sachs." *European Economic Review* 30, pp. 561–564.

Pan-American Union, Inter-American Economic and Social Council. 1958. *Financing of Economic Development in Latin America*. Washington, D.C.: Pan-American Union.

Sachs, Jeffrey. 1982. "LDC Debt in the 1980's: Risk and Reforms." In Paul Wachtel, ed., *Crises in the Economic and Financial Structure*. Lexington, Mass.: Lexington Books.

Sachs, Jeffrey. 1986. "The Debt Overhang of the Developing Countries." Harvard University. Mimeo.

Sachs, Jeffrey, and Harry Huizinga. 1987. "U.S. Commercial Banks and the Developing-Country Debt Crisis." *Brookings Papers on Economic Activity 2*.

United Nations, Department of Economic Affairs. 1948. *Public Debt: 1914–1946*. Lake Success, NY: United Nations Publications.

United Nations, Department of Economic and Social Affairs. 1955. *Foreign Capital in Latin America*. New York: United Nations, Department of Economic and Social Affairs.

Wallich, H. C. 1943. "The Future of Latin American Dollar Bonds." *American Economic Review* 33, pp. 321–335.

Wilkie, James, ed. 1980, 1981, 1985. *Statistical Abstract of Latin America*. Vols. 20, 21, 24. Los Angeles: UCLA Latin American Center Publications.

Wilkie, James. 1974. *Statistics and National Policy*. Supplement 3 of UCLA Statistical Abstract of Latin America. Los Angeles: UCLA Latin American Center Publications.

4 Conditionality and Willingness to Pay: Some Parallels from the 1890s

Albert Fishlow

4.1 Introduction

As the developing country debt problem lingers into its sixth year, two questions remain central: why countries, with only modest exception, have not unilaterally written down the debt or reduced debt service; and why conditionality has yielded such relatively meager results in the way of economic performance.

Answers to both questions, deriving from analytic models, have not been lacking. Utility-maximizing willingness-to-pay models suggest that debtor countries, as badly off as they are now, would suffer even further loss from more aggressive stances. Since current resource transfers are negative for many, that result implies that interruption of debt service would either evoke costly penalties or future loss of access to beneficial capital inflows.[1]

Another literature relating to stabilization emphasizes the inappropriateness of aggregate demand-oriented policies, on the one side, and the lack of consistent implementation, on the other. In the real world, technocrats blame politicians for their unreliability even as politicians criticize technocrats for the inadequacy of their models.[2]

My purpose here is to shed light upon these two issues, not by rehearsing the contemporary evidence but by referring to the earlier historical experience of Argentina and Brazil in the debt crisis of the 1890s. Both countries were unable to meet their contractual debt service obligations during that decade and were required to adjust as the counterpart of rescheduling of interest and amortization payments. Both resumed payments and again received large capital inflows at the beginning of the twentieth century. The record of the 1890s is in many ways more informative than that of the Great Depression in providing historical precedent. In the 1930s, the debtor developing countries were at the margin of an international decline and political crisis centered in the industrial world. They defaulted with impunity in the midst of a world depression.

What the history of the earlier period suggests is that extended economic sacrifice to permit full repayment had strong backing from a variety of domestic interests, as it continues to do today. There was no single maximizing agent focusing on the external accounts. That support for debt service had a positive basis in conviction in the importance of foreign capital for domestic development, as well as belief in the need to trim public expenditures. On the negative side, there was also a concern for potential intervention and loss of sovereignty, as had befallen other debtors like Egypt and Turkey that had received debt relief at the expense of foreign control over public revenues. Debt also was, as it sometimes is today, a rallying point for those out of power; the economics of debt service could be subordinate to the politics of opposition.

The conditionality imposed in the 1890s contains similarities and differences in comparison with present practices. The basic similarity resides in the ascription to domestic policy errors the primary blame for debt service difficulties. International market conditions were given short shrift, whether commodity prices or capital availability. That domestic lack of capability justified an external expertise and oversight. The basic difference is the historical emphasis on the internal transfer problem. Exports could take care of themselves, in part because the long-term trends were confidently expected to be upward. An essential part of the policy prescription, indeed, was appreciation of the exchange rate, not real devaluation.

In section 4.2 I indicate the response of creditors to the two countries' crises, the conditions they imposed and the extent of their implementation by the debtors.[3] In section 4.3 I briefly lay out the elements of the internal debate about alternative strategies to confront the debt crisis in the two countries. In section 4.4 I draw some parallels with the current situation.

4.2 External Actors and the Debt Crises of the 1890s

Argentina

The story of the Baring crisis of 1890, and its partial basis in excess holdings of Argentine paper for which there was no ready market, is well known. Rapid intervention by the Chancellor of the Exchequer and the Bank of England prevented a major financial collapse by guaranteeing Baring's liabilities and thereby permitting orderly reorganization of the firm. The Bank's willingness to play its role as a lender of last resort did not forestall a diminished ardor for overseas investment that rapidly came over the capital market. Not only did Argentine issues immediately move to substantial discounts on the London market, so also did those of other peripheral countries. Many were forced to reduce their debt service in the years that followed.

Correct dating places the Argentine problem much earlier than the Baring crisis in November 1890, however. Former Finance Minister José Terry, in his contemporary view, asserts that the die was cast much earlier: "Until the end of 1887 it was possible to save the patient: in 1888 it already was no longer possible."[4] Since 1885 the country had experienced a rapid monetary expansion that had been based on inconvertible issue. This domestic impulse could be absorbed only because of record inflows of capital to finance government and private investments in infrastructure. Imports outstripped exports and rose to new highs.

But the prosperity showed signs of reversal. Railway net profits had peaked in 1888, and the gold premium on paper pesos rose to 94 percent in 1889 despite continuing foreign investment. And in that year new loans were being contracted at a much reduced rate on the London market. At home, in March 1890 the official banks required a large new emission of notes to be put at their disposition to avoid their failure. Such was the economic deterioration that popular unrest forced the president to resign in August. The new administration, led by the former vice president, Carlos Pellegrini, sought to maintain itself current in its debt service, to the extent of converting notes to gold and remitting to the Barings to try to help alleviate their mounting illiquidity.

After the crisis broke, there was new urgency emanating from Britain for a prompt solution to Argentina's economic problems. The stratagem of guaranteeing the liquidation of Baring Brothers required the restoration of the good credit of Argentina and the marketability of its portfolio of Argentine securities. An international committee of bankers headed by Lord Rothschild had been formed to oversee continuing interest payments on the governmental securities.

It was clearly apparent that there was a potential problem in sustaining them. Federal debt service represented more than 50 percent of governmental receipts; even larger provincial debt service probably was a higher percentage of provincial income. And there was also the cedulas, or mortgage notes of the Land Bank. Together estimated external debt service around 1890 amounted to close to 40 million gold pesos, or something like 40 percent of total exports.[5]

The Rothschild committee considered three alternatives: insistence upon immediate domestic reforms without finance, pressure for adjustment coupled with a small loan to keep current, and a more liberal funding loan over a longer period to induce policy changes. The committee, dominated by the English bankers, opted for the last. Such generous treatment precipitated the French and Germans to abandon participation, in part because the Morgan loan of January 1891 was seen as a device to shore up the price of Argentine securities and facilitate the Baring liquidation. Such was the speculation of *The Economist*. If that was the case, it did not succeed; securities prices continued to slide after the agreement. But neither did the Argentine economy show signs of improvement under the aegis of the loan.

The funding loan failed for two reasons. One was that domestic policy was not wholly on the side of restraint. Although new internal consumption taxes were imposed, import duties, the most important source of revenues, fell dramatically with declining imports and a rising gold premium. Overall, 1891 revenues were down 50 percent from their 1889 level. On the other side, expenditures could not as fully be compressed.

Nor could implicit government guarantees not be honored. First came an internal loan, undersubscribed, to try to save the offical banks. To no avail. With the disarray in domestic credit occasioned by the failure of the Banco Nacional and the Provincial Bank of Buenos Aires and suspension of five private banks, a further emission of 50 million pesos was made to found a new national bank in October 1891. The condition of the funding loan that 15 million pesos be incinerated each year for the three years of its duration was amply violated. The British press even speculated about the appropriateness of having the new bank run by foreigners, given the incapacity of the Argentines.[6]

More generally, deflation was not a popular remedy. An inflationary environment had been favored by landowners whose debts, fixed in nominal cedulas for the most part, had diminished with rising domestic prices. As export producers they stood also to gain from the rising gold premium, or real devaluation. It was difficult, in the midst of a real decline in output, to reverse the strategy, especially with a presidential election to be held in April 1892.

If domestic policy was not up to the task, neither was the level of international finance. The second reason for the failure of the funding loan was an inadequate transfer of resources. Although the £5 million made available annually for three years was considered generous, its level pales in comparison with the average annual £40 million in 1888–89 or even the reduced £15 in 1890. The Rothschild formula covered merely the interest directly owed by the federal government, excluding the considerable obligations of the provinces, cities, cedulas, and private enterprises. The loan thus covered only about a third of foreign exchange requirements for full debt service. Inevitably, full service could not be sustained, and arrears on other obligations mounted. Still, such was the deterioration in foreign exchange availability that total imports had to fall dramatically—by more than 50 percent in 1891. What the loan did was to make continuing debt service by the federal government viable, but without permitting a margin for economic recovery.

Underlying both circumstances was the fact that the developmental cycle had not run its course. Intervention would have had to be much more substantial to contribute to a still earlier recovery. As it was, the data on railway receipts are suggestive of a less severe and prolonged downturn than other peripheral economies experienced during the 1890s. In part that was because real wages adjusted downward under the pressure of devaluation and afforded increased profitability of domestic production and exports.

The Rothschild arrangement was unpopular because it signified paying debt with debt and because of the onerous conditions it apparently imposed:

The loan was realized ... with more than depressing conditions for the honor of the country and of the government. Its product exclusively dedicated to the service of the other foreign debts; the coupons of the loan to be received in customs in payment of tariffs; the goverment obligated to deposit daily in the bank, in a special current account, the funds necessary for the service of the loan, able to be audited by agents of the creditors; the government also obligated not to contract other loans or to grant new guarantees for three years; the goverment obligated to withdraw from circulation 15 million pesos per year in inconvertible notes; the government obligated ....[7]

Despite the reality of nonconformance, the newly elected government made a readjustment of debt arrangements a priority. It occurred on the basis of a maximum ability to pay, offered originally at £1,5 million and modestly increased to £1,565 after discussions with the creditors. The *Arreglo Romero* was concluded in 1893 and substituted a set period of reduction in service obligations in place of the increased indebtedness and full payments of the earlier formula. For five years interest payments were to be reduced by an average of 30 percent and amortization suspended until the beginning of 1901. Despite an initially cool reception in both London and Buenos Aires, the agreement held.

Debt relief was not universally popular. A unification scheme proposed in 1895 to consolidate the defaulted provincial debt and railway guarantees at a discount did not succeed. Some wished the provinces to work out their arrangements without imposing on the national fisc, but others were concerned lest the credit of Argentina suffer by failing to meet its obligations. It was in this context that the Congress passed a requirement that interest payments be resumed a year ahead of the *Arreglo* schedule. Eventually, between 1897 and 1900, arrangements for reducing the provincial obligations at a write-down of almost half were successful; new recission bonds also were issued to replace the railway guarantees.[8]

The key contribution of the *Arreglo* was to cut short a potentially dangerous debt overhang that threatened future public sector capacity. The cost of sustaining payments was substantial. Not only did the funding loan carry a 6 percent coupon, but the market was evaluating it at a very high discount. Argentina needed some temporary interest relief and permanent debt reduction even while the beneficial consequences of earlier investments were providing increased exports and public revenues. Given the large military expenditures in middecade as relations with Chile deteriorated, such assistance was especially timely.

Creditors acceded, and the country grew into its obligations and into a stable monetary environment with the establishment of a fixed gold premium in 1899. There was soon a large new influx of resources: between 1901 and 1915 it is estimated that 47 percent of gross fixed investment was foreign financed.[9] "In 1914, the Argentine Republic, having emerged from the depths of one of the most spectacular modern crises only a few years before, enjoyed a credit rating exceeded by none except the old creditor nations of Europe."[10]

Brazil

The abolition of slavery and end of the monarchy in Brazil set in motion in the early years of the Republic in the 1890s a very large increase in domestic monetary expansion and credit. In an inconvertible monetary system this led to an inevitable rise in the price of foreign exchange as well as increased domestic prices. Speculation became rampant during the *Encilhamento*, until the market crashed in 1891. Thereafter, in November, the Congress was closed, touching off a reaction leading to deposition of the president and replacement by his vice president.

The obvious similarities with the Argentine situation differed in one fundamental respect. Brazil continued to be able to service its external debt, in large part because it was able to contract new loans in the London market, most prominently in 1893 and 1895 but also a short term advance in 1896. Although domestic circumstances remained unsettled with civil war in the south and continuing federal deficits as a consequence, money supply growth was slowed and some consolidation of the banking system occurred. Still the decline of the milreis persisted and deficits were increasing.

As the time of the inauguration of the next president in 1898 approached, it was apparent that declining import revenues made it impossible to sustain continuing debt service at levels of half of the budget. Nor did Brazilian prospects for continuing finance afford bright possibilities as exports were in a state of decline as a result of falling coffee prices. President-Elect Campos Salles, when discussing the financial situation with Brazil's bankers, the Rothschilds, was strongly advised against a moratorium: "besides the complete loss of the country's credit the measure could greatly affect Brazil's sovereignty, provoking reactions that could arrive at the extreme of foreign invasion."[11]

Instead, the formula ultimately agreed upon after negotiations in London, was a funding loan to permit the continuation of interest payments through new debt. The loan amounted to more than £8 million, covering prospective government interest expenses on the external debt for three years. Amortization of outstanding loans was also suspended for 13 years, further reducing needed payments. On its side, Brazil agreed to undertake no new borrowing, internal or external, and to withdraw from circulation treasury notes at an exchange of 18d (the market rate was about 7d) as a counterpart to the issue of the funding bonds. The notes were to be deposited with three foreign banks in Rio and destroyed, unless the exchange rate had risen in the interim to validate their conversion. The receipts of the Rio custom house were pledged as a guarantee for service of the funding loan, with the government rejecting the demands to pledge the additional revenues of the central railway and the Rio waterworks.

The solution was viewed as appropriate to the temporary problems in which Brazil found itself. As the Rothschilds wrote Campos Salles after agreement had been reached: "Unhappily, for several years, Brazil has passed through a crisis as much political as financial and, in these circumstances, it is not surprising that with the great fall that the exchange rate has experienced it should have produced financial difficulties which, we like to believe, are not more than passing." But it was also clear that the success of the arrangement depended upon full compliance: "... but the advantages for Brazil of the projected plan will depend on the exact observance of all its details ...."[12] Such was the improved state of financial markets in the late 1890s, and the sanguine response to the Brazilian problem, that the 5 percent bonds sold at par; the 1895 5 percent issue had been priced at 85.

The next four years saw implementation of a conservative fiscal and monetary policy. Collection of part of import duties in gold was restored, and domestic indirect taxes were increased. Expenditures were compressed. Credit was restricted. The consequences of such an orthodoxy were not entirely benign.

Among their most dramatic effects was the banking crisis in 1900. The government failed to effect a timely new emission of liquidity but led instead to the failure of the Banco de República and its effective nationalization. Finance Minister Joaquim Murtinho defended such a distasteful course of action for one committed to the survival of the fittest by the implicit government guarantee of deposits. And he differentiated his policy from the old simple provision of liquidity.[13] Other banks were not so privileged and failed as part of the price of restoring a new order and discipline in financial markets.

This difficult period elicited strong and negative reaction from contemporaries. The *Jornal do Povo* of Rio de Janeiro in 1891 credited the policies with "three years of complete stagnation and the unquestionable decline of industrial productivity." Campos Salles himself commented that "my government is better received abroad than here."[14] Later critics have also dealt harshly with the consciously deflationary and Darwinian views of Murtinho. A series on imports of machinery and other capital goods from the industrial countries shows severe compression during this period.[15] But rising tariffs imposed by fiscal requirements may have been a source of some relief to the industrial sector.

The success of the policy was consciously measured not by domestic popularity, but by appreciation of the milreis, which stood by 1902 at 12 pence. More rapid domestic expansion resumed, aided by improved coffee prices and rubber exports, and also a new inflow of foreign capital in the decade preceding the first world war. New investments in infrastructure, including urban renovation of Rio and improvement of its port facilities, were undertaken.

A *Caixa de Conversão* was authorized in 1906 to stabilize the price of the milreis. But by 1913 less favorable international circumstances and increased government expenditures imperiled continuation of the quasi-gold standard. While negotiation proceeded on a new loan to shore up reserves, the first world war intervened. Brazil finally left the gold standard and was forced to resort to a new funding loan in 1914.

Conditionality

The conditions imposed by creditors in the 1890s derived from a direct application of the quantity theory to domestic inflation and exchange rates. Excessive monetary issue was seen to be at the root of the debt service problem. In both Argentina and Brazil, large increases in the money supply had occurred in the wake of efforts to extend banking systems and satisfy the credit needs for economic and geographic expansion. Clearly, accommodation had gone too far and produced high domestic inflation and, as a consequence, depreciation of the exchange rate.

That depreciation played a central role in creating a debt service transfer problem for the public sector. Foreign exchange was now more expensive, while nominal revenues did not keep pace. The latter were almost exclusively derived from specific tariffs that had been determined on the basis of past exchange rates. Since interest payments were the principal expense, amounting to a third and more of outlays, and governments could not meet them out of current revenue, deficits resulted, giving rise to domestic floating debt and even more monetary issue.

The funding loans to continue payment of interest relieved the central governments of securing the foreign exchange equivalent. But precisely in order to ensure fiscal discipline, the government was pledged to use its revenues to purchase and destroy domestic currency. The transaction was equivalent to capitalization of interest along with a counterpart payment in currency that would be taken out of circulation. Governments would gain access to those domestic resources by increasing their incomes while limiting expenditures.

Fiscal order was thus a central requirement. That meant new internal consumption taxes as a supplementary source of revenue, as well as increased duties. Collection of some proportion of tariffs in gold were a way of ensuring the latter. It was equivalent to adjusting specific duties to exchange rate depreciation so that nominal receipts rose in proportion. Tariff rate increases were a discontinuous way of accomplishing the same.

This exclusive focus on exchange rate appreciation and domestic discipline may seem to belie the distinction between developmental and revenue defaults that I earlier advanced in differentiating Argentina and Brazil from Egypt, Greece, Peru, and Russia.[16] After all, appreciation, if real, would prejudice export growth and import substitution and hence work adversely on balance of payments adjustment. Real devaluation is a centerpiece of current adjustment efforts.

While the proximate aim was restoring public sector debt service capacity in both revenue and developmental defaulters, there was an important difference. The latter were seen able to grow into their responsibilities because real capital accumulation had occurred. Appreciation could be pursued because the interruption of debt service occurred against a trend growth of trade. Exports would not be greatly disturbed, especially since one was restoring recent relative prices after a sharp depreciation. Precisely because they were developmental defaulters, the balance of payments was a secondary matter.

What therefore was indicated was temporary capitalization of debt service while time and more orthodox domestic management worked their beneficial effects. Debt relief was unnecessary. When provided, as in the *Arreglo Romero*, it was intended to be for a limited duration and for modest amounts. By contrast, the debt overhang in revenue defaulters like Egypt, Turkey, and Greece was so large that substantial relief was necessary and provided, but at the price of intervention in ensuring collection of reduced subsequent service.

This recipe for development defaulters foresaw return to fiscal health as a precursor to exchange convertibility and the discipline of the gold standard. Then domestic monetary excess would be self-correcting, and public officials constrained. Meanwhile the magic of comparative advantage under free trade would evoke a mutually beneficial specialization and global division of labor.

Neither the diagnosis nor the implementation was complete. The model was inaccurate in two respects. First, it exaggerated the importance of domestic monetary policy in provoking disequilibrium and disrupted debt service. Second, it underestimated the domestic resistance to appreciation and the role of exchange rate devaluation in inducing import substitution as well as increased exports.

Table 4.1 presents statistical results relating the exchange rate to money supply; estimates of the net inflow of capital minus debt service, export receipts, or terms of trade; and British wholesale prices.[17] As the regression shows, in the Argentine case capital inflows as well as trade performance have a significant explanatory impact on the gold premium. It was not only domestic conditions but also the international environment that counted. That was the key insight of John Williams' pioneering study of Argentine trade under inconvertible currency. Accepting the linkage between the exchange rate and public debt service, debt service difficulties thus also had a balance of payments component in the short term. Indeed, in the key period 1888–91, 60 percent of the depreciation realized can be allocated to the increase in the money supply and 40 percent to the abrupt decline in

Table 4.1
Regression results

Dependent variables	Independent variables					$\bar{R}^2$	$D-W$
	Real export receipts[a]	Terms of trade[a]	Money supply[a]	Capital inflow minus debt service	Foreign price[a]		
Argentina, gold premium (1884 = 100)[a]							
Least squares							
1884–1900	−0.54 (5.34)		0.64 (11.28)	−0.0018 (3.84)	−1.18 (2.64)	0.95	2.49
1884–99		−0.50 (2.18)	0.51 (5.70)	−0.0013 (2.07)	−0.18 (0.23)	0.91	1.89
Instrumental variables[b]							
1885–1900	−0.62 (3.84)		0.73 (2.21)	−0.0011 (0.25)	−1.22 (1.71)	0.91	2.01
Brazil, milreis per pound[a]							
Least squares							
1877–97[c]	−0.63 (3.00)		0.87 (8.13)	0.0051 (0.91)	−0.86 (2.33)	0.92	1.95
1877–97[c,d]		−0.16 (1.75)	0.60 (6.33)	−0.0029 (0.93)	−1.20 (2.41)	0.96	1.77
Instrumental variables[b]							
1877–97	−1.31 (1.38)		1.03 (1.80)	−0.0134 (0.29)	−1.67 (1.77)	0.78	1.57

Sources:
Argentina
Gold premium: Ford, *Gold Standard*, p. 139.
Value and price of exports: Diéguez, "Crecimiento e Inestabilidad."
Import price: British export price deflator from Albert H. Imlah, *Economic Elements in the Pax Britannica*, New York, 1969, pp. 94ff.
Money supply: *Extracto Estadístico, 1915* (average of preceding and current year).
Capital account: Williams, *Argentine International Trade*, pp. 45, 101, 136, 154.
Foreign price: B. R. Mitchell, *Abstract of British Historical Statistics*, Cambridge, 1962, pp. 474–75. The Sauerbeck-Statist wholesale price index was used.

Brazil
Milreis per pence, value of exports, price of coffee, and import price: *Anuário Estatístico, 1939–40*, pp. 1353–54, 1358, 1378. (Fiscal year averaged until calendar year series begins in 1888.)
Money supply: Carlos M. Palaez and Wilson Suzigan, *História Monetária do Brasil*, Rio de Janeiro, 1976, table A.3, pp. 442ff (end of June values).
Capital account and foreign price: Franco, *Reforma Monetária*, pp. 47–48. (Debt service was calculated from table A-3, p. 47.)
a. Expressed in logarithms.
b. Instruments: time, lagged real exports, lagged money supply, foreign prices.
c. Residuals corrected by a first-order moving averages process.
d. Residuals corrected by a one-period autogressive process.

capital inflows after a great boom. Conversely, it took more than reductions in money supply; growth in exports and/or improved terms of trade were needed to underwrite appreciation in the absence of access to capital markets.

In the case of Brazil, capital flows were not of the same critical importance in provoking default. Despite a reduction in the wake of the Baring failure, as we have seen, foreign loans continued to be contracted. Contagion was less significant than it has sometimes been made out to be. This did not make the balance of payments irrelevant in provoking the discontinuity in debt service. Rather, the key external factor was the sharp decline in coffee prices that rendered the balance of payments progressively more precarious over the course of the 1890s and contributed to the erosion of the exchange rate from 1895 to 1898.

In focusing upon exchange rate appreciation as the cure, moreover, the inevitable short-term adjustment of the balance of payments was thrown back primarily on income rather then relative price effects. Countries had not only to restore fiscal order but to cut back imports since the revenue problem was symptomatic of a deeper international disequilibrium. The recommended deflation was even more difficult than a gold standard remedy in which domestic prices must fall while the nominal exchange rate remains constant. The needed speed of realigning imports and exports only made the problem worse.

In giving short shrift to relative prices and the balance of payments, external creditors failed fully to comprehend the adjustments set in motion by the depreciation-appreciation cycle and the measures required to restore fiscal balance. Depreciation brought real devaluation as the price of tradables rose more rapidly than wages. Contemporaries, such as J. P. Wileman writing about Brazil, commented extensively on the effects.[18] In conjunction with increased tariffs to enhance revenues, there was an important impulse to domestic industrialization, and not merely to increased exports. The Economist rails against Argentine "protectionism" as export surpluses were achieved in record fashion by the end of the 1890s. Even Joaquim Murtinho, extreme in his defense of comparative advantage, could not avoid raising the gold content of tariffs to 25 percent in 1900. Import duties as a percent of imports rose from 28 percent in 1898 to 53 percent in 1906.

In both countries a strong impulse to industrialization is to be found in the crisis of the 1890s, and with it the creation of a domestic industrial interest. This sector found common cause with exporters in resisting the appreciation of the orthodox model. In both Argentina and Brazil there was a return to convertibility well short of the previous rate through the creation of a conversion account. That stable rate could be maintained because of favorable results both in export receipts and in resumed capital inflow.

There were natural limits to the deflationary experience that emerged domestically, that is, without cutting off ties to the international market. Even before these were reached in the Argentine case, it was possible to renegotiate on the basis of a professed inability to pay. That was the tack taken by Finance Minister Juan Romero. Capitalization was rejected in favor of direct relief, much augmented later by a reduced valuation of the provincial debt when it was consolidated with the national.

In Brazil, deflationary policy was more rigidly followed after 1898. But it is wrong to give conditionality full credit. Domestic sentiment had been moving in that direction, and the Congress had legally authorized reduction in monetary emission in 1896. Slackened domestic activity was punctuated by a severe financial crisis in 1900. And appreciation of 50 percent did occur between 1898 and 1902 before new, more expansive policies became the order of the day.

Rhetoric added to the conditionality debate. Heated, but frequently irrelevant, discussions over the extent of foreign intervention through pledges of customs revenues dominated analyses of substantive consequences. These nationalist politics were not always effective in altering actual policy; Murtinho prided himself in his capacity to turn a deaf ear. But these outcries, like the interests of exporters and manufacturers, partially diluted the extremes of the deflationist recipe.

In the end a rising international economy ended the need for restraint. Assistance from investment bankers and restrictive internal policy contributed but did not fully resolve the debt problem in the 1890s. Externally recommended retrenchment had its limits, both economic and political. More fundamental structural adjustment would have required a more suitable theory and a stronger domestic consensus. A broader view of the importance of external factors as well as the role of internal policy would have helped. It might have prompted larger resource flows than became available and led to support for a reformism that might have proved more enduring.

4.3   Internal Responses to the Crises

Although the focus of the last section has been upon the design of creditor policy during the debt crisis of the 1890s, it has already broached the question of debtor response. Here we examine the internal discussion in more detail. Despite significant downturns in incomes and extensive resource transfers, Argentina and Brazil preferred to satisfy their creditors rather than opt for unilateral moratoria. There are three fundamental reasons.

The first is the favorable international context. Trade, including primary products, was still in a state of rapid expansion, and capital markets offered continuing access. Depression could be seen as temporary and cyclical, with a recovery on the horizon and more foreign capital awaiting. There was a reward to bearing the burden.

Second, the burden was explicitly shared. Investment bankers stood in an intermediary role as counselors to countries and advisors to bondholders. This institutional linkage was flexible enough to alter conditions and to countenance national independence. Arrangements could be made to satisfy some creditors while others, holders of Argentine cedulas and provincial bonds, for example, had to wait. Agreements required the imprimatur of existing bondholders, but investment bankers, aided by market quotations, took on the responsibility of persuasion; that task, of course, was aided by evidence of conditionality that would make future debt service continuous.

Third was a conscious internal perception that satisfaction of debts was a necessity. Implicit calculation, within this international and institutional context, led to that conclusion. Benefits and penalties always added up to validate such behavior, whatever the apparent attractions of more nationalist alternatives. For the Latin American elite in these successful late developers—as shown by their capacity to attract productive foreign investment—there was simply no contest. The sanctity of contract was an important domestic principle as well. At a sectoral level, exporters and importers who had obvious stakes in international integration were joined by import-substituting industrialists who reaped advantage from export surpluses and increased protection. The latter was an inevitable concomitant of debt service, as noted earlier.

The expansion of the international economy and the role of investment bankers have already been discussed extensively elsewhere. My emphasis here therefore is upon the internal debate. While the commitment to pay was easily the dominant view, it was not the only one.

The majority position derived both from the benefits of continuing foreign investment as an integral part of the development and modernization experience as well as the penalties of potential loss of sovereignty. Those in favor of servicing the debt did not abandon the rhetoric of nationalism to their opponents. Such sentiments are accurately and concisely conveyed in the 1890 presidential message of Carlos Pelligrini, who accepted the Rothschild accord shortly thereafter:

Not to have paid these [debt] services with that punctuality, the government would have had to declare the country bankrupt, producing such a terrible reaction in our European creditors that there would not been limits to the general indignation directed against us, and they would have closed forever those markets, resulting in the shame of our nation and the rapid decadence of our social state.[19]

More than shame could be the outcome. Actual intervention was frequently cited as a possibility, exactly as had occurred in the cases of some prominent defaulters like Egypt and Turkey. The British press did nothing to avert such speculation. The *Financial News* of May 31, 1891, asked "... but it is evident that the experience and the financial knowledge of the [Argentine] Government are totally inadequate for the task and it ought to be prepared to recognize that only foreign experience will permit it to realize the necessary changes. Why then does not President Pelligrini not recognize the situation and accept some form of control over income? The beneficial effect of such control evidences itself in Eqypt and Turkey."[20]

Later in the decade, as Brazilian leadership contemplated its options in 1897–98, according to the compiler of Campos Salles' correspondence, there were three options: "(1) suspension of debt service; (2) reduction of interest; (3) arrangement of a large loan. The first two hypotheses put at risk the very national sovereignty, with the country subject to foreign intervention against which it would be impossible to defend."[21]

Such a concern was exaggerated. The Foreign Office was not prepared to venture widely. And British economic interests, and even those of the bondholders formally organized into the Corporation of Foreign Bondholders, would not be well served by treating developmental and revenue defaulters alike. Argentina and Brazil were not Egypt and Turkey on either strategic or economic criteria. But the apparent threat reinforced the determination to find negotiated and amicable solutions through loans rather than unilateral suspension. These were epitomized by the Rothschild agreement in Argentina in 1891 and the Brazil funding loan in 1898.

Neither decision was fully accepted internally. Both were opposed for two reasons. One was the imposition of foreign claims on national revenues that secured the new loans. The other was a solution rooted in increasing debt when a balance of payments problem of largely external origin made it impossible to service the debt already owed. Argentine discord manifested itself in political rebellion in 1891 and formation of the Radical party. The more nationalist *Arreglo Romero*, with its insistence on reduced debt service, responded to such sentiments. In Brazil the opposition did not get beyond proposals of alternatives.

There, Rui Barbosa, the ex-minister of finance responsible for the great domestic expansion of credit after the founding of the Republic, played a leading role as editor of *Imprensa*. In its pages, he argued that less onerous arrangements were possible and specifically pointed to the *Arreglo Romero* as an alternative route. The argument against that strategy is of interest. As late as 1902 Alcindo Guanabara, in his history of the Campos Salles administration, argued that the precedent "is one that we did not want to see imitated." He ascribed to it the lack of foreign investment observed in Argentina in the 1890s, asserting that creditors "submitted to the reduction of interest that was imposed on them, *but closed to them the door*."[22] Yet the great boom in renewed capital inflow was just over the horizon and was not blocked by the Argentine decision.

Argentine policy moreover was not unilateral. Romero's original offer was modified, slightly, in deference to creditor claims. The amount provided was based on a realistic calculation of the national government's ability to pay; the provincial debt did not even enter. The Rothschild committee counseled acceptance. The plan met initial and continuing opposition from Pelligrini and his supporters, however, who argued that Argentine credit-worthiness was severely and unnecessarily impacted; the country could pay what it owed if domestic management were correct. In 1895 those forces were able to defeat a proposed consolidation of the debt that amounted to significant reduction of provincial debt, and they imposed an acceleration of one year in resuming interest payments. Internal politics and external debt are nothing new. What is, however, is the strong overt support for full debt service.

Debt problems worked consistently against incumbents. So Pelligrini himself discovered in 1901 when he led the fight for debt consolidation, only to have presidential support withdrawn. Economic interests were complex and intertwined. Exporters and landowners were eager to see expanded credit and exchange rate depreciation, but they also benefited from the improvements to infrastructure made possible by foreign investment. So long as conditionality could be somewhat softened, and appreciation checked, debt service could be tolerated. Repudiation was not a serious option. As property owners, the elite was not unaware of the inconsistency of reneging upon external claims while defending the propriety of internal ones.

There was thus a tendency toward conservatism that weakened national negotiating positions. The ease with which the *Arreglo* was accepted, and the erosion of provincial debts, suggests that a more forceful stand might have yielded other concessions. But the very premise was continuing debt service, not reassessment of the willingness to pay. New loans made sense in the 1890s when the disruption in international capital markets was cyclical and temporary, and countries could be expected to grow into their debts.

4.4   Parallels with the Debt Crisis of the 1980s

This discussion of the 1890s provides basis for a contemporary comparison in the two salient dimensions of conditionality and willingness to pay.

Conditionality requirements, although obviously different, share important similarities. First, the implicit economic models advanced by creditors tend to place principal blame for debt servicing difficulties upon the domestic excesses of the debtors and to prescribe accordingly. That is the significance of a case by case approach. A common focus is reduction of the public sector deficit, since there must be scope for the predominantly public debt to be paid. But current theory also centers upon the balance of payments in a way that historical application did not. A second similarity is in the appeal to more, but limited, debt to permit continuity of debt service as a key element in the solution to the debt problem.

In both regards the application of conditionality was, and is, a serious simplification. Clearly, both then and now, domestic policy has contributed to debt service problems. The Argentine boom of the late 1880s and the Brazilian expansion of the early 1890s have their counterparts in the oil profits of the 1970s. But there is also an external dimension, if only in the abrupt end to favorable conditions of foreign inflow and/or high export prices. Regardless of how one got into a debt problem moreover, the task of getting out is necessarily conditioned by the international and domestic circumstances governments confront later and not earlier.

In this respect the difficult international environment in the 1980s of slowing trade growth and adverse terms of trade may well have provoked a sharper decline in real exchange rates and real income than in the 1890s.[23] Current export surpluses moreover may be less a boon in stimulating domestic activity than a present cost in reducing saving available to finance investment and competitive capability. And in terms of the impact of domestic activity on the income distribution, the historical buffering mechanism of varying immigration has no counterpart in the present period.

Getting public sector deficits down was, and is, complicated by the large share of interest payments in total expenditure. Retrenchment in other outlays is even more difficult now when the private sector takes its cues in larger part from public expenditures. There is not simply a crowding out demand effect but also a crowding in supply effect. At the heart of the matter is how rapidly the public sector can be expected to adjust.

Finance is intended to facilitate adjustment both by offering incentives to follow the right policies and also by affording a longer period for structural change. Here is where the solution of more debt has typically proved inadequate, whether in the 1890s or under the aegis of the present

Baker Plan. It is simply not generous enough. Financial assistance that only guarantees the continuity of debt service can inhibit rather than encourage fundamental reform. In the Brazil of 1898, *Imprensa* wrote: "Our illness cannot be cured with financial arrangements. It comes from economic evils whose cure is long. The accord has remedied nothing. Let us amend it: we will pay you, not in new debt, but in money. Only you will receive not ten as now, but two or one."[24] Identical sentiments resound in contemporary debtor countries, and with even better reason.

Debt service reduction was less critically important when growth trends were more assured on the basis of expanding primary exports and cyclical recovery was assured. Nor did governments have to satisfy demands for immediate improvements in living standards at the risk of electoral defeat. The politics of the 1890s was hardly a politics of the masses.

That circumstance made an elite disposition to the continuity of debt service easier to defend. But even today governments do not like to default, and go to considerable lengths to avoid moratoria. It is not easy to argue that the substantial net resource outflow from debtor countries of the last five years, without major interruption, is a utility-maximizing outcome. Like the intervention feared in the 1890s, the costs of default tend to be exaggerated. But the benefits also are considerably diluted. Lesser debt service cannot be put to good use because the gains are feared to be temporary, and the uncertain environment is not conducive to private investment. Unilateral action can provoke unproductive nationalism and promote internal conflict. All groups do not fare equally. The Peruvian experience is enlightening.

In trying to understand why debtor countries have not formed a debtors' cartel or taken more aggressive stands, these internal aspects have been given insufficient attention. They lead to a more complicated politico-economic calculus. Interests are not uniform. Behind the facade of a national negotiating position are divergent assessments of the risks different groups are willing to take in order to achieve creditor concessions and divergent calculations of the gains that could be achieved. Within the debtor countries many share the perception that reforms can be achieved only under duress, and these persons welcome external monitoring and pressure.

A prime, and valid, reason for sustained debt service in the past was the importance of continuing access to capital markets. Even then it could be exaggerated, in support of a domestic interest, as when the Arreglo Romero was feared to deprive Argentina of creditworthiness for 30 years. Where once that argument was internalized within the debtor countries, one now hears it much more frequently from the creditors. That makes the concern more suspect. Self-interest is more reliable than altruism.

The capital market of the 1970s that led to the current debt problem was by its nature temporary and incapable of replication. It was neither part of an underlying international division of labor or rooted in a sustainable pattern of flows from continuing surplus countries. Flows to developing countries from commercial banks were symptomatic rather of balance of payments disequilibrium and institutional inadequacy of public recycling. It is poor policy to shore up that financial structure indefinitely.

Even in the past, country performance seems to dominate good behavior. That is the central argument of the careful study in chapter 3 by Jorgenson and Sachs of the effects of Latin American default in the 1930s. Faithful debt service, and even attractive foreign investment codes, do not compensate for the absence of profitable opportunities. Today, as in the past, these are based on productive potential, now less on natural resources and more on industrial promise. To the extent that a debt overhang and its service inhibit performance, it can be in the interest of both the debtors and creditors to search for new formulas. Even though the 1890s attempts in Argentina and Brazil were not wholly successful, they evidenced a novel private response to the debt crisis that public intervention now should be able to improve upon.

Notes

1. For a survey of the recent theoretical literature, see J. Eaton, M. Gersovitz, and J. Stiglitz, "The Pure Theory of Country Risk," *European Economic Review* (June 1986).

2. A comprehensive discussion of the Fund's underlying approach to stabilization can be found in *Theoretical Aspects of the Design of Fund-Supported Adjustment Programs*, International Monetary Fund Occasional Paper No. 55, 1987. A more critical view can be found in a set of country studies organized by WIDER, whose synthesis volume, by Lance Taylor, will soon be published by Oxford University Press.

3. More complete treatment of the historical record and analysis of the influence of internal and external factors on the balance of payments can be found in my "Lessons of the 1890's for the 1980's," forthcoming in English and already published in Portuguese in *Pesquisa e Planejamento Econômico* (December 1987).

4. José A. Terry, *Contribucion a la Historia Financiera de la Republica Argentina,* Buenos Aires, 1910, p. 26.

5. For evidence on the magnitude of Argentine debt and its service, see José Terry, *Contribución*, p. 28, and H. E. Peters, *The Foreign Debt of the Argentine Republic,* Baltimore, 1934, p. 45.

6. See the discussion of press reaction to founding of the Banco de la Nacion in Horacio Juan Cuccorese, *En Tiempo Histórico de Carlos Pellegrini,* Vol. 2, Buenos Aires, 1985, pp. 128ff.

7. Terry, *Contribución*, p. 28.

8. See Peters, *Foreign Debt*, p. 47, note, for a comparison of original and consolidated values of the provincial debt.

9. Carlos Días-Alejandro, *Essays on the Economic History of the Argentine Republic*, New Haven, 1970, p. 31, uses ECLA estimates.

10. Peters, *Foreign Debt*, p. 49.

11. Quoted in Steven Topik, *The Political Economy of the Brazilian State, 1889–1930*, Austin, 1987, p. 36.

12. Translated from the letter in French from the Rothschilds cited in Alcindo Guanabara, *A Presidência Campos Sales*, reprinted Brasilia, 1983, p. 41.

13. See *Relatório do Ministério da Fazenda, 1901*, p. L.

14. Quoted in Topik, *Brazilian State*, p. 38.

15. An import series on real capital imports is presented in Wilson Suzigan, *Indústria Brasileira*, São Paulo, 1986, app. 1. Strong criticism of Murtinho's policies can be found in Carlos Manuel Palaez and Wilson Suzigan, *História Monetária do Brasil*, Rio de Janeiro, 1976, pp. 181ff.

16. "Lessons from the Past: Capital Markets during the Nineteenth Century and the Interwar Period," *International Organization* 39, 3 (Summer 1985), pp. 402ff.

17. This is Table 1 from my "Lessons of the 1890's." Further discussion concerning method and results can be found there.

18. Wileman's book, *Brazilian Exchange*, Buenos Aires, 1896, now reprinted by Greenwood Press in 1971, is a classic contemporary study of inconvertible currency. Wileman's emphasis upon a quantity theory approach much influenced Murtinho.

19. Quoted in Cuccorese, *En Tiempo Histórico*, II, p. 88.

20. Quoted in Milciades Pena, *Alberdi, Sarmiento, El 90*, Buenos Aires, 1970, p. 15.

21. Celio Debes, *Campos Salles*, Rio de Janeiro, 1978, II, p. 448.

22. Guanabara, *A Presidência Campos Sales*, p. 220. Italics in the original.

23. Reliable estimates of aggregate income movements in the 1890s are unfortunately not available. Brazilian estimates by Contador and Haddad, and a later variant by Raymond Goldsmith, are quite unreliable, being largely based upon nominal trade and monetary stock series deflated by unrelated price indexes. An Argentine series starts only in 1900. We do know that Brazilian decline from 1980 to 1984 was more severe than from 1929 to 1933, whereas in Argentina the Great Depression had a slighly larger impact. See Rosemary Thorp, ed., *Latin America in the 1930's*, London, 1984, app. 1, and ECLA, *Preliminary Overview of the Latin American Economy, 1987*, table 2.

24. Quoted in Guanabara, *A Presidência Campos Sales*, p. 215.

5   Brazilian Debt Crises: Past and Present

Eliana A. Cardoso and Rudiger Dornbusch

Deficits innumerable, annual, perennial, everlasting and ever increasing deficits!
In these three syllables is comprehended all the mystery of Brazilian finance, the head and front of its offending.

Wileman (1896)

Brazilian debt problems have troubled world capital markets for more than 150 years. A major lesson from that history is the extraordinary repetition of events. The same themes, even the very same language, reemerge every time a sudden halt to lending brings about illiquidity, funding loans, moratoria, and then, soon, renewed lending.

Sometimes the precipitating events are domestic, as in the nineteenth century. At other times, as in the 1930s or the 1980s, a sudden deterioration of the world economy makes a previously accumulated debt overly large and burdensome. The exact details differ, but the broad outlines are always the same. Our interest is to highlight these common features, but we also emphasize how access to the world capital market has served as an essential element in a development strategy. That access was important in the nineteenth century, and it was essential again in the 1970s. This discussion raises the question of where development finance will come from, now that bank lending has dried up.

Our discussion is in five parts. Sections 5.1 through 5.3 report on Brazilian debt history: we start with a discussion of the late nineteenth century, then cover the interwar experience, and, finally, the run up to the 1980s debt crisis. Section 5.4 asks what went wrong with the muddling through strategy initiated in 1982. The chapter concludes with the issue of how to reconcile growth with debt service and offers a proposal.

5.1 Lessons from the Past

Before studying the Brazilian debt crises, it is useful to reflect on two questions: What is the source of debt crises? How are debt crises ultimately resolved?

We start with a conceptual framework. Equation (1) shows the financing of external interest payments by three alternative sources: a noninterest current account surplus (NICA), new debt issues the proceeds of which pay the interest (and amortization) on existing debt, and other net capital inflows, specifically direct foreign investment.

$$\frac{\text{Interest}}{\text{payments}} = \text{NICA} + \frac{\text{Net increase}}{\text{in debt}} + \frac{\text{Other net capital}}{\text{inflows}} \tag{1}$$

A debt crisis can arise for one of four reasons, which often emerge in combination. First, domestic fiscal and/or political disorder translates into trade deficits or a reduction in the noninterest current account surplus.

Second, world economic shocks to a country's terms of trade deteriorate export earnings or increase import costs, or shocks to a country's markets reduce export revenue.

Third, nondebt capital inflows that used to finance interest payments and trade deficits suddenly dry up.

Fourth, rolling of debt (principal and interest) is disrupted by a loss of confidence on the part of the world capital market. Taussig (1928) and Kindleberger (1984), in particular, have emphasized the cutoff of external loans as the precipitating factor in major debt crises.

It is apparent that these disturbances tend to come together: When a country's terms of trade deteriorate, investment opportunities are much less attractive, and hence investment capital from abroad dries up. Knowledge of a financial problem ensures that competitive bondholders will be leery of buying new debt issued to tide the country over the difficulty.

The inevitable outcome, as Brazil's financial history amply demonstrates, is a funding crisis and an interruption of debt service. In terms of equation (1) this is equivalent to "involuntary interest capitalization."

Next, how do debt problems go away? Domestic adjustment programs almost invariably are an essential part of restoring confidence on the part of creditors. But a favorable turn of the world economy (whether through war or improved terms of trade) is equally critical. There is no precedent in Brazilian history for one of these factors alone being enough.

Third, reduction of the debt burden by an adjustment of terms is often part of a return to the capital market. This was clearly the case in the 1942 debt consolidation.

With this background we have all the ingredients to study the debt crises of the 1890s, 1930s, and 1980s.

An Overview of the 1890s

Brazil went into debt in her very infancy. The history of the Brazilian Empire is one of budget deficits financed by external and domestic borrowing. Minister Ouro Preto's report on the budget situation at the time of the proclamation of the Republic shows that taxes and other revenues during the time of the Empire covered only 30 percent of total expenditures. The rest was financed by debt which the Brazilian Republic later inherited.

When the Brazilian Republic was declared in 1889, the external public debt already amounted to £33 million. Ten years later, with an external public debt of almost £50 million, the first debt crisis was brought about by falling coffee prices.

Rippy (1977) notes that in the 60 years following Brazilian independence from Portugal in 1824, English investors preferred Brazil as a field of investment to any other Latin American country because Brazil was politically more stable. By 1890, however, the English already had a larger stake in Argentina.

More than half of the British investment in Brazil was in government bonds. Although some of the Brazilian states failed to meet their obligations, the Brazilian national government had an excellent record. Capital invested in Brazilian bonds brought good returns: the average annual nominal yield seldom dropped below 4 percent until after 1931.

Direct investment was insignificant before 1840 but then grew particularly fast in 1840–75, and immediately before World War I. Using the *South American Journal* as a source, Rippy (1977) observes that British investments in Brazil were less diversified than in Argentina. They were concentrated in railway enterprises, with public utility investment next in size. The average nominal yield of the British capital invested in Brazilian railways remained above 5 percent per annum, except for a few years during the depression of 1890s.

Table 5.1 shows the stock of foreign capital in Brazil between 1885 and 1913.[1]

Until 1900 almost all capital inflows were of British origin, but by 1905 the stock of direct investment from the U.S. and European countries was

Table 5.1
Stock of foreign capital in Brazil, 1885–1913 (millions of £)

	Direct investment	Public debt	Total
1885	24.4	23.2	47.6
1895	40.6	39.0	79.6
1905	75.1	88.3	163.4
1913[a]	255.9	151.7	407.6

Sources: Stone (1977, table 6) and Abreu (1985, table 1). There is a discrepancy between the two sources concerning British loans in 1895. Stone's numbers, which are reported in our table, exceed Abreu's by almost £20 million.

Table 5.2
The balance of payments in Brazil, 1890–1913 (millions of £, accumulated end-of-period flows)

	1890–99	1900–1904	1905–1909	1910–13
Current account	−39.1	35.4	14.0	−48.4
Trade balance	28.8	70.3	83.7	38.7
Freight and insurance	32.5	18.0	26.5	30.0
Remittances and travels	8.7	4.9	7.2	8.1
Interest and amortization	26.7	12.0	36.0	49.0
Capital inflows	30.0	12.0	76.3	135.9

Source: Goldsmith (1986, table III-9).

already 40 percent of the total. Nevertheless, British capital continued to represent more than 80 percent of the stock of public debt until 1913.

Capital inflows came in waves that were in large measure dictated by the supply of savings in the United Kingdom. Net transfers of resources from abroad were positive in the 1890s, negative between 1900 and 1909, and positive again in the years preceding World War I. Table 5.2 shows estimates of the balance of payments between 1890 and 1913.

Three kinds of disturbances dominated the experience of the 1890–1913 period:

1. Sharp movements in the world price of coffee and the evolution of the rubber trade.

2. Domestic financial instability that expressed itself in budget deficits and money creation.

3. Movements in the availability of external credit which at times dampened the extent of domestic inflationary finance but also acted as an independent source of disturbance to the economy.

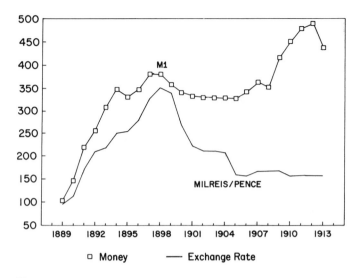

Figure 5.1
Money and exchange rate (1888 = 100). Source: Instituto Brasileiro de Geografia e Estatistica

Figure 5.1 highlights the behavior of the money stock and the exchange rate. Three broad periods can be distinguished: The first one, starting in the 1880s, was marked by extreme domestic instability and inflation. The years of the *Encilhamento* were characterized by very high inflation which was more than 30 percent per year in 1891 and 1892. With reinforcement by a dramatic fall of coffee prices in 1896–1900 to less than half of 1891–94 prices, exchange depreciation was massive. This period lasts to 1898.

Contrary to common belief, the Baring crisis and external credit rationing were not decisive factors in the Brazilian experience of the 1890s. Fishlow (1988) observes that external loans continued to be contracted during 1893 and again in 1895–97. Transfers of resources from abroad were positive until the eve of the 1898 Funding Loan. The threat of Brazilian default in 1898 was brought about by continually falling coffee prices. Table 5.3 shows the price of coffee between 1891 and 1913.

In the second phase, between 1898 and 1905, a funding loan and a shift from money to debt finance introduced deflation. The currency appreciated and was then stabilized in 1905. The crisis of the second half of the 1890s culminated with the 1898 Funding Loan, whose conditionality terms were as harsh as those imposed by an IMF agreement. By 1903 the price of coffee had fallen to 36 percent of its level ten years before. Deflation and depression lasted until 1905.

Table 5.3
Inflation and price of coffee in Brazil, 1891–1913

Period	Inflation (average %)	Price of coffee in London (1888 = 100)		
		High[a]	Average	Low[b]
1891–94	24	130	112	98
1896–1900	2	92	61	47
1901–1905	−5	63	55	47
1906–1913	2	122	82	58

Sources: IBGE, *Series Estatisticas Retrospectivas*, and Goldsmith (1986).
a. The highest yearly index during the period.
b. The lowest yearly index in the period.

In the third phase, from 1906 to 1912, world trade prices were exceptionally favorable—coffee prices doubled between 1906 and 1912. This was a period of prosperity. The recovery of coffee prices, the rubber boom, and capital inflows in the form of portfolio as well as direct investment helped sustain growth. This period came to an end when coffee prices collapsed in 1913–14. Once again, in 1914, a new funding loan was required.

Next, we look at each of these phases in more detail.

From the *Encilhamento* to the Crisis

In the late 1880s the money supply expanded rapidly in response to demands for increased credit. Pressure for monetary expansion came from the abolition of slavery in 1888. More money was needed to sustain a new wage-based labor market, as well as to permit cheap credit, compensating landowners for the capital losses from the emancipation. The argument that the existing stock of paper currency was too small for Brazil, owing to the great size of the country, the limited use of cheques, and the general habit among small traders of keeping large sums of money on hand instead of depositing them in banks, was advanced. Supporters of the gold standard protested: How was the required volume of currency to be determined?

After the proclamation of the Republic, the expansionist doctrine was supported by the Finance Minister Rui Barbosa, and the supply of money almost doubled in 1890. A series of decrees authorized additions to the volume of inconvertible paper money. London disapproved:

Of the issue of new financial decrees by the Brazilian Government there is no end, scarcely a week passing without their number being added to.[2]

... some of the States are said to be in difficulties, but as the *Rio News* points out "they are always in trouble and at this very moment spending money as though they had inexhaustible resources" .... Capitalists on this side of the world, we should think, hesitate very considerably before lending the Finance Minister of Brazil ten millions sterling to assist him and his Government in the kind of "rake's progress", upon which they appear to be so anxious to enter.[3]

Brazil was said to be following the example of Argentina, where events leading up to the Baring crisis are described by Hyndman (1892) as follows:

The history of the loans to the Argentine Republic, now that it has become history, is surprising, indeed. A country which had a national debt of £10,000,000 in 1875, contrived to raise it to £70,000,000 in 1889 .... All the money markets were competing with one another for a share of these good things. London, Paris, Brussels, Berlin, each was ready to outbid the other for the privilege of taking up ventures and floating loans which, at any other time, would have been regarded as very doubtful security, when the nature of the country, the character of the population, and the instability of its political institutions were carefully considered ....[4]

In Brazil, the government financial policy resulted in a proliferation of new banks, at the same time that new companies were started in every branch of commercial and industrial enterprise. Their shares were sold at constantly increasing prices as soon as they were issued. As had just happened in Argentina, "railways, docks, tramways, waterworks, public buildings, mansions, all were being carried on in hot haste ...." A boom took off. *The Economist* commented:

As capital cannot be attracted, the printing presses are to be set to work, and new issues of inconvertible paper currency poured out. In that way temporary relief may be afforded, and fresh fuel will be headed upon the fire of speculation. But what the ultimate result of this policy must be, we see in the case of Argentina, and it is time that all who have a stake in Brazil should be called upon to take note of the direction in which she is drifting.[5]

The comparisons with Argentina finally aroused the protest of a correspondent from Rio de Janeiro:

Permit me to say that a comparison of the finances of Brazil with those of the Argentine Republic is as absurd as to compare the resources natural and otherwise and the trade of the two countries. The Brazilians are a different race of people, and the administration of public affairs has always been a reasonably honest one. The credit of this country has always been maintained at a high level. There is, doubtless, speculation by officials in Brazil, but there has never been such dishonesty as in the Argentine Republic, where an honest official of high or low degree was, and is now, the exception to the general rule.... The prosperity of Argentina during the past 15 years, so much vaunted, has been almost wholly fictitious. Since 1882, more than £120 million of foreign capital has been poured into that country—a great part of which has been stolen by corrupt officials, and as much more planted in public works that will never be remunerative....[6]

But *The Economist* was convinced of the correctness of its prediction and went further in its comparisons with Argentina:

Those interested in the stability of Brazilian finance are beginning to fear, and not without some cause, that the same policy of currency inflation that has brought the Argentine Republic to grief is being pursued by the Brazilian Government.[7]

Economic and political instability were, in fact, on the rise. At the end of 1891, the Marshall da Fonseca dissolved the Congress and proclaimed martial law throughout the country. For some time it had been known that considerable tension between the executive government and the Chambers existed, principally on matters of financial policy. The policy of the government was to increase the already largely inflated stock of paper currency by further issues. But the Congress demanded that the flood of inconvertible currency should cease and that a check should be put upon the action of the Banco da Republica, which was indulging in excesses somewhat similar to those of Argentine banks. The dispute ended in rupture, and for a short while, the promoters of the expansionary policy held the field.

A Committee of the Chamber, appointed to inquire into the affairs of the Banco da Republica, concluded that excessive issue of paper money had promoted stock exchange gambling, which had withdrawn capital from legitimate enterprises and led to a serious depreciation of the currency. The Banco da Republica had played a prominent in promoting this speculation, part and the committee recommended that it should be required to reduce different accounts and to limit the issue of notes. The minister of finance was opposed. He believed that if a halt was put to money creation, a crisis would ensue. Moreover he believed that there was no need to hold gold against the notes and that the credit of the state was sufficient to guarantee conversion of the notes. Nevertheless, the Congress, by a majority of 100 to 12, passed the second reading of a bill restricting the issues of paper money.

The company mania subsided, and the first burst of wild speculation passed. For many bubble companies, the day of reckoning had come. Shares that once sold at a high premium now could not find buyers at less than half the paid-up capital. Banks ceased to pay interest on deposits. The process of liquidation was underway.

The Economist commented:

Although the finances of Brazil have fallen into serious disorder they have not yet lapsed into anything like the deplorable condition of those of Argentina and Uruguay. Besides, ..., on her recent outburst of extravagant speculation, it is with her own and not with borrowed money that Brazil has been dealing.[8]

As figure 5.1 shows, the milreis underwent rapid devaluation. Again the comparisons with Argentina are inevitable. Whether the peso depreciated because of the overissue of banknotes in Argentina or because of the sudden halt in new foreign lending is still debated in the literature. A monetarist position tends to attribute the depreciation to the new bank laws passed in Argentina in 1887, but Williams (1920) claims that cutoff of the capital flow produced the depreciation.[9] Similar questions arose in the case of Brazil. Fishlow (1988) argues that capital inflows did not affect the behavior of the Brazilian exchange rate in the 1890s, and Cardoso (1983) shows that the monetary expansion was not enough to explain the behavior of the exchange rate, which was clearly influenced by the price of coffee.

External confidence was shaken not only by the expansionary policies but also by the political instability that led to the resignation of the Marshall da Fonseca. Rebellion and military repression came in 1893 and 1894. Despite mounting internal and external problems and the negative effects of the Baring crisis on evaluation of Latin American creditworthiness, Brazil did not default and continued to have limited access to foreign loans. *The Economist* reproduced an extract from Rio News in connection with the Brazilian loan issued by the Rothschilds in 1893:

... the general scheme is for the government to guarantee these loans in return for the use of the proceeds not required by the borrowing companies. For instance, a railway company borrows enough for completion of an extension which may require several years to construct, and the treasury undertakes to guarantee the loan for the privilege of having the use of the money until required. Should it be inconvenient for the treasury to advance the funds required at any time, means will of course be found to delay the construction. These companies, therefore are to be used for obtaining loans for the treasury, which loans are not to figure in the public indebtedness of the country .... Employing round numbers, the loan yielded £3 million. This, at the current rate of exchange should have yielded the company $57.84 million, but we are informed that the treasury had taken the loan at 20d, or at a cost of $36.15 million, the company thus losing the important sum of $21.69 million.... We cannot believe that these gentlemen (the directors of the company) are such blind and hopeless fools as this operation implies, consequently the treasury must have given something more than the bare 20 pence announced by the Press.[10]

Fishlow (1988) points out that the government continued to meet its foreign obligations, despite increasing debt service owing to exchange depreciation. Government debt service more than doubled between 1892 and 1894, amounting to more than 100 percent of the trade surplus. External resources were required to help meet interest payments and amortization. In 1895 a new Brazilian loan was offered for public subscription. The loan was for 6 million and was to bear 5 percent interest, the issue price being 85 percent. *The Economist* commented on the terms of the loan:

It is clear from this that the financial position of the country has become utterly unsound, and that if strenuous and successful efforts be not made to economize in every possible direction, Brazil will follow some of its neighbors into the ranks of the insolvent.[11]

The milreis continued its decline until 1898, and matters went from bad to worse. The hope that financial affairs in Brazil would improve with the advent to power of the new president, Campos Salles, soon gave place to the question of whether national bankruptcy could be avoided. The exchange rate had collapsed, adding very heavily to the domestic cost of providing for service of the foreign debt. No wonder, then, that Brazilians bonds fell (figure 5.2). *The Economist* predicted ruin:

The recent mails to hand from Brazil show that default in the service of the foreign debt is regarded locally as only a question of time. The differences in

Figure 5.2
Monthly prices of Brazilian bonds: 1890–1914 (price in pounds sterling; issued 1888; 4.5 percent). Source: *Commercial and Financial Chronicle*, various issues.

opinion refer only to the causes of the present situation and the method in which the crisis is to be met.[12]

One current of opinion ascribed the impending default almost solely to the fall in coffee prices, and called upon European financiers to come forward and save the credit of the country. It pointed out the disasters likely to follow a default in the debt service and the railway guarantees and believed that European financing would not be so blind to its own interest as to allow it to take place.

The Economist argued the opposing view, reproducing an extract from *Rio News*:

Years ago it was pointed out that the policy which the public men of Brazil were pursuing would certainly lead to bankruptcy. They have known that large deficits were being realized every year, and that their extravagance would certainly increase them. But they live in a fool's paradise and would not see the fatal termination of such a policy.... If we are not mistaken, we shall soon be hearing that it is the duty of foreign banking houses to help us out of our difficulties by loaning us more money. Such a claim would be worse than absurd. Brazil has no one to blame for her financial troubles but her own public men.[13]

As it became evident that the financial position of the Brazilian government was desperate, the rearrangement of the debt took the form of a funding loan. The plan provided for funding of the interest on external debt and the internal gold loan of 1879 for a period of three years, and also for certain accounts payable annually for railway guarantees. During the period of moratorium, holders of the bonds and guarantees would receive 5 percent bonds in lieu of the stipulated amounts in gold. As part of the funding arrangement, the government was to deposit with three foreign banks in Rio de Janeiro the equivalent of these bonds in paper money, at the exchange rate of 18d per milreis. The paper money was either to be destroyed or, if and when the exchange rate was favorable, used to buy foreign exchange at 18d to the milreis to be remitted to London. The theory was that the excess of paper money was one of the causes of the fall in the exchange rate. Reducing the outstanding paper currency would cause the exchange rate to appreciate. If the appreciation went far enough to admit the purchase of exchange at 18d, it would be possible to accumulate a gold fund that would then be available when the payment of interest in cash was to be resumed three years later.

Some time later, *Rio News* commented:

Whilst, it is indisputable that by a series of well considered measures Government is gradually introducing order into financial chaos and improving its finances, yet the economical situation is no better, but, in truth, more desperate than ever, and scarcely likely to improve for some time to come, until, in fact, coffee ceases to fall, and the rise that must come some day recommences.[14]

Joaquim Murtinho, the Brazilian Minister of Finance, interpreted the crisis as a result of excess money creation.[15] He attributed the economic crisis to the decrease of the value of Brazil's most important product, coffee. The decline of coffee prices in turn was attributed to overproduction which was explained by the enormous issuance of paper money that excited the fever of speculation. Thus, according to Murtinho, the inflation of the currency constituted the root cause from which all the economic ills of Brazil had sprung. His main conclusion was that the progressive increase of the volume of paper money was the determining factor in the simultaneous depreciation of its value and of the fall of foreign exchange. Even *The Economist* found Murtinho's position exaggerated:

He is thus a very stalwart of the quantitative theory of money, a theory which, in our opinion, he presses to an undue extreme.... It would be interesting to know what the finance houses here who negotiated those loans have to say with regard to Dr. Murtinho's assertion that they knew their proceeds were to be entirely devoted to paying the interest on previous issues. If they had that knowledge they must have been aware that a collapse was inevitable, and that consequently investors who responded to the appeals made to them were certain to suffer loss. But, however that may be, the long catalogue of financial abuses given by Dr. Murtinho shows that infinitely greater reforms than a mere tinkering reduction of the paper currency are needed to put the finances of the country in the way to rehabilitation.[16]

The widely shared view was that Brazilian problems were rooted in large government deficits. Wileman (1896), a classic source on this period, notes:

Deficits innumerable, annual, perennial, everlasting and ever increasing deficits!

In these three syllables is comprehended all the mystery of Brazilian finance, the head and front of its offending.

It is a truism that without deficits there would be no national debt and no inconvertible government issue, because, debt, deficits and inconvertible paper money are all, in a sense, synonymous.[17]

And as long as cuts in the deficits were not imposed, just burning paper money was not seen as a solution:

Whence the Brazilian Government were obtaining the money with which to withdraw notes from circulation, in accordance with the provisions of the funding Loan, has been somewhat of a mystery, as there is no surplus of revenue available for the purpose, but on the contrary a chronic deficit.... The government has been only substituting one form of paper debt for another, and as the new debt bears interest, whereas the old did not, the financial position, instead of being bettered, is being made worse.[18]

Despite criticism from abroad as well as unpopularity and rebellion at home, Murtinho's tight monetary policy, combined with large improvements in the trade balance (in part due to the beginning rubber boom), stabilized the exchange rate after 1903. The cost was economic recession. But soon afterward, rising coffee prices and a favorable balance of payments would attract a new surge of foreign investment and renewed loans. Prosperity returned in the second half of the 1990s and would last for the next half decade.

By 1911 the public debt had increased to £145 million; the second debt crisis, as well as the second funding loan, was imminent. Finance Minister Rivadavia Correa noted:

In finance the essential fact is that debts are paid with funds obtained from new loans. This has been the rule for us for already many years. What is new is that this time the loan is made by the same people to whom we owe the overdue interest.[19]

5.2 The 1930s Crisis

Brazil did not miss out on the 1920s. The first American issue was sold in 1921. Prior to World War I, Brazil had raised her foreign loans in London. Sixty percent of the external obligations outstanding in 1930 was still denominated in sterling. By then, the external public debt had risen to £250 million (more than 1 billion U.S. dollars) and it was time for yet another debt crisis, a moratorium, and shortly afterward, the third funding loan. But in the next few years regular debt service could not be maintained even with a restructuring. As a result of the depression, service was suspended in 1931–32. Application of part of the reduced funds available for debt service to the market purchase of bonds, depreciated by the default, became common.

Table 5.4 shows Brazilian public debt and debt service in the interwar period. The dramatic increase in the debt service ratio (counting only public debt and not including important private debt and income from direct investment) explains the liquidity problem.

In barely 40 years the bondholders were forced to accept three voluntary abatements of their contractual claims, marked by the fundings of 1898, 1914, and 1931. In February 1934, a "readjustment plan" named after Finance Minister Osvaldo Aranha was put into effect. It effected a unilateral scaling down of payments. In previous difficulties a funding loan had

Table 5.4
Brazilian trade and debt in the interwar period (millions of $)

	External debt[a]	Debt service[a]	Debt service ratio[b]
1926	1053.0	60.3	13.1
1927	1012.4	62.3	14.5
1928	1108.3	69.2	14.6
1929	1125.6	76.3	16.7
1930	1204.1	74.7	24.0
1931	1037.7	68.4	28.3
1932	1112.5	73.0	40.4
1933	953.1	78.5	35.0

Sources: Werhahn (1937) and *Estatisticas Historicas do Brasil* (1987).
a. Public debt only.
b. Ratio of public debt service to merchandise exports.

provided the extra resources to satisfy existing creditors partially. This was the first time that debt service terms were unilaterally reduced, and some payments suspended.

Starting in November 1937, there was a complete suspension of debt remittances. Brazil's dictator Getulio Vargas explained:

We stopped the service of the external debt, moved by circumstances beyond our control. This does not mean the rejection of earlier commitments. All we need is time to resolve difficulties that we did not create and to readjust our economy, transforming potential wealth in resources that will permit us to repay, without sacrifices, our creditors. Gone are the days when our obligations were written abroad, at the discretion of banks and intermediaries.[20]

Not until 1940, with the help of World War II, was partial debt service resumed, under a modified version of the previous schedule. This involved a further cut in the original rates of payments.

In late 1943 Brazil implemented a unilateral exchange offer to consolidate debt service in a manner that is highly suggestive of possibilities today. The American press reacted with sympathy, as shown in an article in *Barron's*: "In retrospect, we find that Brazil always paid on its foreign obligations when it was able to do so."[21]

Not everybody, however, would agree with such a statement. A notable exception appeared in *The Economist*:

The whole story (of the Brazilian reschedulings) confirms the belief, expressed here more than once, that Brazil's intention has throughout been to escape from her obligations as lightly as possible and that she was enabled to do so by persistent disagreement between the representatives of America and Britain, and by the inability or unwillingness of the British authorities to play any effective part in securing reasonable terms.[22]

The 1943 plan consolidated the entire Brazilian debt, stretched the maturities by 40 to 60 years, and adjusted down both principal and interest. Creditors were offered a choice between two plans:

Plan A: There would be no reduction of principal, but interest rates would be reduced from more than 6.5 percent to 3.375 (and less) with a provision for a sinking fund. Debt service (interest plus sinking fund) amounted to between 2.9 to 5.1 percent of principal per year.

Plan B: For every $1,000 of original bonds, bondholders would receive a cash payment of between $75 and $175, a new bond with a face value of $800 (or $500 in some cases), and a coupon rate reduced to 3.75 percent. The bonds had no fixed maturity but were entitled to a sinking fund. Interest plus sinking fund amounted to a combined debt service rate of 6.4 percent. In addition, the Brazilian government guaranteed the service of state and municipal bonds assenting to plan B, should the individual debtor fail to make the required remittances.

Dollar issues constituted only about one-third of the foreign indebtedness of Brazil. The bulk of the obligations consisted of sterling loans, and the amount of service funds allotted to British creditors was based on the 65.8 percent of total debt held by them.

Once again, *Barron's* and *The Economist* disagreed as to which of the plans offered better terms. *The Economist* believed that option A, retaining the nominal capital intact, was the better option to take in the case of bonds with a low market value.[23]

Barron's stated that much more favorable treatment was available under option B, which could be accepted only through the last day of 1944. It also explained the reason that option A was offered at all considering that option B was far superior. Since the creditors were given one unfavorable and one favorable choice with a time limit, the number of assents was probably higher than it would have been otherwise. And Brazil, no doubt, would find it worthwhile to offer better terms for its external creditors if the external debt could be cut from $837.7 million to $521.5 million, assuming 100 percent acceptance of option B.[24]

By early 1946, 78 percent of the bondholders had assented to the exchange offer. Plan A had been chosen by 22 percent of the bondholders,

Figure 5.3
Monthly prices of Brazilian bonds: 1927–60 (relative to price of U.S. long-term bond).
Source: *Commercial and Financial Chronicle,* and Federal Reserve Board.

Table 5.5
The bond price in New York ($ per $100 face value)

	1939	1940	1941	1942	1943	1944	1945	1946
Low	10.4	11.3	11.5	16.9	23.0	39.0	51.9	43.3
High	19.8	18.9	18.3	20.3	33.8	50.5	63.5	68.0

Source: *Commercial and Financial Chronicle.*

and 56 percent had opted for plan B. Figure 5.3 shows the monthly
maximum price in New York of a Brazilian bond[25] with original terms of
6.5 percent interest and a 1957 maturity date. After 1943 the price refers to
the same bond, now stamped for plan A, interest adjusted to 3.375 percent
and the maturity stretched to 1979. (Throughout, the price is expressed
relative to the price of a 30-year U.S. government bond with a 6.5 percent
coupon.) The interesting point here is that after the 1943 downward
adjustment in terms, with repudiation threats removed, the bond actually
increased in value. Table 5.5 further brings out this point further by showing
the annual high and low quotations on the bond.

The increase in the bond price reflects a combination of three factors.
First, the fact of a settlement eliminated the fear of more significant debt

reduction of even near-repudiation. By comparison, in 1944 Mexico settled at 10 cents on the dollar, without payment for 30 years of interest arrears! Second, the wartime improvement in Brazil's external balance created objective conditions for debt service. Third, the already likely prospect of European depreciation would reduce the value of external debt denominated in francs or sterling for a country that had developed significant trade relations with the United States. Each of these three factors is reflected in the strengthening of the market for Brazilian bonds.

From a rock bottom in 1940, prices increased over the next ten years more than sevenfold, yielding a compound rate of return (interest plus capital gains) of 125 percent per year! As a result Brazilian loans are seen as unusually attractive. This analysis, however, leaves out the financial consequences for widows and orphans who sold out at the bottom.

5.3   The 1982 Debt Crisis

Brazil's debt problems did not end in 1943. New debt difficulties emerged in the early 1960s and again in the 1980s.

From the 1940s to the 1970s

Figures 5.4 and 5.5 show the real debt per capita and the debt/export ratio[26] between 1929 and 1986. The relatively low and decreasing levels of external debt recorded in the first postwar quinquenium are a legacy of the prewar experience. The 1943 plan helped reduce the size of the debt from its peak level of more than $1 billion in the early 1930s to some $600 million in 1946. In addition a strong postwar recovery in Brazil's export prices postponed the need to explore new sources of external credit.

In the early 1950s, however, the country experienced huge trade deficits, which resulted primarily from the relaxation of import controls to permit stockpiling of materials during the Korean War. Those imports were initially financed by commercial arrears which were, in the following year, refinanced by short- and medium-term loans. By 1953 the external debt had doubled to more than $1 billion. Figure 5.6 shows the trade balance (as a fraction of GDP) for the 1913–64 period. It is apparent that the postwar deficits form an entirely new pattern.

By now, recourse to the world capital market and foreign resources in order to finance an ambitious industrialization drive had become necessary. Total capital inflows, both direct investment and loans, increased sharply after 1955, especially with suppliers' credits. At the end of 1961, a time of political unrest, the external debt stood at double its 1955 level, and the

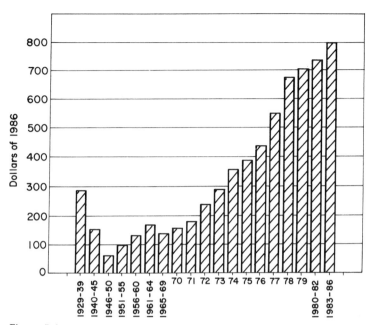

Figure 5.4
Brazil's real debt per capita, 1929–86.

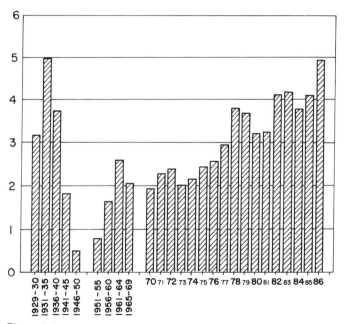

Figure 5.5
Brazil's debt/export ratio, 1929–86

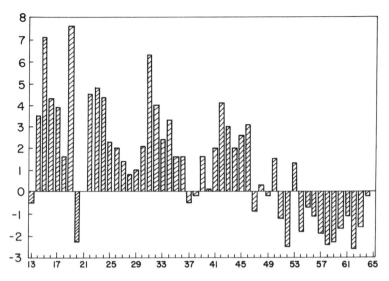

Figure 5.6
Brazil's trade surplus, 1913–65 (percent of GDP). Source: Goldsmith (1986).

country was ready for yet one more external crisis. As the economic situation deteriorated, capital inflows virtually ceased. The World Bank, previously an important source of official resources for Brazil, did not authorize a single loan between 1960 and 1964.

Debt rescheduling and new credits[27] became available after the military coup in 1964. Thereafter the government consciously embarked on a policy of tapping private capital markets to underwrite rapid expansion.

Two main features distinguish the postwar evolution of Brazil's balance of payments on current account. First, this balance was almost continually unfavorable. Between 1950 and 1986 there was a surplus in only eight years. Second, the deficit on current account, which was relatively small until 1969, increased sharply after 1970.

The Origins of the 1982 Crisis

The existence of a large deficit on current account up to 1983 was regarded as normal, because developing countries are importers of capital. The deficits rose sharply after 1970 and created one of the preconditions for renewed debt problems.

But the existence of debt is not enough for financial troubles. Always and invariably, world economic deterioration needs to come about to complete the picture of too much debt service and too little foreign exchange. We next look at how world economic developments helped bring about the 1982 crisis.

When the debt crisis erupted in Mexico in the summer of 1982, and in all of Latin America shortly after, three common sources of the debt problems could be easily identified:

First, the world economy was very badly off: economic activity was more depressed than at any time since the Great Depression. Interest rates were at their highest levels in decades. The real price of commodities were sharply depressed, and the dollar was overly strong. Recovery of the world economy was certain. As a result there was an expectation of cyclically rising manufactures exports, rising real commodity prices, declining real interest rates, and even of an early fall of the dollar. This favorable perspective for the world economy suggested that the burdens of debt service would almost surely vanish.

Second, debtor countries had mismanaged their economies beyond belief; overvalued exchange rates, pervasive budget deficits, unproductive spending, and capital flight had absorbed scarce foreign exchange resources and stood in the way of better trade performance and debt service ability. The possibility of using resources more efficiently implied, of course, that debt service would not necessarily be at the cost of reduced standards of living.

Third, a return to voluntary lending could only be envisaged if debtor countries made the best efforts to cooperate with the system, adjusting and servicing debts to the fullest extent possible. Debtor countries agreed to do their utmost to promote a return of voluntary lending, so as to be in a position to call on foreign saving for development finance. There was no doubt that foreign lenders would resume lending, once creditworthiness (defined objectively in terms of debt ratios) was restored.

These three problems applied quite uniformly to all Latin debtors, even though the proportions in which each was responsible for the troubles of the region or for each individual country differed. Not surprisingly, observers disagreed on the weight assigned to each of these considerations. Characteristically, U.S. officials saw the mess in the debtor countries as the cause of the debt crisis:[28]

... the debt crisis just did not happen in 1982 or was not the result of the increase in the oil price shock of 1979–80 or the rise in the dollar exchange rate. The cause of the debt crisis had its domestic origins in the economic policies of the debtor countries and so what we are seeing and what we will continue to see is a change in these policies—budget deficits, excessive government spending, government interference in the markets, price controls, and so on....

Table 5.6
World macroeconomic indicators

	Real commodity prices (1980 = 100)[a]	Libor (%)	Inflation (%)[b]	World activity (%)[c]
1960–69	115	5.2	1.0	6.2
1970–79	115	8.0	11.4	3.4
1980	100	14.4	13.0	0.0
1981	96	16.5	−4.1	−7.0
1982	89	13.1	−3.5	−3.3
1983	98	9.6	−3.3	3.3
1984	101	10.8	−2.5	6.5
1985	88	8.3	−0.4	3.0
1986	72	6.9	13.7	1.0
1987	63	6.8	12.8	2.2

Source: IMF and Economic Commission for Latin America.
a. Measured in terms of manufactures export prices of industrial countries.
b. Rate of increase of industrial countries' unit export values.
c. Industrial production.

Latin American observers, by contrast, gave far too little weight to their own dramatic mismanagement and the resulting debt accumulation. World macroeconomic developments, shown in table 5.6, are seen by them as the outstanding source of problems.

The Brazilian Case

Brazil's case is interesting in that it does not meet the image of capital flight, overvaluation, or massive inefficiency in the public sector.[29] Increased interest rates and sharply augmented debt burdens are the most immediate cause of the foreign exchange shortage. If not for the Mexican crisis, rolling over of debts and some domestic restraint and cleaning up might well have made the problems disappear into the background.

Table 5.7 shows the impact of external shocks on the Brazilian external debt. The data reported draw on a counterfactual analysis developed in detail in Cardoso and Fishlow (1988) to determine by how much the external debt increased compared to what it would have in the absence of external shocks. Between 1978 and 1982 the *actual* current account shifted by $13 billion toward a deficit. The counterfactual analysis demonstrates that the current account deterioration and the resulting increase in in-

Table 5.7
Contribution of external shocks to debt accumulation, 1978–82 (billions of $)

	Oil (1)	Export volume (2)	Interest rates (3)	Total debt shock	Net debt outstanding
1978					36.2
1979	1.8		0.3	2.1	46.4
1980	5.7	0.6	1.1	7.4	57.7
1981	7.1	1.4	2.5	11.0	68.0
1982	6.1	2.4	5.9	14.4	83.5

Source: Eliana Cardoso and Albert Fishlow, *The Macroeconomics of the Brazilian External Debt*, Chicago University Press, table 3.1, in press.
Note: The calculations are based on the 1978 oil price, 1978 real interest rates (in terms of the U.S. deflator), and export performance is based on deviations from an export regression.

debtedness can be explained, for the most part, by the impact of the slowdown in exports, the increased real interest rate, and higher real oil prices. These calculations do not even include the impact of reduced real commodity export prices or the interest on the extra debt that was due to the shocks.[30]

The table shows that between 1978 and 1982 a cumulative sum of $35 billion—three-quarters of the total net debt accumulation—can be accounted for by the adverse external environment. The fact that external shocks can explain so much of the debt accumulation does not, of course, imply that there was no Brazilian policy mistake involved.

The policy mistake is well explained by Finance Minister Delfim Neto's memorable phrase: "Debts are not paid, debts are rolled." Nevertheless, relatively permanent shocks need adjustment, not financing. The Brazilian policy mistake, if any, was failure to adjust to external shocks. But then in 1982 everybody was busily explaining how the world economic shock was transitory.

5.4   What Went Wrong with Muddling Through?

The muddling through strategy initiated by the Federal Reserve, the Treasury, and the IMF in 1982 was predicated on the assumption that a return to creditworthiness (via adjustment and a more favorable world economy) would come fast, visibly, and without extreme costs for either borrowers or lenders. This view was shared by some observers. Cline (1984), who was foremost in setting out a framework and forecasts, saw

Table 5.8
Cline's 1983 forecasts for Brazil and actual outcome (billions of $, except as noted)

	Current account[a]	Noninterest current account	Interest[a]	Debt increase[b]	Debt/exports[c]
Cline's forecast	−3.4	5.8	9.2	4.1	2.0
Actual	−3.0	8.0	10.8	27.3	4.2

Sources: Cline (1984, table 3.3), IMF, and Banco Central.
a. Annual average 1983−86.
b. Cumulative increase in total debt, in billions of $, 1982−86.
c. Ratio of net debt to exports.

Brazil, in particular, as one of the countries with a favorable outlook in its ability to return to creditworthiness. Table 5.8 shows forecasts for Brazil laid out by Cline (1984) in 1983. The baseline scenario assumed the following 1983 to 1986 averages: a growth rate of industrial countries of 2.6 percent, $30 a barrel of oil, Libor (London Interbank Offer Rate) at 9 percent, and a cumulative 10 percent dollar depreciation.[31]

Although the current account deficit was approximately what had been predicted, the debt accumulation and increase in the debt/export ratio turned out to be far larger than the forecast. The difference in the debt accumulation arose from the fact that Brazil experienced large capital outflows (in part connected with debt-equity swaps), whereas the Cline scenario anticipated substantial inflows. More recently, capital flight has become an additional source of capital outflows. The serious discrepancy between the actual debt/export ratio and Cline's forecast was due to the fact that Cline assumed a doubling of the value of merchandise exports, whereas even in 1986 the export level was only 10 percent above that of 1982.

Developments of the past five years proceeded in a very different direction from the 1982−83 expectations. It is clear that a return to voluntary lending to Brazil is not on schedule. Even though in 1986, a return to the capital market seemed possible, at least in the rhetoric of the creditors, the chances today are once again quite remote. The 1987 moratorium and domestic disarray, including more than 600 percent inflation, were enough to disabuse any lender of the notion that the debt strategy was on course.

Today the muddling through strategy, even with Baker Plan enhancements, is widely considered to be a failure. The problem was not with growth in industrialized countries. The 1982 IMF economic outlook in the base scenario, to use a specific benchmark, anticipated a growth rate of 2.2

percent on average for the period 1984–86, whereas the actual growth rate was 3.1 percent. However, there were four factors that clearly diverged from the 1982 scenario.[32]

First, real interest rates were expected to decline much further than they did. The outlook was for real interest rates to average only 2 percent in 1984–86 (using the U.S. GNP deflator to measure inflation). In fact, however, real rates averaged 5.4 percent, and even in 1987 they still uncomfortably exceeded the early expectations. Given the sensitivity of major debtors to an increase in interest rates, this represents a major deterioration in the outlook. (This is compounded by the fact that Brazil's spreads did not actually decline, unlike those of other major debtor countries.) The chief reason for high interest rates was the U.S. budget deficit.

Second, real commodity prices were expected to recover from what was thought to be a cyclical low. However, they kept on falling, even from their 1982 levels. By early 1987 the real price of non-oil commodities was at the lowest level since the 1930s. It had become increasingly clear that much of the decline was not cyclical but was rather an irreversible decline in real commodity prices due to capacity expansion and commodity-saving innovation and substitution on the demand side. For agricultural goods, in particular, immense productivity growth and increasing self-sufficiency of many traditional importers, as well as price support policies in industrial countries, had led to worldwide oversupply.

Third, there was the unexpected (but historically well-known) "transfer problem." This is the catchall phrase that describes problems that result from the attempt to transfer resources representing a significant share of GDP from debtors to their creditors.[33] There are three aspects of the transfer problem that deserve emphasis. First, the effort in the budget to service debts (including interest) rather than to roll them strains budgetary resources and leads to inflationary money creation. If domestic debt is issued to acquire the resources for external debt service, then the domestic debt accumulation foreshadows debt and deficit problems that are merely postponed. Second, the effort to transfer resources abroad requires an improvement in competitiveness that is itself inflationary.[34] It is more inflationary, the stickier are real wages. Moreover these two factors interact: the need to depreciate the real exchange rate in order to transfer resources abroad raises the real cost of debt service measured in terms of the domestic tax base.

The third aspect of the transfer problem concerns the manner in which the transfer is financed on the resource side: the required trade surplus may come out of reduced consumption (public or private) or out of reduced investment. When investment declines, as has been the case in Latin America, there is concern about sustainable growth. The notion that the transfer could be financed by asset sales, thus apparently avoiding any crowding out, is an illusion, as Simonsen (1985, 1986) has forcefully pointed out.

Finally, cartel fatigue is now pervasive. The precarious cohesion of the creditor cartel is increasingly being tested as reschedulings are becoming open-ended and the mirage of an early return to normal fades away. Differences between large and small banks and, now, even between large- and medium-sized banks are becoming more stark. Differences between European Banks, those in Japan and the major U.S. banks are also apparent. Congress increasingly takes the view that the current handling of the debt problem is not in the public interest. Staffs of the multinationals, though perhaps not their management, admit openly to the implausibility of muddling through. Every new rescheduling is said to be the last that could possibly be done, but the next one is already on the calendar.

While the previous four factors have undoubtedly worked to the detriment of a steady, smooth disappearance of the debt problem there has been at least one favorable factor, namely, oil prices. Oil prices, in Brazil's case, provided an important offsetting good news. From a level of $34 in 1982, world oil prices declined to an average of only $25 in 1983–86. By 1987 the price was a mere $18. The favorable oil price helps explain how, in 1985, the entire Brazilian interest bill could be paid out of trade surpluses.

More recently, since 1987, sharply increasing commodity prices further contributed to alleviating the debt service problem at least with regard to the external transfer problem. But despite sharply rising commodity prices in world markets, in early 1988 prices of those commodities of interest to Brazil had not yet returned to their 1983 levels.

5.5   The Current Situation

The situation today is captured well by the large discount for Brazilian debts in the secondary market. Brazil has emerged from the moratorium of 1986, but the attempt to regularize relations with her creditors has no counterpart in domestic macroeconomic improvements. Hence the chances of uninterrupted external debt service must be viewed as slim. With inflation running in mid-1988 far above 500 percent and with public debt growing in real terms, rolled from day to day, the debt problem cannot be said to be on the road to improvement—hence the discount on external debt in the secondary market.

Table 5.9
The discount in the secondary market for Brazilian debt (in U.S. $)

7/85	7/86	1/87	7/87	9/87	6/88
$.75	$.73	$.74	$.57	$.39	$.51

Source: Salomon Brothers.

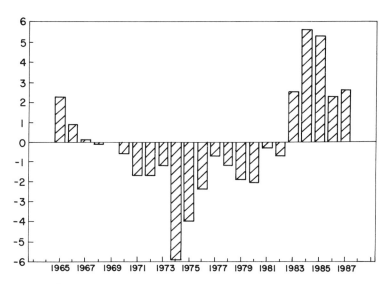

Figure 5.7
Brazil's transfer of resources, 1970–87 (percent of GDP). Source: Banco Central, *Brazil Economic Program*, June 1988, p. 53.

Much of the problem with external debt today reflects the disastrous state of domestic macroeconomics and an unwillingness to pay. The objective ability to service debt, in the long run, is much less in question than the willingness of the government to perpetuate the political and economic mistake of continuing the muddling through strategy.

Debt service raises three issues among others. The first is the net resource flow abroad. Figure 5.7 shows that since 1982, Brazil has been transferring resources abroad at an average rate of more than 2 percent of GDP. In the absence of increased saving, this transfer must come at the expense of domestic iunvestment. Second, the inability to correct the budget implies that much of the external debt service is now financed either by inflationary money creation or by increases in domestic public debt. The real value of the domestic public debt is 60 percent higher today than in 1982.

Table 5.10
Macroeconomic indicators for Brazil, 1970–87 (annual average %)

Period	Real growth per capita	Inflation rate (IGP-FGV)	Investment/GDP	Resource transfer abroad/GDP
1970–75	7.4	23	22.8	−2.54
1976–80	4.5	57	22.5	−1.87
1981–85	−0.7	173	18.5	2.5
1986	5.3	65	20.5	2.3
1987[a]	0.4	416		2.6

Source: Banco Central.
a. Estimates.

Thus a domestic public debt problem arises as a by-product of the attempt to contain the growth of external indebtedness.

Third, the transfer of resources abroad requires a real exchange rate that has depreciated far more than would be the case with a balanced non-interest account or even a deficxit. As a result there are adverse effects both on the standard of living and on the budget. In the budget the real depreciation will tend to raise the value of external debt service in terms of the tax base and hence create an even worse plublic finance problem.

The transfer problem highlights the domestic costs of bringing about, in the budget and external balance, a premature transfer of real resources toward the creditors. The costs take the form of depressed living standards, hyperinflation, sharply reduced investment, and hence the prospect of reduced long-term growth opportunities. The insistence on cash collection of the past five years has aggravated these transfer problems dramatically. Even in Brazil, where foreign resources had on balance been wisely invested at least until the late 1970s, the costs were significant as is apparent from table 5.10 which shows the deterioration in macroeconomic performance in the 1980s.

Per capita income is barely above the 1980 level (of course that performance is far better than elsewhere in Latin America), investment has declined, and inflation is proceeding at unprecedented rates. Domestic mismanagement accounts for much of this poor performance, but there is little question that the external environment also played a role. In particular, the policy of allowing domestic debt to increase to service external debt has evolved into a now massive fiscal problem. The possibility of a default on *domestic* public debt is widely recognized and is reflected in a drastic shortening of the average maturity of the domestic debt to only a few days. This is, of course, the setting in which a funding crisis can emerge.

There is little doubt that domestic policy mistakes account for a large part of the current difficulties. This does not of course imply that external debt service can or should go on unchanged, with all adjustments falling exclusively on the home economy. Creditors stand to gain from an improved Brazilian macroeconomy, and they should accordingly be made to participate in the reconstruction effort. The major adjustment must come in domestic public finance, but creditors should contribute by financing domestic investment in the critical transition period. We now sketch the key features of such a proposal.

5.6   A Debt Proposal

Are there ways in which the long-term interests of debtors and creditors can be reconciled? The answer is yes! A scheme that recycles a large part of the interest payments in the country does away with the need for trade surpluses and the resulting crowding out of investment. This would thus make it possible to have investment and growth and yet provide creditors with debt service, albeit in investments that cannot be repatriated for the time being.

Practically, this could be achieved by adopting the following procedure. A trade surplus of perhaps 1 percent of GDP would be used to service a minor part of the debt, mostly trade credit and debts to governments and multilateral agencies. A minor portion of these resources might also be used, in the form of auctions to buy up the claims of small foreign creditor banks who are willing to accept deep discounts.

The major part of the debt would be paid in investment certificates (Baker certificates)—cruzados that are in part automatically loaned to the government to finance public sector investment and in part can be used to finance loans or acquisition of assets in Brazil. The only restriction on the disposal of Baker certificates or the investments they generate would be that they could not be transferred out of Brazil. In combination with a serious fiscal reform, this shift in debt servicing would restore normal growth and investment and thus provide maximum assurance of an ultimate transfer of resources to the creditors.

This scheme basically gives Brazil some years to restore a normal macroeconomy before resuming resource transfers abroad. It emphasizes that debt service is ultimately best guaranteed by investment and growth.

Appendix

Table 5A.1
External debt

Period	Total debt (billions of current $	Real debt per capita (in 1986 $)[e]	Debt/income (index 1970 = 100)[f]
1929–39	1.190[a]	287	582.3
1940–45	0.855[a]	153	255.8
1946–50	0.600[b]	60	81.9
1951–55	1.227[c]	96	107.4
1956–60	2.201[c]	131	123.5
1961–64	3.545[c]	168	133.5
1965–69	3.755[c]	138	103.1
1970	5.295[c]	156	100.0
1971	6.622[c]	179	105.9
1972	9.521[c]	239	129.4
1973	12.572[c]	291	141.3
1974	17.166[c]	355	162.2
1975	21.171[c]	389	173.1
1976	25.985[c]	438	181.9
1977	35.737[d]	551	224.2
1978	48.111[d]	675	268.4
1979	56.104[d]	706	268.2
1980	64.648[d]	712	254.0
1981	75.511[d]	742	280.7
1982	83.265[d]	751	288.6
1983	91.632[d]	779	314.8
1984	102.039[d]	815	319.3
1985	105.126[d]	795	294.9
1986	110.572[d]	798	280.6

Sources: (a) Marcelo de Paiva Abreu, "Brazilian Public Foreign Debt Policy, 1931–1943," *Brazilian Economic Studies*, no. 4, IPEA: Rio de Janeiro, 1978, table 1 figures were converted to dollars. (b) John T. Donnelly, "External Financing and Short-Term Consequences of External Debt Servicing for Brazilian Economic Development, 1947–1968," *Journal of Developing Areas* (April 1973), pp. 411–30. (c) Banco Central do Brasil: long- and medium-term debt. (d) Banco Central do Brasil, long-, medium- and short-term debt. (e) Nominal debt deflated by U.S. implicit price deflator for GNP, *National Income and Product Accounts of the U.S.*, U.S. Department of Commerce. Brazilian population before 1950 from Villela e Suzigan, *Politica de Governo e Crescimento da Economia Brasileira, 1889–1945*, IPEA/INPES, Rio de Janeiro, 1973. After 1950, IMF, *International Financial Statistics*. (f) Obtained by dividing the index of the real debt per capita by the index of the real GDP per capita.

Table 5A.2
Brazilian debt and deficits

	1982	1983	1984	1985	1986
PSBR[a]	15.8	19.9	23.3	27.5	10.8
Operational deficit[b]	6.6	3.0	2.7	4.3	3.7
Total debt/GDP	28.8	45.0	47.7	49.2	46.9
Resource transfer abroad[c]	−0.6	2.4	5.6	5.1	2.5
Share of external debt in total debt	55.5	64.1	60.4	59.3	59.11

Source: Banco Central do Brasil, *Brazil Economic Program*, Vol. 17, June 1988.
a. Public sector borrowing requirement, percent of GDP.
b. Percent of GDP.
c. Nonfactor Current Account, percent of GDP.

Table 5A.3
Brazil: 1987 structure of the external debt

	Billions of $	%
Total	110.4	100.0
Official institutions	28.3	25.6
International organizations	13.7	12.4
Governments	14.6	13.2
Private Lenders	82.1	74.4
Banks	75.0	68.0
U.S. banks	(22.2)	(20.1)
Other	7.1	6.4

Source: Banco Central.

Notes

We thank Peter Lindert for helpful comments. Tim Vogelsang provided valuable research assistance.

1. Rippy (1977), Edelstein (1982), Feis (1965), Stone (1977), Avramovic (1964), and Wileman (1969) discuss capital flows to Brazil during the nineteenth century.

2. *The Economist*, November 29, 1890.

3. *The Economist*, October 4, 1890.

4. H. M. Hyndman (1892) *Commercial Crises of the Nineteenth Century*. Reprinted by Augusts M. Kelley, New York, 1967.

5. *The Economist*, January 10, 1891.

6. Letter from Mr. Gibson to *The Economist*, December 13, 1890.

7. *The Economist*, January 10, 1891.

8. *The Economist*, October 24, 1891.

9. See Williams (1920), Kindleberger (1985), Fishlow (1988) and Cardoso (1988).

10. *The Economist*, May 27, 1893.

11. *The Economist*, July 20, 1895.

12. *The Economist*, April 23, 1898.

13. *The Economist*, April 23, 1898.

14. Reproduced in *The Economist*, August 26, 1899.

15. See the *Brazilian Review*, October 3, 1899.

16. *The Economist*, October 29, 1899.

17. Wileman (1969), p. 179.

18. *The Economist*, October 7, 1899.

19. Quoted by Claudionor de Souza Campos, *Divida Externa*, Rio: 1946, our translation.

20. Quoted by Valentim Boucas, *Historia da Divida Externa*, Rio: 1950, our translation.

21. *Barron's* National Business and Financial Weekly, April 20, 1942, p. 18.

22. *The Economist*, December 18, 1943, p. 817, "Squeezing the Lender." In the following issue, December 25, pp. 833–34, *The Economist* further criticizes the Brazilian settlement and states: "... the British authorities were unwilling or unable to put any pressure on the Brazilian government in favor of a less inequitable settlement. And it is an open secret in the city that the reason for the authorities' reluctance was the fact that Washington would not permit it .... To put the question quite bluntly, the British holder of Brazilian obligations has been made to sacrifice to Pan-Americanism .... There are higher things at stake than Brazilian bonds. Least of any journal in the country would *The Economist* object to anything that smoothes the path of British-American cooperation, even if it involves some sacrifice. If this is Washington's idea of a fair bargain, there is nothing to be done but to acquiesce."

23. *The Economist*, December 23, 1944, p. 852.

24. *Barron's*, January 31, 1944, p. 8.

25. Weekly prices of Brazilian Bonds are found in *The Commerical and Financial Chronicle*.

26. Sources are given in the appendix.

27. Bitterman (1973) provides a description of the 1961 and 1963–64 consolidations.

28. Statement by Ciro DeFalco, U.S. Treasury, before a conference cosponsored by the Joint Economic Committee and the Congressional Research Service *Dealing with the Debt Problem of Latin America*, p. 76.

29. See Dornbusch (1985a, b), Simonsen (1986), and Cardoso and Fishlow (1987).

30. For an alternative calculation, broadly consistent with the estimates reported here, see Dornbush (1985). It is shown there that in the period 1978–82 a $34.9 billion increase in debt, compared to the counterfactual scenario, can be attributed to higher oil prices and increased interest rates. This number is virtually identical to the estimate in the text, although it was arrived at in a very different fashion.

31. The actual 1983–86 averages are 3.5 percent growth, $24.5 a barrel of oil, Libor at 9 percent and 8 percent cumulative dollar depreciation.

32. See IMF *World Economic Outlook*, April 1982 for the initial scenario.

33. See Fraga (1985), Dornbusch (1985a, 1989), and Webb (1988) for a discussion of the transfer problem in relation to debt service and for comparisons between the experience of Weimar Germany and Brazil.

34. We are of course abstracting from the possibility of achieving a gain in competitiveness by an absolute fall in wages and prices by deflation. In the context of inflation rates between 50 and 200 percent, a reversion to nineteenth-century adjustment modes seems unlikely.

References

Abreu, M. de Paiva. 1978. "Brazilian Public Foreign Debt Policy, 1931–1943", *Brazilian Economic Studies* 4, IPEA: Rio de Janeiro.

Abreu, M. de Paiva. 1985. "A Divida Publica Externa do Brasil, 1824–1931," *Estudos Economicos* 15, 2 (May) pp. 167–89.

Avramovic, Dragoslav. 1964. *Economic Growth and External Debt*. Baltimore: Johns Hopkins Press.

Bittermann, Henry. 1973. *The Refunding of International Debt*. Durham: Duke University Press.

Boucas, Valentim. 1950. *Historia da Divida Externa*. Rio de Janeiro.

Calogeras, J. Pandia. 1910. *La Politique Monetaire du Bresil*. Rio de Janeiro: Imprimerie Nationale.

Campos, Claudionor de Souza. 1946. *Divida Externa*. Rio de Janeiro.

Cardoso, E., and Fishlow, A. 1989. *Macroeconomics of Brazilian External Debt.* NBER volume on Debt of Developing Countries, forthcoming.

Cardoso, E., and Fishlow, A. 1983. "Exchange Rates in Nineteenth Century Brazil: An Econometric Model." *Journal of Development Studies* 19, 2 (January), pp. 170–78.

Cardoso, E., and Fishlow, A. 1988. "Lessons of the 1890s for the 1980s: Comments." In R. Findlay (ed.), *Debt, Stabilization and Development.* Basil Blackwell.

Castro Carreira. Liberato. 1889 *Historia Financeira e Orcamentaria do Imperio do Brasil desde a sua Fundacao.* Rio de Janeiro: Imprensa Nacional.

Cline, W. 1984. *International Debt.* Cambridge: MIT Press.

Donnelly, J. T. 1973. "External Financing and Short-Term Consequences of External Debt Servicing for Brazilian Economic Development, 1947–1968." *The Journal of Developing Areas* (April), pp. 411–30.

Dornbusch, R. 1985a. "External Debt, Budget Deficits and Disequilibrium Exchange Rates." In G. Smith and J. Cuddington (eds.), *International Debt and Developing Countries.* World Bank.

Dornbusch, R. 1985b "Policy and Performance Linkages between LDC Debtors and Industrial Nations." *Brookings Paper on Economic Activity* 2.

Dornbusch, R. 1987, "Stopping Hyperinflation: Lessons from the Experience of Germany in the 1920s." In R. Dornbusch, S. Fischer and J. Bosson (eds.), *Macroeconomics and Finance: Essays in Honor of Franco Modigliani.* Cambridge: MIT Press.

Dornbusch, R. 1989. "Background Paper." In *The Road to Recovery.* Taskforce reprint of the Twentieth Century Fund, New York.

Edelstein, Michael. 1982, *Overseas Investment in the Age of High Imperialism.* New York: Columbia University Press.

Feis, Herbert. 1965. *Europe The World's Banker, 1870–1914.* New York: Norton.

Fishlow, A. 1988. "Lessons of the 1890s for the 1980s." In R. Findlay (ed.), *Debt, Stabilization and Development.* Oxford: Basil Blackwell.

Feldstein, M. 1986. "International Debt Service and Economic Growth: Some Simple Analytics." NBER Working Paper No. 2076.

Feldstein, M. 1987. "Latin America's Debt." *The Economist,* June 27.

Fraga, A. 1986. *German Reparations and Brazilian Debt: A Comparative Study.* Princeton Studies in International Finance, International Finance Section. Princeton University.

Goldsmith, Raymond. 1986. *Desenvolvimento Financeiro Sob Um Seculo de Inflacao.* São Paulo: Harper and Row do Brasil.

Instituto Brasileiro de Geografia e Estatistica. 1986. *Estatisticas Historicas do Brasil.* Rio de Janeiro: IBGE.

Kindleberger, Charles. 1984. "The 1929 World Depression in Latin America From Outside." In R. Thorpe (ed.), *Latin America in the 1930s.* London: Macmillan.

Kindleberger, Charles. 1985. "Historical Perspective on Today's Third-World Debt Problem." ch. 12, pp. 190–211, and "International Propagation of Financial Crises," ch. 14, pp. 226–39. In *Keynesianism vs Monetarism.* London: George Allen & Unwin.

Maddison, A. 1985. *Two Crises: Latin America and Asia 1929–38 and 1973–83.* OECD.

Marques Moreira, M. 1986. *The Brazilian Quandary.* New York: Twentieth Century Fund.

Ministerio da Fazenda, Republica do Brasil. 1987. "The Financing of Economic Development in the Period 1987–1991." Brasilia, March 31.

Nogueira Batista, P. 1983. *Mito e Realidade da Divida Externa Brasileira.* Rio de Janeiro: Paz e Terra.

Pelaez, Carlos manuel e Wilson Suzigan. 1976. *Historia Monetaria do Brasil.* Rio de Janeiro: IPEA/INPES.

Rippy, J. Fred. 1977. *British Investment In Latin America, 1822–1949.* New York: Arno Press.

Simonsen, M. 1985. "The Developing Country Debt Problem." In G. Smith and J. Cuddington (eds.), *International Debt and the Developing Countries.* World Bank.

Simonsen, M. 1986. "Brazil." In R. Dornbusch and L. Helmers (eds.), *The Open Economy: Tools for Policy Makers in Developing Countries.* World Bank.

Stone, Irving. 1977. "British Direct and Portfolio Investment in Latin America before 1914." *Journal of Economic History* 37, 3 (September), pp. 690–722.

Taussig, F. W. 1928. *International Trade.* New York: Macmillan.

Webb, S. 1988. "Comparing Latin American Debt Today with German Reparations after World War I." U.S. Department of State, Planning and Economic Analysis Staff. PASA Working Paper No. 5, February.

Werhahn, P. 1937. *Kapitalexport und Schuldentransfer im Konjunkturverlauf.* Jena: Verlag Gustav Fischer.

Wileman, J. P. 1896. *Brazilian Exchange: The Study of an Inconvertible Currency.* Buenos Aires: Galli Bros. Reprinted in 1969, New York: Greenwood Press.

Williams, John H. 1920. *Argentine International Trade under Inconvertible Paper Money, 1880–1890.* Cambridge: Harvard University Press.

6 Interpreting the History of Mexico's External Debt Crises

Vinod K. Aggarwal

The rescheduling of external debts has a long history in Mexico, dating back to its independence from Spain in the 1820s.[1] This chapter provides an analytical interpretation of the negotiations concerning these debts, with an eye toward improving our understanding of the prospects for resolution of Mexico's current debt problems. I also hope that it will shed some light on the debt-rescheduling process in general.

Empirically, the analysis points to important parallels in the pattern of Mexican borrowing, problems in debt servicing, the government's efforts to seek debt rescheduling, and the ultimate resolution of the debt crises. For example, as in the 1970s, when oil was discovered in Mexico in the early 1900s, bankers eagerly sought to lend to Mexico. At the same time the government was eager to receive this foreign capital as a means of accelerating development. Overborrowing and overlending combined to create a fragile financial situation. The bankers' fear of a possible Mexican default led them to reduce their lending—ironically precipitating the very situation they sought to avoid. Their action only served to aggravate Mexico's precarious financial position, fostering a worsening crisis as lack of confidence led to capital flight.

Resolution of debt crises in both the nineteenth and twentieth centuries ran the gamut from frequent conversion plans, efforts to secure new loans, and committees to investigate and recommend changes in fiscal and monetary policy. The negotiations themselves were characterized by issue linkages to trade and immigration and active participation by the U.S. government in the ultimate resolution of the debt crises.

In light of these parallels, this chapter develops a theory to provide a political-economic explanation of debt-rescheduling strategies. I start with the premise that sovereign debt rescheduling cannot be analyzed simply along standard, purely financial economic lines. I show how we can systematically analyze domestic pressures and international political considerations that interact with more commonly examined financial factors. In addition this approach helps in providing insight into both short- and long-term strategies employed by Mexico and its lenders to improve their bargaining situation.

Section 6.1 provides an overview of Mexican borrowing and debt rescheduling, which dates back to the 1820s, and draws parallels to Mexico's current debt problems. Section 6.2 presents a model that examines debt rescheduling and the international and domestic political and economic factors likely to affect debt-rescheduling strategies and outcomes. Section 6.3 uses this model to analyze two key Mexican debt rescheduling episodes that took place in the 1830s and the 1880s and to briefly examine the current crisis. Finally, section 6.4 evaluates the utility of the model and reexamines the parallels and differences in past and current rescheduling episodes.

6.1   Mexican Debt in Historical Perspective

For analytical purposes, we can consider four epochs in international lending and rescheduling over the 160 years since Mexico became an independent country. The first epoch begins in the 1820s and ends in the 1870s, the second overlaps in part with the first and runs from the 1860s to the onset of the first world war, the third from the interwar period to the post-World War II resolution of debt problems, and the fourth from the 1970s to the current debt negotiations.[2] In all of these epochs there have been important similarities with respect to the lending process, Mexico's problems in servicing its debts, actors' negotiation strategies, and the ultimate resolution of debt problems.

With respect to the lending and borrowing process, two common patterns emerge. On the supply side the cycles of lending are related to the degree to which banks could float bonds among the public or were flush with deposits.[3] Inadequate analysis by the banks of the long-term prospects for repayment by debtors appears to be the rule rather than the exception. Mexico's desire to seek foreign funds is related to the government's almost perpetual inability to secure sufficient funds domestically as domestic spending continually outstripped revenues. Discovery of large oil reserves at various times only whetted the government's appetite for foreign loans as Mexico was seen to be a more attractive investment site.

Turning to problems in debt servicing, Mexico has continually faced difficulties in generating trade revenues. Its difficulties are aggravated by its mono export dependence and the ease with which industrialists can engage in the export of capital because of Mexico's long border with the

United States. Any economic downturn or political instability generates immediate capital flight that governments over the years have found nearly impossible to control.

With respect to the central focus of this chapter, debt rescheduling, both the negotiations and final outcomes show important similarities. Bondholders and banks have attempted to organize to pressure Mexico and have frequently allied with lenders to other countries. For its part, Mexico has followed a strategy of repeatedly concluding rescheduling agreements that it rarely implements for long. During the negotiations, both Mexico and its lenders have often sought to link debt matters to trade, direct investment, and immigration. Finally, on the creditor government side, the United States has played a key role in every negotiating episode, both by advancing funds directly and through pressure on lenders.

In the remainder of this section, I will examine the origins of Mexico's debt and the rescheduling negotiations in detail for each epoch. My focus is on past parallels to the current problems which Mexico has encountered.

Epoch 1: 1820 to 1880s

The first epoch of lending to Mexico—and to Latin America in general—began with its independence from Spain in 1821 after 11 years of revolutionary turmoil.

In 1824 Mexico contracted its first bond loan of £3.2 million ($16 million) through the London financial house of Goldschmidt and Company. Mexico received only $6 million of this amount in cash, the rest being lost to discounting of the bonds, money withheld for bond servicing, and commissions. Another bond loan issue for the same amount was contracted the following year in London through Barclay, Richardson, and Co. For both loans, it pledged one-third of its customs duties as security.

By 1827, however, Mexico stopped coupon payments on the bonds and bondholders found themselves thrown into negotiations with successive Mexican governments over the resolution of the defaults. It was not until an era of relative peace and a strong government under President Porfirio Díaz in 1885 that Mexico's leaders worked out a comprehensive scheme of financial readjustment to settle these early foreign loans. Several parallels to the current negotiations in the ensuing periods of bargaining are striking.

Mexico took a first step toward settling its debts in the early 1820s by discussing a secret plan to repurchase its bonds at their depressed price (owing to the political unrest in the country) and to resell them at the inflated price that would have come about as a consequence of the artificially "increased" demand. Such a repurchase idea has been considered with respect to the bank loans in the current era.[4] Mexico—as well as other debtors—has often been accused of using part of the new funds it has received to purchase its discounted debt on the secondary market rather than to service debt at face value.

Negotiations continued throughout the 1830s until Mexico agreed to capitalize overdue interest on the initial loans through the issuance of new bonds. After servicing the new bonds for only a year, Mexico again defaulted on its debt. In a novel twist on debt-equity swaps (the exchange of debt for assets), shortly after the Mexico–Texas war the Mexican government sought to adjust its debt while securing support for its effort to regain and maintain its northern territories. It proposed that British bondholders be given land in Texas, Sonora, the Californias, and elsewhere. This proposal garnered little support among London bondholders: they were not interested in obtaining questionable territory, and they were not eager to emigrate to Mexico.

In the 1840s, in parallel with its ongoing negotiations with bondholders, Mexico was induced to conclude an agreement on the so-called English Convention Debt, which was to provide restitution to British nationals in Mexico whose property had been damaged. This accord eventually brought the British government more directly into the bondholders-Mexico negotiations, posing a hazard for Mexican efforts to resist bondholders' attempts to be repaid.

In 1846, Mexico found itself at war with the United States. The subsequent peace treaty of 1848 left Mexico without a third of its territory in "exchange" for $15 million and an agreement by the United States to assume Mexican obligations to U.S. nationals' claims against Mexico. The prospect of securing a portion of these funds for payment of obligations on their bonds encouraged the London bondholders to send a mission to Mexico for further negotiations. Although the British courts ruled that the bondholders were entitled to a portion of these funds, the British Foreign Office cautioned the bondholders about pressuring Mexico. Uncertain of British intentions in light of these conflicting signals, the Mexicans decided to conclude an agreement that would give the bondholders $4 million in exchange for all interest arrears. Dissension among the bondholders led to delays in the agreement. As in more recent discussions, domestic politics played a key role in debt renegotiations. The Mexican Congress unilaterally reduced the offer to only $2.5 million and called for the reduction of interest on the old bonds to only 3 percent from the previous 5 percent.

Faced with such actions, and fearing further reductions, the bondholders quickly agreed to the new proposal. Mexico thus managed to cut its annual liabilities by one-half. Yet continued political instability left Mexico in desperate need of funds. In an example of issue linkage to trade, in 1857 Mexico agreed to a treaty that would have given it a $15 million loan in exchange for granting the US commercial trading concessions. But dissension with the U.S. government led to disagreement over the treaty and in the end the Americans disavowed it. Similarly, in the 1980s the United States has actively pressed Mexico to join the GATT and open up its markets.

In the meantime unrest in Mexico broke into open civil war. In an effort to secure diplomatic recognition, both the Conservatives and Liberals promised favorable debt settlements. Benito Juárez's eventual success in the civil war failed to end Mexico's financial problems. When the Mexican Congress called for a suspension of national debt payments in May 1861, the British ambassador to Mexico was instructed to call upon the British navy for support if the Mexicans refused to consider appropriate redress.

As rumors circulated that the Spanish, French, and British might intervene militarily in Mexico to secure payments on the various debts, the United States took an active role in the negotiations. It tried to undercut the likelihood of foreign intervention by offering to pay Mexico's creditors in exchange for a lien on its public lands and mineral rights. The European powers immediately voiced strong opposition to this plan. As the United States became more heavily involved with its own civil war problems, this effort came to an end.

Although Britain and Spain participated in the initial invasion of Mexico, they did not share French objectives of territorial conquest and quickly withdrew their troops. The French pressed onward on their own. By 1863 they managed to defeat the Mexican army, and install Ferdinand Maximilian as emperor of Mexico. Maximilian quickly arranged a conversion and interest capitalization of the London debt and floated an eight million pound loan somewhat unsuccessfully. By 1865 Mexico under Maximilian had incurred a debt of Mex$138 million pesos but had received only Mex$25 million pesos in actual cash![5]

After 1865 Maximilian encountered greater difficulties in maintaining his position as the head of the Mexican government in the face of growing political opposition and a dire financial crisis. He had pledged almost 99 percent of revenues to service the foreign Debt, leaving only 1 percent of all customs revenues for the government's own uses. Facing this dire situation, Maximilian resorted to forced loans and new taxes but failed to raise government revenues.

More ominously, rumors circulated that the United States was considering military action to drive the French out of Mexico.[6] When the United States sent an army to the Mexican border, Napoleon III, facing his own problems with Prussia began withdrawing his forces from Mexico. In early 1867, with Maximilian's foreign support eroding, Juárez launched an offensive against the monarchy. By May of that year, Maximilian surrendered and was summarily executed.

Returning after five years in exile, Juárez took an aggressive stance with Mexico's creditors, repudiating Maximilian's loans and disavowing the international character of Mexico's Convention Debt obligations. Going further, in 1868 Mexico began to repurchase its foreign bonds at heavily discounted prices (about 20 percent of their original value). In 1869 a representative of the London bondholders recommended a new approach to debt rescheduling. He proposed an agreement whereby the principal on the debt would be cut by nearly one-half if Mexico would secure a U.S. guarantee for the payment of this reduced amount by pledging a portion of its territory, an idea similar to the recent Mexican debt/U.S. Treasury bond plan. Experience with the Americans had not been very satisfactory, however, and the plan was rejected.

In 1873 the bondholders tried to pressure Mexico by blocking a railway bond flotation on the London stock exchange. Although this effort failed, it apparently generated enough uncertainty among Mexican officials to induce Lerdo to open negotiations with the bondholders. But Díaz revolted against the government, arguing that Lerdo has "sacrificed Mexico's best interests."[7]

Díaz's ascension to the presidency in 1877 marked a new era in Mexican history known as the *Porfiriato*. After preliminary efforts to resolve the debt overhang failed, in 1884 Díaz instructed a newly formed commission to prepare a comprehensive plan of financial readjustment, including a bond adjustment proposal, details of which are given in section 6.3. In June 1886 an agreement was reached based on this proposal.

Overall, the bondholders did not fare badly, considering the constant defaults, repudiations, conversions, and rescheduling agreements. The holders of the London debt bonds were able to recover all of their principal in 1888, with interest averaging 2.3 percent a year on the 1824 bond issues and 1.1 percent on the 1825 bond issues.[8]

Epoch 2: 1880s to the Default of 1913

Following the 1886 settlement, British bankers and capitalists were unwilling to play a part in new foreign borrowing by Mexico. By contrast, the Germans, flush with funds, were more forthcoming. In 1888 Díaz floated a £10.5 million bond issue to German capitalists, beginning a new period of foreign borrowing. Over the next few years, Mexico secured additional loans connected to railroad construction and general revenue expenditures. Toward the middle of the 1890s, however, Mexico's financial condition deteriorated, and new loans were obtained at quite unfavorable rates.

Consolidation of Mexico's internal debt and changes in revenue collection greatly improved Mexico's financial prospects. By 1899 Mexico managed to secure an extremely favorable refinancing of its outstanding debt that reduced its servicing requirements. Most important, as in the late 1970s, the discovery of oil in 1901 set off a major period of borrowing at improved terms. By 1910, 4 percent bonds were marketed almost at par.

Such propitious circumstances were short-lived. In May 1911 Díaz was overthrown by a revolution led by Francisco Madero. The immediate financial effect was a massive outflow of capital from Mexico, forcing Madero to seek a $10 million short-term loan from American bankers in 1911 and a second loan for the same amount in 1912. In February 1913, however, Madero was overthrown by General Victoriano Huerta. Despite American refusal to recognize the Huerta government, bankers agreed to float a £16 million loan in June of that year. Although only a portion of this amount was actually issued, it was sufficient to cover the short-term loans held by American bankers, allowing them to escape from a possible Mexican default on their loan.

Responding to Huerta's dissolution of the Mexican Congress in October 1913, U.S. President Wilson decided to force Huerta out of office by blocking his access to foreign funds. Faced with an inability to raise additional funds, Huerta declared a moratorium on debt servicing on December 23, 1913. Despite American efforts to prevent loans to Mexico, Huerta managed to obtain funds from Mexican banks controlled by foreign capital and also was able to sell the remaining unissued bonds he had contracted for in 1913. This allowed him to stay in office and pay for war materials to continue his civil war against Venustiano Carranza, a revolutionary governor of Coahuila who opposed Huerta's presidency. In the meantime, however, the United States allowed Carranza to purchase American weapons. After an incident with an American vessel in April 1914, Wilson ordered the occupation of the port of Veracruz. Under mediation from Argentina, Brazil, and Chile, Huerta was forced to resign from office. Carranza forcibly took power from the provisional president, Francisco Carbajal, in August 1914. Although Carranza's government was recognized by the United States in 1915, Mexico remained in dire financial straits and was unable to raise additional funds internationally.

Epoch 3: 1920s to 1940s

In 1919 an international committee of bankers on Mexico was constituted, with an eye to reorganizing Mexican finances to encourage resumption of debt service. After Carranza was overthrown by General Alvaro Obregón in 1920, more serious negotiations got underway.

But two factors led to a rapid breakdown in the negotiations. First, Mexico's insistence on new loans as part of its agreement to resume servicing met with opposition from the bankers' committee. Second, the Mexican government decided to impose a tax on oil exports as part of its effort to raise revenues. It suggested that oil companies purchase discounted Mexican bonds on the open market (about 40 percent of their face value) and use these to pay the tax.[9] Bankers opposed this proposal because it would undercut the payments on their bonds and put them in an awkward position with their clients. As a consequence negotiations broke down in 1921.

After renewed efforts Mexico finally concluded an agreement with its bankers in September 1922 that provided for a rescheduling of about $700,000 in principal and interest payments.[10] Yet the agreement did not provide for an additional inflow of new money, a key objective of President Obregón. The accord quickly unraveled as de la Huerta, the Mexican finance minister who had negotiated the agreement, led an armed revolt against President Obregón. By June 1924 Mexico announced a suspension of the freshly negotiated agreement, in part owing to a sharp decline in revenues from the oil tax connected to growing foreign competition and the exhaustion of easily accessible wells. Further negotiations led to an amended agreement in 1925 that reduced Mexico's immediate obligations for the years 1926 and 1927 by more than 50 percent. Still, these concessions did not prove sufficient as Mexico's oil revenues continued to fall, and no provision was made for new money. Instead, as has been the case in recent negotiations with the major banks, the committee continued to advance Mexico short-term loans, allowing it to cover its servicing obligations over the next two years.

By the end of 1927 Mexico once again suspended debt servicing, pending conclusion of a new agreement with its bankers. This time (paralleling the recent role of the IMF), the bankers sent a committee of experts to Mexico to examine its economic problems in greater detail before further adjustments would be made. The report submitted by J. E. Sterret and J. S. Davis in May 1928 called for a comprehensive attack on the debt problem that would deal not only with Mexico's foreign obligations but its domestic debt as well. After further negotiations, an agreement to issue a 45-year refunding issue was concluded. It provided for a very favorable reduction in the amount owed for interest arrears (5.5 percent of the amount).

The ensuing depression did not contribute to financial solvency. After initially failing to ratify the agreement, the Mexican Congress passed a law in 1932 declaring the accord to be invalid. This default remained in force under President Lázaro Cárdenas from 1934 to 1940. Although nonbond claims of foreign nationals were negotiated during this period, discussions of the bond debt resumed only in 1942.

The resulting agreement was highly favorable to Mexico as the U.S. government actively intervened in the talks. The context of World War II was clearly fundamental in creating this auspicious climate for the Mexicans as the United States agreed to Export-Import Bank assistance to Mexico, a trade agreement, and various other credits and collaboration accords. The debt agreement called for major interest rate concessions, in some cases with agreement to pay 0.1 percent of the original value on interest arrears! Overall, taking into account provisions for debt resumption and repayment of a portion of the principal amount, it has been estimated that a debt of over $500 million was eliminated for slightly less than $50 million.[11]

Epoch 4: 1970s, 1980s, and Beyond

More than 30 years passed before bankers had forgotten Mexico's earlier debt problems. In the current case the majority of its debt has been held directly on the books of banks rather than among the bondholding public at large but the parallels to past debt negotiations continue. Although forced to turn to the IMF in 1976 as a result of problems brought on by import substitution industrialization and an overvalued peso, Mexico managed to escape the Fund's tutelage as a consequence of the oil boom of the late 1970s and early 1980s. The optimism about Mexico—and its ability to secure loans at declining interest spreads—is reflected in the enthusiasm of one banker who noted: "Maybe no one's making a fortune here any longer, but you've got to be in Mexico. This is where the action is."[12]

By 1981 falling oil prices dimmed the lights on the party: in 1981 alone Mexico's foreign debt grew from $55 billion to $80 billion.[13] Moreover average maturities on loans were reduced to the point where over 20 percent were shorter than one year. With massive capital outflow putting pressure on the peso, Mexican authorities devalued the currency by about 30 percent in February 1982. Despite this action Mexico was unable to staunch its loss of reserves and was forced into the now famous August 1982 financial crisis.

During the first set of negotiations until February 1983, Mexico and the banks were forced to cope with the immediate crisis. In August 1982 Finance Minister Jesús Silva Herzog met with IMF and U.S. government officials in an effort to secure funds. He managed to secure a commitment for about $3 billion from the United States, including $1 billion in commodity credits, $1 billion as prepayment for Mexican oil, and about $1 billion as an emergency bridge loan. The United States drove a hard bargain on the oil agreement, securing a 20 percent discount and a $50 million negotiating fee.[14]

The next Mexican step was to encourage concessions from the banks by declaring a moratorium on principal repayments for 90 days. Although negotiations appeared to be moving smoothly, President José López Portillo's nationalization of the banks on September 1, 1982, and the imposition of capital controls threw a wrench into the discussions. Under pressure from the Federal Reserve and other central bankers, Mexico agreed to an IMF program on November 10, 1982. But most significant, Jacques De Larosière, head of the IMF, made the IMF loan contingent on the banks' participation in a jumbo loan of $5 billion in new money to Mexico to prevent their being repaid at the IMF's expense. By December 2, 1982, Mexico and the banks reached an agreement on the new money.[15] The banks managed to secure reasonably high fees as well as a favorable interest rate while Mexico was compensated in part by a continued moratorium on principal repayments to the end of 1984.

The next step began in April 1983 with Mexican efforts to reschedule its debt and ended with a major agreement negotiated in September 1984 (the official signing of this agreement was in March 1985). During 1983 Mexico successfully met its IMF targets, repaid its bridge loan, and managed to secure a major public sector rescheduling of almost $19 billion. Moreover by December the banks agreed to an additional $3.8 billion in new funds on more lenient terms than in the previous year.

In 1984 Mexico began efforts to secure a longer rescheduling of its debts. By September of that year, it secured an agreement in principle for a long-term rescheduling of about $50 billion with maturities of 14 years and no rescheduling fees. But bankers were wary of signing the agreement until

Mexico and the IMF reached agreement on the targets for the third year of its IMF accord. After a good faith payment on a portion of the principal of its $5 billion loan and new budget cuts in February 1985, Mexico managed to reach agreement with the IMF on March 25, 1985. Soon thereafter, the agreement with the banks was initialed, with over 550 banks participating in the multiyear rescheduling.

From mid-1985 until the March 1987 signing of the $6 billion commercial bank package, Mexico faced severe problems. A divisive election in July 1985 put pressure on the ruling party's (PRI) ability to control dissent; the Mexico City earthquake in September 1985 proved financially, physically, and politically costly; and the dramatic decline in oil prices in January of 1986 forced Mexico to seek large new loans.

Although the PRI won the 1985 elections handily, charges of corruption and electoral manipulation hurt Mexico's image—and its credit rating. In September problems were aggravated by the Mexico City earthquake. With respect to the negotiations, however, this catastrophe had a mixed political and financial impact. On the one hand, official handling of the reconstruction was seen as one more example of governmental incompetence and corruption; on the other hand, since the problems Mexico faced were not of its own making, the IMF found it difficult to force additional austerity on the government. More importantly from the banks' perspective, the unique nature of Mexico's problems permitted them to take a more lenient stance toward it without setting a precedent for other debtors—a persistent fear on their part in all the reschedulings.

By late September Mexico raised its estimated needs for new loans from $2–$3 billion to almost $5 billion. Capital flight began to worsen toward the end of the year and was further aggravated by the sharp fall of oil prices in mid-January of 1986. In June 1986 the peso fell over 30 percent in one week while negotiations dragged on with the banks and the IMF. In late July the IMF provided a relatively softer package. It called for additional loans if oil prices fell further and concessions on how the public sector debt would be computed in exchange for an informal commitment on Mexico's part to continue the opening of its economy and privatization of several sectors.

Shortly after this agreement, negotiations began with the commercial bankers on their contributions (approximately $6 billion of the total $12 billion package). In the meantime the United States pressed other central banks and the lead commercial banks to come up with a $1.6 billion short-term bridge loan to tide Mexico over. Although this effort proved successful, many banks continued to balk at the large $6 billion commitment.

Although they missed an initial September 30 deadline, pressure on chairmen of the commercial banks from Paul Volcker of the Federal Reserve, De Larosière of the IMF, and Barber Conable of the World Bank encouraged the tentative October 1 agreement. Most significantly, Mexico secured a promise for up to $1.7 billion tied to changes in Mexico's economic performance, and an additional $720 million for the same purpose from the IMF.[16] Soon thereafter, Mexico and the banks agreed to a rollover of an additional $11 billion in private sector debts.

Raising the money from the hundreds of banks with loans to Mexico proved more difficult than ever before. The first deadline of October 31, 1986, passed without success as regional banks balked at the additional commitment. As a consequence disbursements from the IMF and the World Bank were delayed until November when 90 percent of the funds had been raised. The final agreement was not actually signed until April 3, 1987.[17]

Most recently, Mexico offered a bond conversion plan in December 1987. In exchange for a sharp reduction in the nominal principal of their loans, banks would receive a guarantee on principal payments (though not on interest) because Mexico would back the new bonds with U.S. Treasury bonds that it purchased. During the offer period, Mexico continued to seek disbursement of the remaining amount of the $6 billion jumbo loan (about $1 billion), leading some bankers to express their annoyance with the bond plan since it would lead to bank losses on previous loans. By March 1988, when the offer expired, however, the J. P. Morgan led plan came to very little, with the proposal yielding only a reduction of about $1 billion— rather than the $10 billion predicted by some analysts.

We now turn to a general model to analyze Mexico's debt rescheduling in sections 6.2 and 6.3.

6.2   Modeling Debt Rescheduling

We have seen strong similarities across epochs in the way that Mexico and its lenders have negotiated over the costs of rescheduling. Other debtors in Latin America and elsewhere have engaged in negotiations with their creditors that partially resemble the Mexican case.[18] From the parallels presented in the last section, the role played by international and domestic political and economic factors in determining outcomes is evident. But is there a systematic means of combining these various factors to explain and predict rescheduling outcomes across cases and over time?

This section attempts to address this question by constructing a simple general model to help in predicting how much debtors will be willing to adjust their economy and the degree to which lenders are likely to make concessions.[19] To this end I show how bargaining between debtors and lenders can be modeled as a game with payoffs that represent their valuation for policy combinations of lending concessions and economic adjustment. In addition I briefly discuss how actors may draw upon unused power resources to alter their or their opponents' payoffs in negotiations.

As a first step in deriving debtors' and lenders' payoffs, I postulate that actors in a debt-rescheduling game are likely to have the following basic goals. Debtors' leaders will wish to (1) avoid their country's bankruptcy, (2) avoid politically disruptive economic policies (austerity policies), and (3) maintain long-run access to lending and to markets to buy and sell goods and services. Lenders in a crisis want to (1) minimize the commitment of additional funds, (2) avoid write-offs by pressing debtors to pursue economic adjustment so that they will maintain debt servicing, and (3) avoid retaliation and maintain good relations with debtors for possible future profitable lending opportunities. Both debtors and lenders must of course decide how to value each of the goals in making policy choices, an issue we will turn to shortly.

Although bargainers can theoretically consider a large number of issues in negotiations, their attention has generally focused on a few key aspects of policy. Debtors are concerned with the degree and ways in which they will be forced to promise and implement adjustment in their economies in exchange for lending concessions. They must also decide whether, and to what extent, they will service their debts.[20] Specifically, I define debtors' strategies as being a choice to pursue (1) no adjustment of their economy, (2) some adjustment, or (3) a high degree of adjustment. Lenders face a choice among three strategies of loan concessions that they can offer the debtors. For analytic purposes, we distinguish among no, "some," and "many" concessions. These can involve reductions of the interest rate charged on rescheduled debt, the amount of debt they are willing to reschedule, the amount of new funds and trade credits advanced, and the grace period that they offer the debtors before payment must recommence.[21]

Since we wish to be more precise about how actors rank their preferences in light of competing objectives, we next turn to a simple model to analyze how actors are likely to develop such rankings. We will then consider some hypotheses on how actors in different situations (defined by international and domestic economic and political factors) will weight their goals under different possible circumstances.

In general, debtors would like to receive the highest lending concessions possible, while making no or few adjustments of their own. Similarly, lenders hope to secure a commitment from debtors for the maximum amount of adjustment (consistent with their interest in ensuring debt servicing), while making the fewest lending concessions. However, we also postulate that debtors and lenders would be interested in maintaining good relations with their counterparts in light of possible retaliation and their future need for money.

The Utility Equations

We assume that it is possible to quantify lending concessions by the lenders to a debtor, the domestic adjustment undertaken by debtors, and the concern that the debtor and lenders have with maintaining good relations (goodwill) with each other. Let L, A, G, and H represent, respectively, lending concessions, domestic adjustment, and debtors' and lenders' concern with goodwill.[22] The preference ordering of the debtor and lenders can be obtained by calculating the values of debtor, U_D and lender, U_L. These are the utilities of the debtor and lenders, respectively, for different policy combinations of adjustment and loan concessions. Their utilities can be represented as follows:

$$U_D = aL - bA + cG$$

$$= aL - bA + c\left(\frac{A}{L} - 1\right), \tag{1}$$

$$U_L = yA - xL + zH$$

$$= yA - xL + z\left(\frac{L}{A} - 1\right), \tag{2}$$

where a, b, and c are the weights assigned to the three goals by a debtor, x, y, and z are those assigned by lenders, and all weights are greater than zero.

Before examining how we should decide what weights to use in these equations, we consider how the utility functions work. The way the equations are structured, a debtor's utility for a particular policy combination of adjustment and lending concessions is equal to the algebraic sum of the weighting of three goals: the benefits of loan concessions, L, the costs of adjustment, A, and the value of maintaining goodwill, G. Similarly, lenders' utility for different policy combinations will be equal to the sum of the weighted utilities for three goals: the benefits of a debtor agreeing to adjust, A, the cost of providing loan concessions, L, and the value of maintaining goodwill, H.

The intuitive interpretation of the terms G and H, which represent the actors' concern with goodwill, is that actors are aware that the arena in which they are interacting might expand. For example, if banks are worried that rescheduling negotiations might get linked to security or other "games" in which they might be weaker, they will avoid playing too aggressively in order to prevent such linkages.[23]

These points can be illustrated by considering the numerical values assigned to the different options and the resulting utility calculations:[24]

$L = 3$ when lending concessions are high,

$\quad = 2$ when lending concessions are medium,

$\quad = 1$ when lending concessions are low;

$A = 3$ for high degree of adjustment,

$\quad = 2$ for medium degree of adjustment,

$\quad = 1$ for low degree of adjustment,

In light of the assigned values, the values for goodwill will range as follows: G ranges from 2 (when A is 3 and L is 1) to $-\frac{2}{3}$ (when A is 1 and L is 3); H ranges from 2 (when L is 3 and A is 1) to $-\frac{2}{3}$ (when L is 1 and A is 3).

As an example, let us evaluate a policy choice by a debtor of HC, HA (high concessions, high adjustment) versus HC, NA (high concessions, no adjustment) and, for simplicity, assume that the values of a, b, and c are 1 (i.e., each of their goals is equally weighted). Then we have

U_D for $HC, HA = 1 \times 3 - 1 \times 3 + 1 \times (\frac{3}{3}) - 1$

$$= 3 - 3 + 0$$

$$= 0,$$

and

U_D for $HC, NA = 1 \times 3 - 1 \times 1 + 1 \times (\frac{1}{3}) - 1$

$$= 3 - 1 - \frac{2}{3}$$

$$= 1\frac{1}{3}.$$

This illustrates the simple idea that with weights of 1 each for a, b, and c, the debtors will prefer HC, NA (with a value of $1\frac{1}{3}$) to HC, HA (which only has a value of 0).

The Weighting of Actors' Goals

We next turn to an examination of how actors are likely to weight their basic goals in different international and domestic situations. In evaluating the factors that might possibly affect actors' considerations, we are faced with almost endless possibilities. To develop a manageable integrated approach, we consider three variables drawn from the political science and economics literature: an actors' overall power position, issue specific power (which will vary with cognitive understandings of the issues involved in the negotiation), and the strength of their domestic coalitions.

With respect to overall capabilities, we examine issues such as trade, political stability, immigration, and security concerns. For example, debtors unable to do without trade may be more reluctant to take precipitous actions for fear of retaliation. Regarding issue-area strength or weakness, we focus on actors' resources directly connected to the debt-rescheduling area. As we shall see, the issues involved in negotiations can be manipulated by actors to improve their bargaining position.

With respect to domestic considerations, debtors' leaders will never be anxious to incur adjustment costs. In some cases, however, depending on their coalitional stability, the political cost they will be forced to bear will be lower. Debtor countries' negotiators must consider whether an agreement to pursue economic adjustment (to increase prices, lower wages, etc., as the IMF might demand) will lead to domestic turmoil. One way to predict whether adjustment will lead to political chaos is to measure the debtors' coalitional stability.

Finally, for lenders, we judge the extent to which they have a stable coalition, rather than focusing on their internal stability. Although differences among lenders will be considered where relevant, the group focus will be my point of departure.

As a first step in gauging the effects of different constraints on actors' goals, we identify the various individual situations based on domestic and international factors. For simplicity, the different possible situations can be characterized by dichotomizing the values of the three factors of overall capabilities, debt resources, and domestic coalitional strength. Table 6.1 illustrates the possibilities.

Table 6.1
Individual situations (*IS*)

Issue and overall capabilities	High coalitional stability?	
	Yes	No
Issue strength, overall weakness	*IS*1	*IS*2
Issue weakness, overall strength	*IS*3	*IS*4
Issue strength, overall strength	*IS*5	*IS*6
Issue weakness, overall weakness	*IS*7	*IS*8

The eight individual situations in the table refer to combinations of the values of the three variables. For example, *IS*4 would appear to describe the case of Argentina in the 1980s—an unstable coalition, few debt-related resources, but overall strength in negotiations with the banks.

How are actors likely to weight their goals in different individual situations? To deduce the weights, I consider both the independent effect of each of the three factors of coalitions, debt resources, and overall capabilities and the possibility that they may have an interactive effect in influencing actors' preferences. Although the detailed arguments for the rationale behind the values specified in the charts in appendix C can be found elsewhere,[25] I present some examples here. For example, we can hypothesize that, in general, the greater the coalitional stability of debtors' governments (focusing on incumbency expectations and the ability to control opposition), the lower the costs associated with adjustment policies. Higher debt-related capabilities should also lead to a decreased need for additional lending concessions on the debtors' part. And finally, greater overall capabilities will decrease debtors' concern with maintaining goodwill.

Similarly, stable coalitions will decrease lenders' fear of "free riders." And if lenders are financially secure (if they have high debt *H* related capabilities), they are likely to be more aggressive in their demands. Finally, lenders who are weak in overall capabilities will be more concerned about maintaining goodwill than those who are able to resist coercive efforts by their counterparts in the negotiations.

Examples of Preference Orderings

The weights are presented in appendix C. For illustrative purposes, I present some examples of how they can be used to generate payoffs. Specifically, I assign numerical weights of 1 through 5 to the classifications of low, low–medium, medium, medium–high, and high values, respectively. Consider the following illustration, based on the values that debtors and lenders place on basic goals as well as their weightings:

Debtor's individual situation: 7

Debtor: coalition stable, issue weak, overall weak

Debtor's weights: borrowing need, $a = 5$, adjustment unwillingness, $b = 2$, goodwill, $c = 5$

Lender's individual situation: 6

Lender: coalition unstable, issue strong, overall strong

Lender's weights: lending unwillingness, $x = 5$, assets concern, $y = 1$, goodwill, $z = 1$

Let us calculate a few examples for debtors' and lenders' valuation of different possible outcomes. First, for the debtor,

$$U_D = aL - bA + c\left(\frac{A}{L} - 1\right),$$

$$U_D \text{ for } NC, NA = 5 \times HC - 2 \times NA + c \times \left(\frac{A}{L} - 1\right)$$

$$= 5 \times 3 - 2 \times 1 + 5 \times (\tfrac{1}{3} - 1)$$

$$= 9.67,$$

where HC = high lending concessions and NA = no adjustment.

$$U_D \text{ for } NC, NA = 5 \times NC - 2 \times NA + c \times \left(\frac{A}{L} - 1\right)$$

$$= 5 \times 1 - 2 \times 1 + 5 \times (\tfrac{1}{1} - 1)$$

$$= 3,$$

where NC = no lending concessions.

These two examples show the most- and least-preferred policy combinations for a debtor in individual situation number 7. That is, the debtor values the combination of high lending concessions and no adjustment

(HC, NA) at 9.67 and no lending concessions and no adjustment (NC, NA) at 3. In this case, because of the debtor's concern with goodwill and relatively high willingness to undertake adjustment, it fears a collapse of the negotiations and would even be willing to undertake adjustment (at least for some time) even without any lending concessions. This latter point can be illustrated by calculating the value it ascribes to a policy of no lending concessions and some adjustment:

$$U_D \text{ for } NC, SA = 5 \times NC - 2 \times SA + c \times \left(\frac{A}{L} - 1\right)$$

$$= 5 \times 1 - 2 \times 2 + 5 \times (\tfrac{2}{1} - 1)$$

$$= 6,$$

where SA = some adjustment.

The apparent counterintuitive (and seemingly incorrect) result of the debtor being more willing to undertake adjustment, even without lending concessions, than simply to have no adjustment or loan concessions is actually a desirable property of the utility function. It comes in part from the importance assigned by the debtor to goodwill, thus indicating the concern that debtors in a weak overall position who need money—but who are coalitionally stable—might have with maintaining good relations with lenders.

Consider now two examples for lenders' preferences in situation number 6:

$$U_L = yA - xL + z\left(\frac{L}{A} - 1\right),$$

$$U_L \text{ for } HC, NA = 1 \times NA - 5 \times HC + z \times \left(\frac{L}{A} - 1\right)$$

$$= 1 \times 1 - 5 \times 3 + 1 \times (\tfrac{3}{1} - 1)$$

$$= -12,$$

and

$$U_L \text{ for } NC, HA = 1 \times HA - 5 \times NC + z \times \left(\frac{L}{A} - 1\right)$$

$$= 1 \times 3 - 5 \times 1 + 1 \times (\tfrac{1}{3} - 1)$$

$$= -2.67.$$

This is what we might expect from a more standard economic modeling of lenders' behavior. That is, the worst outcome from the lenders' perspective is when they make high loan concessions while the debtor undertakes no adjustment (HC, NA) for a value of −12. The best outcome is when even in the absence of loan concessions, the debtor agress to high adjustment (NC, HA) for a value of −2.67. But we should remember that this may not always be the case for all lenders—only those who don't care too much about goodwill and who insist on immediate adjustment.

By combining the payoffs that actors assign to different amounts of lending and adjustment, we can construct 3 × 3 games. In each of these games, we first consider the likely outcome of negotiations as played by the two actors under conditions of perfect information and focus on the Nash equilibrium of the game as the solution. Before considering these games, we turn to discuss two other theoretical possibilities that may lead to an outcome other than the Nash solution. In addition we will discuss how actors might attempt to alter theirs or their opponents' payoffs.

First, actors may not have perfect information. Thus the outcome may represent strategic misrepresentation of their payoffs by the negotiator, cheating, or reflect the ability of actors to develop a reputation that leads its opponent to perceive it differently than the actual game payoffs would suggest.

Second, as noted earlier, intervention by creditor governments (CG) could push the outcome to one quite different from that which the actors would have negotiated on their own. Some of the relevant calculations that the CG will make in deciding whether or not to intervene will be: (1) the utility they assign to the expected outcome in light of strategic, political, and financial considerations; and (2) the costs of pushing either the debtor or lenders to their preferred outcome. Although we do not formally quantify creditor governments' decisions in this chapter, we focus on such considerations in the empirical cases.

Turning to a dynamic analysis, we consider the possibility that actors may not simply bargain in light of the static payoffs of the game postulated for them. In brief, I suggest that actors receiving poor payoffs will be more motivated to alter their situations than those faring relatively well. If they choose to pursue changes, they can use power resources to alter the individual situations in which they or their opponents find themselves. These include military power and financial or other economic concessions or threats, appeals to norms and rules, and efforts to secure allies. In sum, then, actors may not continue to play the game they are in for several iterations but at times may attempt to foster changes that will lead to a more favorable game structure in the hope of securing higher payoffs.

6.3   An Analytical Examination of Mexican Debt Negotiations

We turn now to an application of the model to two debt-rescheduling periods in Mexican history: the 1820s to 1840s and the 1880s. These cases are particularly interesting. The first represents the failed initial efforts at negotiating a settlement of the default; the latter period represents a successful resolution of the long-standing conflict over resolving the debt problems that had hampered Mexico for over 60 years. Each case is structured on the basis of the model discussed in Section II: We first identify actors' individual situations to deduce how they are likely to weight their goals to yield preference orderings for adjustment and lending concessions. Then, I analyze the game that the negotiators are in and find the likely outcome of their negotiations—the Nash equilibrium point. Lastly, we examine the negotiations to evaluate the consistency of the model and to identify some of the strategies used by actors to alter the structure of the game. We shall see that variation in domestic and international factors identified by the model are critical for predicting the sharp variation in outcomes in the two periods analyzed here. I also briefly consider the 1980s at the end of this section.

From the 1827 Default to the 1846 Conversion

In brief, during the first period of negotiations, we can classify Mexico as coalitionally unstable, debt-issue area weak, and overall strong. This places it in $IS4$ for debtors in table 6.1. The bondholders were relatively united, but debt-issue weak, and overall weak, placing them in $IS7$. Great Britain, the key creditor during this first period, was unconcerned about the amounts that had been loaned to Mexico. On the other hand, it was anxious about countering the United States and maintaining good relations with Mexico in an effort to secure markets for British industry. The last thing the British wanted was an American excuse to expand into Mexico to "protect Mexican sovereignty." Let us examine the evidence for these classifications.

Preference Orderings
During the time period under consideration, Mexico went through tremendous factional strife, revolutionary uprisings, changes in government

administrations, civil wars, and wars with outside powers. Needless to say, such conditions produced a shaky political situation, frequent leadership changes, and an unstable domestic coalition in Mexico throughout this round.[26]

Agustín de Iturbide had been instrumental in Mexico's revolutionary struggle by switching sides from the colonial officials to the side of the resistance. In 1821 he formed a precarious alliance between the conservative faction and the liberal, more radical faction of revolutionaries supporting the overthrow of Spanish colonial rule. But his decision to install himself as emperor of Mexico in May 1822 shortly after independence destroyed the shaky alliance that had brought him to power. In a parallel twist of fate, Antonio López de Santa Anna, Iturbide's commander in the key port and city of Veracruz, led a liberal uprising against the new monarchy. By February 1823 Iturbide was forced to abdicate his throne. The provisional three-man military junta that came in as the interim government with General Santa Anna's blessing proved no more stable than the "empire." Following passage of a new constitution, creating a Republic of Mexico, Guadalupe Victoria was elected president in 1824. The initial London debt was incurred during Victoria's administration.

Although Victoria managed to complete his presidential term in spite of an attempted coup by his own vice president, he would be the last president to do so until Benito Juárez managed the same feat from 1868 to 1872.[27] The pattern of coups (often by vice presidents from the opposing faction) continued throughout this first period. In the words of one study, "Mexican history from 1833 to 1855 constantly teetered between simple chaos and unmitigated anarchy."[28]

In sum, there was no stable domestic leadership in Mexico during this period. The differences and disputes between the conservative and liberal factions in Mexico remained irreconcilable after the collapse of Iturbide's shaky alliance. In addition, with the formation of the Mexican Republic, political conflicts arose between those who supported a federalist-structured government and those who supported a centralized state. Yet struggles over political ideologies played a lesser role in Mexico's domestic instability than the political ambitions of the nation's leaders who were unable to reach an agreement on power sharing.

Mexico's financial position continued as dismally as its domestic political situation throughout this period. Put succinctly, the government was unable to raise enough revenue to cover national expenditures.[29] Commerce, agriculture and mining, and industry had stagnated throughout the 11-year revolutionary struggle. In addition the new national government needed to repay troops and secure military supplies for the defense of the country.

The trade picture was not much brighter. In 1825, when Mexico floated its second loan, imports were almost five times its exports (Mex$24 million of imports versus Mex$5 million worth of exports). This poor trade performance continued throughout the period. In 1843 imports were still almost double its exports (Mex$22 million versus some Mex$12 million). Combined with the inability of the government to raise sufficient revenues through a levy on sales, import duties, or governmental monopolies, the result was a nearly bankrupt treasury. This sorry state of affairs was reflected in the government budget deficit. In 1822 the Mexican government estimated that its national deficit in the next year alone would run close to Mex$ 20 million. In 1825, even after the foreign bond loans, the budget deficit remained at approximately Mex$8 million.[30]

With respect to its overall capabilities, Mexico was relatively powerful. President Victoria, in power from 1824 through 1828, maintained a standing army of some 50,000 men. Moreover Mexico had little to fear from the retribution of the bondholders. The lenders could not attach any foreign assets since Mexico had few such assets or investments abroad. At this time the bondholders also could not disrupt Mexican trade, commerce, or access to foreign capital.

Most important, the bondholders could not secure assistance by allying with the British government. It could hardly escape Mexico that the British government was going to great pains to make it clear to the aggrieved bondholders (soon after the suspension of interest began in 1827) that it would not intervene on their behalf. The Foreign Office stated that the nonpayment of the bondholders of the Mexican debt was a private matter for which the British government had no responsibility or authority to interfere, except in giving its "friendly support."[31]

During this first period a group of British bondholders formed the "Committee of Mexican Bondholders" that acted as the sole organizational body representing the interests of the lenders. The committee's leader, John Marshall, addressed the claims of the bondholders to the Mexican government and actively sought assistance from the British government in the debt issue.

As to debt-related capabilities—the financial situation of the bondholders in relation to the Mexican loans—the bondholders were fairly weak. Unlike banks and large financial institutions, the bondholders, organized as a group under a committee, did not have reserve funds to cover possible losses on their Mexican loans. In fact the salaries and expenses of the committee members and bondholder representatives were tied to Mexico's debt service payments. Lastly, regarding overall capabilities, as

noted, the bondholders without the active support of the British government were weak. In 1827 the bondholders had to accept Mexico's inability
to make debt payments and could do little to prevent the continuing
default.

The Game

Based on the individual situations of the actors and the evidence, we can
construct the game in which actors found themselves during the first
period as shown in Figure 6.1.

On a purely deductive level, if we examine Mexico's preferences, we
would expect it to play a policy of no adjustment. Regardless of what the
lenders do, it achieves the optimal payoff by not adjusting. If the bondholders could be sure that Mexico would (and could) carry out a high
adjustment policy, then they would not be inclined to make any lending
concessions. But if they expect Mexico to yield only some or no adjustments, then the bondholders will play a policy of high concessions
to obtain the best outcome possible for their interests. In fact, this pair
of strategies—high concessions, no adjustment—is the Nash equilibrium
point of the matrix.

As to the role of the British government, it clearly placed strategic
considerations ahead of its bondholders' demands. These interests were not
closely tied to Britain's own immediate security but instead were connected to its efforts to counter U.S. influence in Latin American commercial
markets. At the beginning of this period there was a low level of creditor
government diplomatic intervention in the debt rescheduling; moreover
the Mexican debt involved a medium level of British security interests.
We would predict that the British government would maintain a neutral
position on the debt rescheduling, favoring neither greater nor lesser
cooperation.

We can analytically distinguish the bargaining during this first period
from the 1827 default to the 1846 conversion into three bargaining rounds.
The first round begins in 1827 and ends with the conversion of 1831.
The second round encompasses the negotiations from that time until 1842
when another debt rescheduling and bond conversion agreement was
carried out. Finally, the third round runs from 1842 to the final debt
conversion and interest capitalization in 1846. Throughout these three
rounds we will see that the actual outcomes correlate well with the model's
prediction of a "No debtor adjustment–High lender concessions" outcome. We will also see that the involvement of the British and other
creditor governments increased from the first to the third round. How-

The 1820s

Lender: *IS*7

Lender: coalition stable, issue weak, overall weak

Lender values: lending unwillingness x: 2 assets concern y: 5 Goodwill z: 5

Debtor: *IS*4

Debtor: coalition unstable, issue weak, overall strong

Debtor values: borrowing need a: 4 adjustment unwillingness b: 5 Goodwill c: 1

	Preference Ordering			
	Cardinal		Ordinal	
	Lender	Debtor	Lender	Debtor
HC, HA	9	−3	6.5	4
HC, SA	6.5	1.67	5	7
HC, NA	9	6.33	6.5	9
SC, HA	9.33	−6.5	8	2
SC, SA	6	−2	3.5	5
SC, NA	6	2.5	3.5	8
NC, HA	9.67	−9	9	1
NC, SA	5.5	−5	2	3
NC, NA	3	−1	1	6

Cardinal Payoff Matrix: 1820s
Debtor (*IS*4)

		HA		*SA*		*NA*	
Lender	HC	9	−3	6.5	1.67	9	6.33
(*IS*7)	SC	9.33	−6.5	6	−2	6	2.5
	NC	9.67	−9	5.5	−5	3	−1

Ordinal Payoff Matrix: 1820s
Debtor (*IS*4)

		HA		*SA*		*NA*	
Lender	HC	6.5	4	5	7	6.5	9
(*IS*7)	SC	8	2	3.5	5	3.5	8
	NC	9	1	2	3	1	6

Figure 6.1

ever, British strategic interests and competition with the other European powers and the United States—rather than pressure from the British bondholders—was the real impetus behind the British government's intervention. Owing to space limitations, the focus is on the final agreements, rather than the negotiation process itself.

Round One

In October 1827 the Mexican government failed to meet interest payments due on its London debt. Despite the default the Mexican government made it clear that it had every intention of fulfilling its obligations in the future and of maintaining Mexico's reputation and credit abroad. As a sign of good faith, in November 1827 Mexico assigned all export duties on gold and silver, as well as one-eighth of all maritime customs duties, to the service of its foreign debt. Moreover, to further appease the bondholders, Congress passed an act in 1828 for the capitalization of all overdue interest on the foreign debt.

These pronouncements of good faith served the important purpose of keeping creditor governments from taking a more active interventionary role. By arguing that they were simply unable to fulfill the terms of their contract—but that they had every intention of doing so at their first available opportunity—they temporarily placated the bondholders and the creditor governments. Eventually, in later years, Mexico used its reputation for being financially unstable to avoid fulfilling its agreements—even when it did have some resources to do so.

Despite these actions further events in Mexico worsened its ability to resume its debt agreements and servicing. Late in 1828 new revolutionary uprisings arose in the Mexican countryside. In early 1829 a virtual civil war took place over the presidential succession. In July 1829 Spanish troops landed at the Mexican port of Tampico, as Spain attempted to recapture its greatest American colonial territory. After early Spanish success the Mexican army repelled the Spanish invasion. And finally, in late 1829, General Bustamante, a former Mexican vice president, led a successful revolution against President Guerrero and was himself installed as president the following year.

In 1830, to show Mexico's good faith in the debt matter, the government invited the bondholders to name their own agents to collect the assigned customs proceeds in Mexican ports.[32] In October 1830, following negotiations between Manning (the committee's representative) and the Mexican minister of finance, the Mexican Congress passed a law allowing the government to enter into an agreement with the bondholders for the issue of new bonds and the capitalization of interest. The arrangement called for the issue of new bonds in satisfaction of all interest due up to 1831 and half of the interest coming due five years thereafter. The bondholders of the Goldschmidt loan received new 5 percent bonds at the rate of Mex$ 1,000 worth of bonds for Mex$ 625 of interest due; the Barclay bondholders received new 6 percent bonds at a rate of Mex$ 1,000 for Mex$ 750. For the payment of the unfunded half of the interest due from 1831 through 1836, one- sixth of the maritime customs duties at Veracruz and Tampico was assigned to be collected by two officials, one named by the government of Mexico and one by the Committee of Bondholders.

The new bonds for the capitalization of interest due prior to 1831 were issued immediately, whereas the new bonds for the capitalization of half of the interest coming due from 1831 to 1836 were to be issued periodically during those years. The new bonds were to bear no interest for five years (until 1836). The agreement increased Mexico's bonded indebtedness by nearly Mex$ 8 million. But it was to Mexico's advantage to have the interest due on the new bonds, representing overdue interest as well as half of the interest that would have been due within the next five years on the London debt, postponed for five years.

In sum, at the end of round one, the bondholders made concessions while Mexico undertook little adjusmtent. The bondholders agreed to accept new bonds and a five-year postponement in a large amount of debt payments owed to them. Mexico received a five-year reprieve by pledging future revenues to their creditors. No painful adjustments on the Mexican government's finances or the Mexican economy were imposed while Mexico's standing and creditworthiness was reestablished.

Round Two
Following the 1830 agreement, the Mexican government issued new bonds in 1831 for the capitalization of unpaid interest due prior to that year. Mexico satisfied its obligations, including the delivery of assigned customs for only one year before failing to meet its debt service and once again defaulting on the London debt. As before, internal strife and poor public finances created problems for Mexico. By claiming it was temporarily unable to meet its debt agreements but that it had every intention of doing so in the future, the Mexican government hoped to maintain its advantageous position against the bondholders.

In 1833 Mexican President Pedraza ordered that, for the time being, 6 percent of the proceeds of the maritime customshouses would be devoted to the payment of interest of the foreign debt. This pledge, however, turned out to mean very little. In 1833, only 4 to 5 percent of these revenues went toward payment of the foreign debt. In 1834 the percentage was reduced to 0.5—only Mex$ 20,678 of the customs duties of the two ports went to Mexico's foreign creditors. In 1835 this amount was reduced to Mex$ 1,309, and finally, in the following year, no interest payments arose from the revenues of the customshouses.[33]

Partially as a result of Mexico's performance and unresponsiveness, certain bondholders began to question the Mexican government's sincerity. To increase their leverage, the bondholders of the Mexican debt consolidated their interests with those of the bondholders of other Latin American states including Columbia, Peru, Chile, Argentina, and the Central American states. Suspecting that the Mexicans were cheating— that is, that the Mexicans were able but unwilling to pay—the new committee began to actively pursue the assistance of the British government.

During this time the Mexican government continued its desperate struggle to find new funds for its newly bankrupt treasury. The government resorted to short-term, high-interest loans from Mexican capitalists, as well as other internal forced loans, but failed to raise enough capital to cover government expenditures. The Mexican government also explored the possibility of loans from the U.S. government or from American private capitalists. Certain American officials showed great interest in such a loan as a means of obtaining northern Mexican territory for the United States. Colonel Anthony Butler, U.S. charges d'affaires, in a letter to President Jackson in 1833, suggested that if such loans were secured upon Mexican territory, the United States might gain title to the land. The U.S. government, however, rejected the idea of any loan-for-territory plan with Mexico because of the situation in Texas.

After the war with Texas, the Mexican government sought to try to colonize the Texas territory in the hope of bringing it back under Mexican control. This plan became closely linked with the debt negotiations when in April 1837 the Mexican Congress directed the president to "proceed to make effective colonization of the lands that ought to be the property of the Republic by means of sales, long leases, or mortgages."[34] The interim Mexican president, José Justo Corro, proposed a new conversion of 1837 in which the holders of the bond issues of 1824, 1825, and 1831 could exchange their bonds for titles to vacant lands in these territories and 5 percent bonds. The land swap idea, as noted in section 6.1, was rejected by bondholders.

The debt negotiations continued during the "Pastry War" with France and in June 1839, the bondholders and Mexico agreed to the bond conversion proposed in 1837. By this arrangement half the bonds of 1824, 1825, and 1831 were converted into new active bonds and half into new deferred bonds. The land purchase offer remained open to the bondholders, but the bondholders shunned the deferred bond-for-land exchange. Although talks of the security assignment for the new bonds continued, practically all of the old bonds were converted by 1841. In February 1842, after considerable pressure from the British minister, calling attention to the losses of the British subjects in this matter, the Mexican government agreed to raise the customs assignments at Veracruz and Tampico from one-sixth to one-fifth.[35]

With this agreement on the bond conversion and customs assignment, the Mexican government once again postponed much of its debt servicing, pledged future revenues to the payments to placate bondholders, and did little actual adjustment. The bondholders, insistent on some adjustment from Mexico, agreed to these concessions with the conversion and to the acceptance of an unreliable source of payments—the customs duties assignment.

Round Three

After concluding the conversion agreement with London debt bondholders, Mexico returned to a more politically important—and dangerous—game settling the claims of foreign nationals living in Mexico. In October 1842 a diplomatic convention was signed by the British minister in Mexico and the Mexican ministers of finance and of foreign affairs. With this convention, the Mexican government acknowledged a liability of Mex\$1,148,630 debt to British subjects for various claims, including past advances of money to the government, sales of goods and property to the government, and other damages incurred by Mexico. (This is the 1841–42 accord that came to be known as the English Convention Debt.)

The actions of the British government in the Convention Debt marked an important change in the creditor government's involvement in the debt issue. The government had used its diplomatic powers to secure the claims of British subjects against Mexico. The British government increased its involvement in the debt issue to the diplomatic and economic level on behalf of the British subjects.

Earlier that year, realizing that the deferred bonds issued in the 1839–1840 conversion would soon begin drawing interest, the Mexican Congress passed a law calling for a new definitive settlement of the foreign debt. According to the new law the settlement could not include the capitalization of interest, interest rates higher than 5 percent, an increase in the amount of the debt, or the hypothecation or pledging of Mexican national property as payment. On this basis a new debt agreement was reached in June 1846, known as the Conversion of 1846. The agreement called for a new issue of 5 percent bonds worth £10,241,650 or Mex$51,208,250. These bonds were applied to the conversion of all existing bonds totaling nearly Mex$50 million. Active bonds were converted at 90 percent of their face value, and the deferred bonds at 60 percent. The remaining new bonds to be issued, nearly Mex$11 million worth, were to be sold for cash for Mexico. As security on these new bonds, Mexico made a general pledge of all revenues of the Republic, and the special assignment of the tobacco monopoly revenue, the duties on exports of silver through all Pacific ports, and one-fifth of import and export duties at Veracruz and Tampico. With this arrangement, the Mexican government reduced its London debt by nearly Mex$ 5 million and, at the same time, obtained nearly Mex$ 11 million to be disposed of for its own account. One observer called the agreement for Mexico, "one of the most advantageous and brilliant financial operations ever effected."[36]

At the end of this round, Mexico had again adjusted very little. The government issued new bonds to reduce the face value amount of its debt, received new bond loan cash for its public treasury, and pledged future, questionable revenues to the bondholders. The lenders, by contrast, had made high concessions. They agreed to a reduction in the amount of the debt, the flotation of an Mex$11 million bond loan to Mexico, and the acceptance of unreliable sources of cash as security on the new bonds.

Summary

The Mexican government throughout the three rounds of the first period continued to assert that it was unable to service its debts. But the bondholders simply could not believe this, suspecting Mexico of cheating. Ironically, in order to appease the bondholders—and in the minds of Mexican leaders—keep creditor powers from pursuing their designs on Mexico, Mexico had no option but to cheat. It concluded agreement after agreement to undertake high adjustment, but a glance at the game they were in indicates that they were uninterested in keeping their pledges. In sum, at the end of the first period, Mexico made few adjustments while the lenders made high concessions.

Because of their weak position, the bondholders acted in several ways to change their situation. Early in the period they attempted to use norms and rules as power resources to improve their situation, arguing that nations must fulfill their private obligations. Such an appeal, as might be expected, had little coercive power, and Mexico remained unresponsive.

The bondholders then attempted to form an alliance with the British government to increase its involvement on their behalf. As we have seen, although the British acted to protect the interests of the bondholders, the government's actions were motivated more by strategic concerns. However, the British government did involve itself with the creation of the English Convention Debt. The Convention Debt brought about the direct diplomatic involvement of the government in protecting the property of British subjects against Mexico. In later periods this new arrangement would prove to be hazardous for Mexico. It was one thing to cheat the bondholders when they insisted on repayment: by themselves, they had little power over Mexico. It was something else entirely to play this game with the British and French governments.

Although the bondholders were pleased at the new British interest in their plight, the implications were more complicated. Debt servicing is a collective good. The creation of the English Convention Debt meant that London debt bondholders would now have to compete with the Convention Debt bondholders for the scarce Mexican funds charged to debt servicing. These actors would begin to "crowd" their interests. The London bondholders must have been even more shocked when they found themselves at odds with their own government over the nature of British diplomatic protection. The British government restricted diplomatic protection to the Convention Debt, arguing that protection was a purely private good. The London debt bondholders, however, were unsuccessful in convincing the British government that protection should be extended to their claims. Without such protection, the London debt bondholders would be in the worst of all possible worlds. They would be competing with other claimants who were protected by the British government for a collective and crowded good—Mexico's debt payments.

Mexico Comes to Terms: Negotiations in the 1880s

Negotiations over the original debt contracted by Mexico in the 1820s were finally resolved at the beginning of the *Porfiriato*. Although many of the policies followed during this time were based on the reforms of Díaz's two predecessors, Juárez and Lerdo, it was Díaz who was able to bring stability to the country and implement these policies to their fullest. He decided to pursue a policy of attracting foreign capital and investment to the country in an effort to spur its economic development. Most important with respect to the debt negotiations, Díaz believed that Mexico would have to come to terms with the bondholders if it wished to secure access to new foreign capital and investment.

Preference Orderings
During the 1880s we can classify Mexico as coalitionally stable, debt-issue weak, and overall weak (*IS7*). We can also classify the bondholders, as united, debt-issue weak, and overall strong (*IS3*).

With respect to domestic politics, the rise of Díaz ushered in a period of true political stability for the first time in Mexico. He introduced a new harsh pacification program to quell rebellion in the countryside and increased the power, jurisdiction, and appropriations for the rurales (the rural police force), which began to play a major peace-keeping role in the countryside. Díaz also did not hesitate to use force to meet force.

Financially, the country was in shambles when Díaz came to power. He inherited an empty treasury, a large foreign debt, and a civil service and military corps that had not been paid. Immediately after his victory over Lerdo, Díaz requested a Mex$500,000 loan from the merchants and capitalists of Mexico City, but this effort was only partially successful. Díaz then turned to a 6 to 10 percent tax on the profits of all classes of property to increase government revenues.

The Mexican economy remained stagnant. Mining and agriculture still had not recovered from Mexico's many wars, and industry remained only a future hope for the country. Trade and commerce suffered from a terrible balance-of-payments problem as the value of imports far outstripped the value of exports.[37] Under Díaz's leadership, however, Mexico's economy gradually grew, industry and trade developed, and the government increased its revenues to cover expenses.

In overall capabilities, Mexico retained its sovereign powers. Díaz, unlike Juárez, made clear his desire to attract foreign, and especially European, capital and investment to Mexico. For him, Mexico's economic growth and well-being depended on the capital of Europe and America. As a result Díaz revealed Mexico's vulnerability to other foreign powers. Moreover the bondholders and their committee, which became affiliated with the Council and Corporation of Foreign Bondholders in 1876, began to try to block Mexico's access to new foreign capital and investment. Although these efforts were only partly successful before the 1880s, the message was clear to Díaz. If he wanted to develop Mexico's economy with foreign investment, Mexico would have to address the outstanding claims of the bondholders.

The bondholders had significantly altered their situation. The affiliation of the Council brought the Mexican bondholders, once again, into an alliance with lenders to other foreign governments. But the Council was a more powerful international financial group than previous committees. Under the Council's leadership, the Mexican bondholders presented a united position toward Mexico. The committee and bondholders, however, continued to lack the financial resources to cover losses on the debt issue and even the expenses of their agents.

More important, however, the bondholders, with the Council, strengthened their overall capabilities. Despite being unsuccessful in 1871 and 1874, it continued its efforts to block Mexico's access to foreign capital markets. Even European and American investors were pressed by the committee and Council not to float loans for Mexican projects. The bondholders were now in a better position to force Mexico to the bargaining table.

The British government continued its nonintervention policy in the debt issue. The bondholders increasingly relied on the representations of the Council, rather than those of the British government, to Mexico. Moreover it was only in 1884 that diplomatic relations between Mexico and Great Britain were restored. (Relations with France were restored in 1880.) Just as important, British security and strategic interests were moving away from North America to events on the European continent. Bismarck's defeat of France in the Franco-Prussian War and the rise of Germany threatened the balance of power on the continent that had existed since the Congress of Vienna. Thus security interests in Europe decreased the British government's concern and interest in Mexico and its foreign debt.

The Game
From our classifications we place Mexico, at the beginning of Díaz's regime, in IS7, and the bondholders in IS3. From our theoretical model we obtain the debt game matrix in figure 6.2.

From the matrix in figure 6.2, we would expect bondholders to play a policy of no concessions. Regardless of whether Mexico adjusts or not, the lenders receive their higher preference by yielding no concessions. For Mexico, the best strategy is to play a policy of high adjustment, a combination yielding the Nash equilibrium.

In 1874 the Council issued a statement to the effect that the bondholders would make every effort to block Mexico's access to foreign capital and investments. Instead of challenging the bondholders' threat and "calling their bluff," Díaz made efforts to improve Mexico's credit standing abroad

The 1880s

Lender: *IS3*

Lender: coalition stable, issue weak, overall strong

Lender values: lending unwillingness x: 1 assets concern y: 4 Goodwill z: 1

Debtor: *IS7*

Debtor: coalition stable, issue weak, overall weak

Debtor values: borrowing need a: 5 adjustment unwillingness b: 2 Goodwill c: 5

	Cardinal		Ordinal	
	Lender	Debtor	Lender	Debtor
HC, HA	9	9	7	6.5
HC, SA	5.5	9.33	4	8
HC, NA	3	9.67	1	9
SC, HA	9.67	6.5	8	5
SC, SA	6	6	5	3.5
SC, NA	3	5.5	2	2
NC, HA	10.33	9	9	6.5
NC, SA	6.5	6	6	3.5
NC, NA	3	3	3	1

Preference Ordering

Cardinal Payoff Matrix: 1880s
Debtor (*IS7*)

Lender (*IS3*)		HA		SA		NA	
	HC	9	9	5.5	9.33	3	9.67
	SC	9.67	6.5	6	6	3	5.5
	NC	10.33	9	6.5	6	3	3

Ordinal Payoff Matrix: 1880s
Debtor (*IS7*)

Lender (*IS3*)		HA		SA		NA	
	HC	7	6.5	4	8	2	9
	SC	8	5	5	3.5	2	2
	NC	9	6.5	6	3.5	2	1

Figure 6.2

as a first step toward Mexico's economic development. Clearly, Díaz realized that Mexico would have to make adjustments before the creditors made concessions.

Analytically, we consider this period as running from Díaz's rise to power to settlement of both the London and Diplomatic Convention debts. Because there were few intermediary agreements, this period consists of only two negotiating rounds, the first lasting until 1884, when a short-lived London debt agreement was reached, and the second lasting to the definitive settlement of the outstanding debts.

Round One

In late 1878 the Mexican government proposed a settlement of the London debt similar to the old canal concession proposal. This arrangement called for a similar conversion and consolidation of the debt, plus 18 other obligations, at the rate of 50 percent. In compensation the interest rate would be increased from 3 to 6 percent on the new bonds, and the creditors would receive a concession on the building of a railroad from Mexico City to the Pacific Coast. The bondholders did not look favorably on this arrangement because of its similarity to the canal plan. As a result Mexico sold the concession to an American concern and stated that it was severing the question of a settlement of the debt from that of public works.[38] Thus Mexico gave up its attempt to tactically link the debt issue to the development of its public works projects.

Despite this failure Díaz continued his efforts to restore Mexico's economic stability and credibility. Accordingly, he created the Banco Nacional de Mexico to stabilize Mexico's financial community, lowered government expenditures by several measures, including lowering his salary as well as those of other officials, and created a committee to formulate a new settlement of the country's foreign debt.

In 1882 an opportunity arose for the bondholders to put their threat to block new loans into action. At that time the Mexican National Railway Company, the American concern that had been granted the concession to build a railway from Mexico City to the Pacific, attempted to float a £2 million bond loan in London. The company was to receive a subsidy of $10,000 per mile of track laid from Mexico, secured on a portion of the customs receipts which the bondholders claimed. The Council protested loudly against the flotation. The London Stock Market refused to revoke the loan. Moreover others argued that the loan actually helped the bondholders by fostering its economic development, and hence increasing its ability to satisfy creditors. The bondholders, however, refused to recognize a substantive link between the development of Mexico by public works projects with its ability to service its debt; they continued to protest the flotation. As a result, although the loan was allowed on the market, few of the bonds were sold, and the loan was quickly withdrawn from the market.

After the bondholders' success, Mexican President González sent a representative to London in the spring of 1883 to settle the debt. After early aborted agreements, the Mexican Congress passed a law on June 14, 1883, stipulating that the external debts of Mexico were to be consolidated and converted into a new 3 percent bond debt. Under this authorization a new agreement was negotiated in September 1884. The agreement was similar to the arrangement proposed in May 1883. A new bond loan of £17.2 million was to be floated for the conversion of the London debt bonds (at a rate of £112 of the new bonds for £100 of the old) and the bonds covering the arrears (at the rate of 52 new for 100 old). The bonds were to have an increasing rate from 2 to 3 percent. The new bonds were to be secured by a pledge of 10 percent of all import duties.

The bondholders accepted the agreement because it was more favorable than any recent proposal. No part of the debt was to be exchanged for a public works concession, and the exchange rate was in their favor. Moreover, they believed that since "the government was more stable than it had been since the intervention, and the revenues were increasing rapidly,"[39] the government would make the payments due on the new bonds.

With this agreement at the end of round one, the bondholders felt they had received a favorable outcome. This agreement, however, was short-lived. The Mexican press attacked the arrangement because its conversion rate was unfavorable for Mexico and because the pledge of specific revenues (10 percent of customs receipts) was in direct violation of the law of July 14, 1883. Because of public opposition the Mexican legislature adjourned in 1884 without considering the agreement, which was then canceled by the Mexican government.

Round Two

In 1884 Mexico and Great Britain moved to restore diplomatic relations. As a part of the reestablishment of relations, Mexico acknowledged liability for the amounts due on the Convention Debt and other claims. In return, Britain agreed not to interfere in the debt issue on behalf of the bondholders.

With Díaz's return to the presidency in 1884, renewed emphasis was
· placed on settling the foreign debt. He created a commission to prepare a
comprehensive plan of financial readjustment. As a part of this readjustment plan, Díaz issued three decrees in June 1885. First, he made all salaries
of civilian and military government workers above Mex$500 subject to
temporary reductions from 10 to 50 percent. Second, he consolidated
the floating debt incurred after 1882 into new 6 percent treasury bonds.
Third, he called for the conversion of all external debts incurred before
1882 to be converted into new bonds with a gradually increasing interest
rate from 1 to 3 percent. The new bonds were to be known as the
Consolidated Debt of the United Mexican States. Moreover the debt was
to be secured not by any specific revenue assignments but by funds in the
Banco Nacional de Mexico received directly from the customshouses at
Veracruz.

In June 1886 an agreement on the London debt was reached on this
basis. The bonds of the London debt were to be converted at the rate of
50 percent of the face value of the old bonds into the new bonds of
the consolidated debt, and the 1864 bonds covering arrears were to be
converted at the rate of 15 percent. In December of that year, a similar
settlement was reached on the Convention Debt, by which the old bonds
were to be converted at a rate of 71 percent of the face value into the new
bonds.

By August 1888, when the conversion offer expired, over 99 percent of
the London Debt and Convention Debt bonds had been exchanged. Overall, the value of the London debt was reduced from £22 million to £14
million of the consolidated debt, and this was eventually paid off two years
later by £5.5 million in cash. The value of the Convention Debt was
reduced to a value of £872,000 of the new debt and was later paid of
by the sum of £350,000.

In sum, during this period, the bondholders used their overall power to
block Mexico's access to new foreign capital, forcing Mexico to make
serious adjustments. President Díaz, the first leader to bring a long period
of stability to the country, sought foreign investment in an effort to
develop Mexico. He implemented important financial reforms and adjustments to foster economic stability within the country and to improve Mexico's creditworthiness abroad. He also realized that the country
would have to make high adjustments, which he implemented, before
the bondholders would make any concessions to settle the debt. As expected from our modeling effort, although Mexico carried out strict eco-

nomic and financial reforms, the bondholders made few concessions to Mexico.

Modeling Debt Rescheduling in the 1980s

Although space limitations preclude extensive discussion of how the model we have developed and applied in the previous sections applies to the 1980s, some observations are worth making. I argued in section 6.1 that there are close similarities in debt rescheduling between the 1980s and earlier epochs. At a minimum these parallels provide justification for using a similar model for modeling Mexican debt rescheduling across different time periods. Let us consider these similarities and differences from the perspective of the model and see what outcomes the model predicts.

Turning first to issues involved in the 1980s negotiations, by and large the issue area for bargaining purposes began with debt matters divorced from issues of trade. In the 1800s trade was more evidently connected to debt rescheduling since Mexican government revenues were tied directly to maritime customs duties. Although this did not help Mexico much in servicing its debt since its general financial weakness did not allow it to use this connection to promote its exports to Britain, in principal at least the connection was more readily evident. In the current negotiations, although some decision makers in the United States have expressed concern about a decline in exports to Mexico and the need to keep markets open in the developed countries to allow Mexico to service its debt, the banks have not taken an active role in either attempting to keep U.S. markets open or in making concessions that would prevent American exporters from being hurt severely for the debt crisis. From their perspective their profits are pitted against those of American exporters and import-competing industries in the United States who face growing pressures from foreign exporters as those countries attempt to gain an export surplus.

With respect to political considerations, the U.S. government is motivated to intervene in the Mexican negotiations for fear of growing immigration from Mexico if it becomes politically unstable as economic conditions continue to worsen. In the nineteenth century, the United States was more concerned about a renewed territorial presence of the European powers on the American continent that could pose a threat to U.S. strategic and economic interests. But whatever the motivation, in both centuries the United States has been motivated to play an activist role in the debt negotiations.

Turning now to the actors involved in negotiations, we have already noted the different role of banks. They now hold debt on their own books rather than playing the role of an intermediary to float bonds. Another key change is the activist role of the International Monetary Fund in the 1980s. Together with the United States, the IMF has played an important role in moderating private debt negotiations. These differences can be easily incorporated into the model.

With respect to actors' goals (which are central to the modeling effort), broadly speaking, they are similar across both centuries. Lenders worry about repayment, are wary of extending new funds, and worry about future retaliation. Mexico would still like to minimize the costs of adjustment and receive additional funds while fearing retaliation as well. Lastly, the United States as a key actor is still motivated to intervene in negotiations for strategic and economic reasons, although the precise resons have varied over time.

Let us now briefly consider what outcomes we might expect in light of current conditions and see if using the same utility equations and weights for different individual situations provides insight into the negotiations.[40] We can consider three periods of negotiations from the August 1982 predicament Mexico and its lenders found themselves in to the present. The first runs from the first crisis until the first big rescheduling package, until February 1983; the second to mid-1985 and the signing of the multi-year rescheduling; and the third from that accord to the present, and encompassing the earthquake, difficult political elections, and a worsening oil market.

The game that Mexico and its lenders found themselves in during the first period, from August 1982 to early 1983, appears in figure 6.3 (lenders in *IS8*—coalition unstable, issue and overall weak; Mexico in *IS7*—coalition stable, issue and overall weak). From the structure of this game, the likely outcome (Nash equilibrium) is a combination of banks' unwillingness to advance further loans, whereas Mexico is willing to undertake adjustments. In practice, this was the case. In light of U.S. strategic concerns and the IMF's fear of financial collapse, the outcome was one where these actors pushed the banks to make a large loan to Mexico by mid-1983.

In the second time period, with the banks now more unified and having additional confidence in being able to raise jumbo loans with participation from almost all banks, following the model, the resulting game (with each actor now in *IS7*) should have been as shown in figure 6.4. Here, the game is a clear case of "chicken" with the danger being an outcome of no

Period 1: Mexico 1982–83
Mexico (IS7)

Banks (IS8)		HA		SA		NA	
	HC	0	9	−3.5	9.33	−4	9.67
	SC	4	6.5	0	6	−2	5.5
	NC	8	9	3.5	6	2	3

Period 1: Ordinal Payoffs
Mexico (IS7)

Banks (IS8)		HA		SA		NA	
	HC	4.5	6.5	2	8	1	9
	SC	8	5	4.5	3.5	3	2
	NC	9	6.5	7	3.5	4.5	1

Figure 6.3

Period 2: Mexico 1983–85
Mexico (IS7)

Banks (IS7)		HA		SA		NA	
	HC	9	9	6.5	9.33	9	9.67
	SC	9.33	6.5	6	6	6	5.5
	NC	9.67	9	5.5	6	3	3

Period 2: Ordinal Payoffs
Mexico (IS7)

Banks (IS7)		HA		SA		NA	
	HC	6.5	6.5	5	8	6.5	9
	SC	8	5	3.5	3.5	3.5	2
	NC	9	6.5	2	3.5	1	1

Figure 6.4

Period 3: Mexico 1985–Present

Mexico (IS8)

		HA		SA		NA	
Banks (IS8)	HC	0	0	−3.5	4	−4	8
	SC	4	−3.5	0	0	−2	3.5
	NC	8	−4	3.5	−2	⟨0	0⟩

Period 3: Ordinal Payoffs

Mexico (IS8)

		HA		SA		NA	
Banks (IS8)	HC	5	5	2	8	1	9
	SC	8	2	5	5	3	7
	NC	9	1	7	3	⟨5	5⟩

Figure 6.5

concessions by either party as each tries to secure its Nash equilibrium (in this case NC, HA for the lenders and HC, NA for Mexico). The game was highly regulated by the U.S. government and the IMF, with the outcome being closer to some adjustment by Mexico and some concessions by the banks, avoiding either the asymmetrical equilibria or, more dangerously, the no adjustment, no concession outcome.

Lastly, we can consider the implications of the current Mexican instability after mid-1985 and the increased problems that the banks have had as some money center banks have taken loan loss reserves or written down their loans (as in the European case) and smaller banks increasingly balked at additional outlays of funds. The game with both actors in IS8 now becomes one of deadlock (with an equilibrium outcome of NC, NA),[42] as shown in figure 6.5. This is a dangerous game from the U.S. government's perspective. Each actor is motivated to play a strategy of no concessions leading to a deadlock. Such actions would challenge the U.S. strategy of coaxing the banks and debtors to continue adjusting. This would threaten the financial health of many banks as well as pose problems for Mexican economic stability. The likely consequences are evident: a fragile international financial system and unrest in Mexico leading to increased pressure to migrate. The recent (October 1988) $3.5 billion bridge loan to Mexico from the United States responds to these new fears. It remains to be seen whether this effort will carry the day.

6.4   Conclusion

This chapter has examined the political economy of Mexican debt rescheduling over the last 150 years and analyzed selected episodes in some detail. Two conclusions based on the empirical and theoretical analysis are worth noting.

First, the parallels between past and current negotiations considered in section 6.1 are quite striking. The rationale for borrowing and lending has remained quite similar even though the form of financial intermediation has undergone important changes. Bankers in both the nineteenth and twentieth century were eager to find profitable outlets for loans despite Mexico's history of defaults. Whether billed to the public as promising opportunities or to the regional and smaller banks as a good investment, the lack of careful consideration of the risks involved in making sovereign loans is notable. On the borrowing side, Mexico often sought loans for general financial and balance of payments rather than for specific development projects. As a consequence it frequently found it difficult to service the debt it incurred.

With respect to debt problems, the recent phenomenon of capital flight and reluctance of bankers in a crisis to lend additional funds has been a common historical occurrence. The bargaining and efforts to resolve defaults also demonstrate important parallels. Debt-equity swaps, conversions, interest capitalization, and eventual write-downs of a large portion of loans have been a pattern that has been replicated time and again. In these negotiations the United States and other creditor governments have played an important role in cajoling both debtors and lenders into various arrangements. The United States, in particular, has been highly involved in providing loans to Mexico because of strategic, economic, and political interests in the region. Lastly, both Mexico and the United States have attempted to link negotiations to trade and other issues from the earliest efforts at debt rescheduling.

From a theoretical perspective, I have attempted to show how a simple model that incorporates both political and economic considerations can be used to deduce game payoffs for Mexico and lenders in debt negotiations. This effort contrasts with that of scholars using game theory as a post-hoc interpretation of negotiations. Instead, by specifying a priori how actors are likely to emphasize their different goals in the negotiations depending on the political and economic constraints they face, I have tried to deduce probable outcomes of their bargaining. Although the model furnishes only relatively broad predictions, I hope that it will provide a useful step in our efforts to understand analytically the complex process of international debt rescheduling.

Appendix A: A Brief Chronology of Mexican Debt

Epoch 1

1824: £3.2 million loan

1825: Second £3.2 million loan

1827: Mexico fails to meet interest payments

1830–61: Frequent interest capitalization and conversions of debt

1864: Maximilian loans: £8 million, £5 million for conversion of arrears and a Fr110 million loan for costs of intervention and French claims

1865: Maximilian Fr250 million loan

1867: Juárez repudiates Maximilian loans

1885–88: Settlement of 1824–25 loans and subsequent conversions

Epoch 2

1888: £10.5 million

1889: £2.7 million railway loan

1890: £6 million loan

1893: £3 million loan

1899: £22.7 million loan

1904: $40 million loan

1910: £11.1 million loan

1913: £6 million loan

1913: Moratorium on payments

Epoch 3

1919: International Committee of Bankers on Mexico formed to discuss rescheduling

1922–30: Various failed efforts to settle earlier debts

1932: Mexican Congress refuses to ratify rescheduling agreements

1942: Settlement of prior debts at sharply reduced amounts

Epoch 4

1970s to 1982: Mexico borrows heavily, total debt $82 billion

1982, August: Mexico declares three-month moratorium, U.S. package of $3 billion

December: $3.92 billion loan agreement with IMF, $5 billion from commercial banks, partial rescheduling of $20 billion (effective March 1983)

1983, February: $433 million bridge loan from BIS

December: $3.8 billion agreement with banks (April 1984 signing)

1984, September: $20.1 billion rescheduling agreement

1985, September: New terms on $43.7 billion rescheduled debt, $6 billion in new loans, $1.7 billion in contingent commitments from banks

1987, December: Bond conversion plan, expires March 1988 with reduction of about $1 billion in debt

---

Note: This is not a detailed chronology of all loans and rescheduling efforts. For details, see Turlington (1930) for epochs 1 and 2, Wynne (1951) for epoch 3, Aggarwal (1987) for epoch 4.

Appendix B: Coding of Lending Concessions and Debtor Economic Adjustment

Lending Concessions

No concessions: same terms, no new funds

Some concessions: rescheduling, some new funds

High concessions: forgiveness, interest rate concessions, new lending

Economic Adjustment

No adjustment: no policy changes

Some adjustment: efforts to cut money supply or fiscal deficit, assignment of part of tax revenue

High adjustment: cut in money supply and fiscal deficit, high assignment of other revenues to lenders

Appendix C: Weights for Debtors and Lenders in Different Individual Situations

Weights for Debtors

a = borrowing need
b = unwillingness to adjust
c = goodwill

	Coalitional stability?	
Capabilities	Yes	No
Issue strength, overall weakness	IS1	IS2
	a: low	a: low
	b: low–medium	b: high
	c: medium–high	c: medium
Issue weakness, overall strength	IS3	IS4
	a: medium–high	a: medium–high
	b: low	b: high
	c: low–medium	c: low
Issue strength, overall strength	IS5	IS6
	a: low	a: low
	b: low–medium	b: high
	c: low–medium	c: low
Issue weakness, overall weakness	IS7	IS8
	a: high	a: high
	b: low–medium	b: high
	c: high	c: medium

Weights for Lenders

x = unwillingness to make loan concessions
y = need for adjustment/servicing
z = goodwill

	Unity of lenders?	
Capabilities	Yes	No
Debt-specific strength, overall resources weakness	IS1	IS2
	x: low–medium	x: high
	y: low	y: low
	z: high	z: medium–high
Issue weakness, overall strength	IS3	IS4
	x: low	x: high
	y: medium–high	y: medium–high
	z: low	z: low
Issue strength, overall strength	IS5	IS6
	x: low–medium	x: high
	y: low	y: low
	z: low	z: low
Issue weakness, overall weakness	IS7	IS8
	x: low–medium	x: high
	y: high	y: high
	z: high	z: medium

Notes

1. I would like to thank Ted Chan for research assistance on the Mexican debt negotiations. For comments on an earlier draft, I am indebted to Om Aggarwal, Barry Eichengreen, Peter Lindert, and the conference participants for this volume. For research support, I would like to thank the Rockefeller Foundation and the Institute of International Studies and Program in Mexican Studies at the University of California, Berkeley.

2. In Mexico's case, the chaos following the Mexican revolution in 1911 prevented the more common international pattern in the third epoch of new borrowing and rescheduling. See appendix A for a brief chronology of lending and rescheduling from the 1820s to the 1980s.

3. See Fishlow (1985) for a discussion of historical patterns of lending and borrowing.

4. Interview with a high Mexican official, April 1987.

5. Turlington (1930), pp. 153–55.

6. Ridley (1970), p. 734.

7. Meyer and Sherman (1987), p. 410.

8. Turlington (1930), p. 6, and Wynne (1951), p. 46.

9. Turlington (1930), p. 283.

10. For secondary source discussions of this agreement, see Turlington (1930), pp. 288–91, and Wynne (1951), pp. 67–70.

11. See Wynne (1951), pp. 97–99 and 106, for the full terms of the settlement of 1942.

12. *Institutional Investor*, December 1980, p. 158.

13. Kraft (1984).

14. See Kraft (1984) for a detailed discussion of the Mexican agreement.

15. For details on this period, see Kraft (1984), and for two analytical accounts of the negotiations, see Charles Lipson (1985) and Aggarwal (1987).

16. See *Wall Street Journal* and *New York Times*, October 1, 1986, for further details.

17. *The Economist*, April 11, 1987, p. 84.

18. For an analysis of negotiations in other cases, see Aggarwal (1990).

19. Although the decision of creditor governments to intervene in negotiations is also a crucial issue, owing to space limitations I omit that portion of the model. Readers interested in the full model and a more detailed discussion of its elements and rationale should consult Aggarwal (1990).

20. For analytic purposes, however, I do not analyze the debt-servicing decision separately in developing preference orderings but assume that increased adjustment will be related to a higher willingness to service one's debt.

21. The coding of debtors' and lenders' choices are presented in appendix B. I should note that the distinctions for both debtors' and lenders' strategies are simply one way of dividing up the continuum of both lending concessions and economic adjustment. One could consider a more refined division of each of these strategies, but our analysis would become increasingly complex and difficult, making predictions more uncertain.

22. We also assume that L and A are real-valued positive numbers. We use two

different variable notations for goodwill since the goodwill of debtors and lenders will be different.

23. As indicated, we have rewritten G as the term $[(A/L) - 1]$ for debtors. The simple interpretation of this is that debtors recognize that lenders will generally favor a higher value for adjustment as compared to additional lending. Thus, as the amount of adjustment that a debtor agrees to undertake increases relative to lending concessions, the amount of goodwill that the debtor "receives" from the lender also increases. I have subtracted one from the ratio of A/L so that when adjustment efforts and lending concessions are equal (HA, HC; SC, SA; NC, NA), the goodwill term will have no effect ($G = 0$). Similarly, goodwill for lenders, H, can be measured by $[(L/A) - 1]$. Since debtors will prefer greater lending concessions to increased adjustment, lenders will secure greater goodwill from debtors as the ratio of lending concessions to adjustment increases.

24. In assigning specific numerical values, I assume that we can compute a cardinal utility function for the different bargainers, and not simply an ordinal utility function. Although the exact values chosen may seem hard to justify, the model I am developing should be seen as an effort to estimate preference orderings, not a "known" estimation of actors' views.

25. See Aggarwal (1990).

26. The following discussion of Mexican politics draws mainly on Bancroft (1914), pp. 376–443, and Meyer and Sherman (1987), pp. 294–354.

27. Although this was Juárez's third term, his first two were as a rival "govern-ment" to Maximilian and his Conservative predecessors.

28. Meyer and Sherman (1987), p. 324.

29. Whereas in 1809, $26 million worth of gold and silver had been mined in colonial Spanish America, in 1821, only $6 million was mined in the new Mexican state. See Meyer and Sherman (1987), p. 304.

30. Turlington (1930), p. 42.

31. British and Foreign State Papers, Vol. 18, pp. 1012–14; Turlington (1930), p. 57.

32. Turlington (1930), p. 58.

33. Turlington (1930), p. 65.

34. Turlington (1930), p. 70.

35. Payno (1862), app., p. 20.

36. Payno (1862), p. 16.

37. Meyer and Sherman (1987), p. 432.

38. Wynne (1951), p. 34.

39. Turlington (1930), p. 193.

40. This modeling discussion should be seen as tentative in light of the abbreviated discussion here. A more systematic analysis of Mexico in the 1980s will appear in Aggarwal (1990).

41. Some might argue that the banks are now in *IS2* because the banks are now stronger in the debt area since they have taken loan loss provisions. It is worth noting that the game outcome only becomes a more severe deadlock in this case (banks in *IS2*, Mexico in *IS8*).

References

Aggarwal, Vinod K. 1987. *International Debt Threat: Bargaining among Creditors and Debtors in the 1980s*. Berkeley: IIS Policy Paper 29.

Aggarwal, Vinod K. 1990. *Debt Games: Strategic Interaction in International Debt Rescheduling*. New York: Cambridge University Press, forthcoming.

Bancroft, Hubert H. 1914. *History of Mexico*. New York: Bancroft Company.

British and Foreign State Papers. Various years. London.

Fishlow, Albert. 1985. "Lessons from the Past: Capital Markets during the 19th Century and the Interwar Period." *International Organization* 39: 383–439.

Kraft, Joseph. 1984. *The Mexican Rescue*. New York: Group of Thirty.

Lipson, Charles. 1985. "Bankers' Dilemma: Private Cooperation in Rescheduling Sovereign Debts." *World Politics* (October).

Meyer, Michael, and William Sherman. 1987. *The Course of Mexican History*. New York: Oxford University Press.

Payno, Manuelo. 1862. *Mexico y Sus Cuestiones Financieras con la Inglaterra, la Espana, y la Francia*. Mexico.

Ridley, Jasper. 1970. *Lord Palmerston*. London: Constable.

Turlington, Edgar. 1930. *Mexico and Her Foreign Creditors*. New York: Columbia University Press.

Wynne, William H. 1951. *State Insolvency and Foreign Bondholders*. Vol. 2. New Haven: Yale University Press.

International Debt and National Security: Comparing Victorian Britain and Postwar America

Charles Lipson

Any exploration of national security and international lending must begin with a profound parallel: foreign lending developed during the nineteenth and twentieth centuries at the same historical moment that the major European powers significantly expanded their global political roles. Indeed, the most important capital markets by far were to be found in those countries that had most self-consciously asserted themselves as international powers, complete with naval forces to protect their long lines of seaborne commerce and, when necessary, sufficient to project power at a distance. Victorian Britain took on this dual role of international military and commercial power, as did postwar America. In Britain's case, the expansion of foreign trade and then international lending largely preceded the extension of diplomatic commitments and territorial expansion. In America's case, political and security commitments were substantially enlarged in the late 1940s and early 1950s. This shift was followed, one decade later, by a surge of direct foreign investment and, a decade after that, by a dramatic expansion of commercial lending to developing countries. It is this broad congruence between the international expansion of commerce, diplomacy, and strategic interests that raises the most serious questions for students of international politics.[1]

In the case of international debt, in particular, these parallels raise at least two fundamental questions. First, did the growth of international finance with its periodic debt crises shape the security policies of industrial states? The issue here is really one of grand national strategy. How do major powers define their global interests and how do they shape policies and forces to secure those interests? The fact that major powers typically have such financial interests abroad (or at least their citizens do) at least raises the issue of how those interests are incorporated into national security policy.[2]

If the first question is "How do international economic interests affect security policy?" the second is "How do military capabilities and diplomacy affect the security of foreign lending?" Do the military and diplomatic resources of powerful countries play an important role in protecting their own lenders abroad? The issue here is essentially one of the political underpinnings for international property rights and contractual obligations.

Foreign loans are, after all, inherently problematic and risky, especially when they involve private lenders and sovereign borrowers. Like all lending, they involve the current provision of credit in return for promises to repay specified amounts in the future. Meeting these distant obligations depends partly on the debtor's economic capacity, partly on its willingness to adhere its bargains, and partly on some agreed interpretation of what the bargain actually entails. Some uncertainty about each of these issues underlies foreign lending. For example, even a carefully drafted loan cannot fully specify the parties' obligations under all possible contingencies. Nor can it ensure that the parties share an understanding of their contractual obligations or display a willingness to meet them. The problems surrounding the commercial viability of such loan arrangements are more familiar but are no less difficult to forecast in practice.

The differences between such sovereign lending and its domestic counterpart are critically important.[3] The central problem is that international loans, unlike domestic credits, lack true third-party interpretation and enforcement. In this important sense, international lending resembles many other issues in international politics: its rules and procedures must be shaped in the harsh and institutionally spare environment of international anarchy.[4] Most fundamentally, the enforcement of claims requires costly direct action by the parties to the agreement or by their allies. Their willingness to incur costs is inherently problematic, as is their effectiveness.[5]

Nor can these problems be solved simply by taking hostages or putting up collateral—even though both have been used from time to time.[6] It is typically impossible to secure sufficient collateral for sovereign loans. To provide collateral, borrowers would need to place substantial national resources beyond their own control, where they could be liquidated, if necessary, to satisfy lenders' claims. Besides the political difficulties of assigning such assets, sovereign borrowers seldom have sufficient securities to pledge. Of course, their physical capital and tax revenues may provide ample collateral, but they are not easily seized if the loan should fall into default. Customs revenues were sometimes seized during the nineteenth and early twentieth centuries, often at great long-term cost, but the rise of modern nationalism has virtually extinguished such creditor remedies.

These inherent features of sovereign lending mean that lenders need to calculate with care how their loan contracts will be supported in case of difficulty. They must think, in Oliver Williamson's terms, about the governance of contractual relations. In the case of sovereign loans, this means that they must first look to themselves, individually and collectively, to protect their contracts from opportunistic renunciation.[7] In addition they may well seek support from their home governments, either to threaten debtors or to provide financial inducements for compliance. Such sanctions and sweeteners are costly, however, and they have larger diplomatic implications. They are not assumed lightly by creditor states, a point that lenders typically understand before they enter into financial arrangements.[8] (Students of international politics, on the other hand, understand this point less well and typically exaggerate the role of home governments in supporting foreign investments. If the role of the state is central to international politics, this does not mean it is equally central to all aspects of international investment.)

To return then, to the basic questions:

How do lenders protect themselves abroad?

How much do they rely upon the protection of their home state?

How does foreign lending shape the definition of national security interests and policies?

To answer these questions, I will compare the extensive international loans of mid- and late-Victorian Britain with those of postwar America. These were surely the most important international financiers of their time, and, as such, they faced periodic defaults and debt crises. By the same token each country was a dominant maritime power, commercially and militarily. Each had global security interests, interests that broadly matched the scope of their lending abroad. What I want to examine here is the inner connection between these global security commitments and economic relationships. To do that, I will consider the extent to which (1) creditors could rely on home governments for support and assistance in case of difficulties in repayments, (2) capital flows were specifically directed by governments to reinforce diplomatic links, and (3) security considerations entered into the overall disposition of debt problems.

7.1 British Diplomacy and British Loans in the Nineteenth Century

The city of London was the world's banker in the nineteenth century. It had competition, of course, chiefly from France and, in the years before World

War I, from the German Empire. But these rivals had less well-developed capital markets and a narrower range of international borrowers. French and German lending tended to be more domestically oriented, perhaps because local investment demand was more extensive and more rewarding. What international lending they did undertake was often directed to European allies, such as Russia, or to areas of special diplomatic interest, such as Turkey.[9]

The British were different. Their market was by far the deepest and most international. Their foreign loans, typically arranged by investment houses such as Barings, were important sources of finance around the world and played a particularly important role in establishing basic economic infrastructure, from railroads and ports to public utilities.[10] The scale of these investments is striking. On the eve of World War I, about half of Britain's new investment in fixed capital was made overseas. The stock of these foreign assets, worth about £4,500 million, outstripped those of Germany, France, the Netherlands, and the United States combined.[11] In Latin America, for example, British lending dwarfed that of other creditors in every country except Venezuela, where the German presence was also significant.

This lending reinforced British trade links, as in Argentina, for example, and helped ensure Britain's primary status in external relationships.[12] But loans were seldom a direct instrument of British diplomacy. Although official interest in a region might indirectly encourage the bond-issuing houses and stimulate investor confidence, there were few mechanisms to channel private investments. Even informal channels were deemphasized, although sometimes used in areas of strategic importance. There was some reluctance to use suasion and some good reasons not to do so, principally the desire to limit government involvement in commerce generally. In addition the Foreign Office understood that indiscriminate protection of Britons abroad would open a bottomless pit of potential liabilities. Limiting those liabilities, and excluding from them the ordinary risks of commerce, had been the announced policy of British foreign secretaries throughout the nineteenth century, from Castlereagh and Canning after the Napoleonic wars to Salisbury and Lansdowne at the end of the century.[13]

These internalized restraints meant that the government had little direct influence over capital flows. It had almost no tools to redirect investments, aside from the indirect effects of making areas more salient and safer. Certainly there was no public substitute for private lending. There was no equivalent to modern loans by foreign aid agencies and no multilateral public agencies to underwrite investments abroad or supervise debt repayment.

Britain's separation of private finance and public diplomacy was by design and deeply ingrained. First, it conformed to the basic character of government involvement in Britain's domestic economy, which was itself sharply limited. Laissez faire at home reinforced the separation of commercial and diplomatic interests abroad.[14] Foreign circumstances were obviously more complicated, not least because some rivals were latecomers to international economic competition and were more inclined to help their citizens to the detriment of British firms. This tension grew during the late nineteenth century, and was particularly acute in the case of Germany. But Germany was not alone. Most industrializing countries on the Continent, plus Japan and the United States, were becoming serious economic rivals. As Michael Edelstein notes, these governments were typically more active in support of foreign commerce:

During the first three quarters of the nineteenth century, British expansion was largely a quiet, uncompetitive affair. In the last quarter of the nineteenth century expansion again took place within what can only be termed an international scramble. Britain's rivals were Belgium, France, Germany, Italy, Japan, Portugal, Russia, Spain, and the United States; most of these nations were either among the most advanced industrial economies of the day or were making strong, government-supported efforts to move in that direction.[15]

Such competition posed real problems for British diplomacy. There were conflicts with German economic interests in China, for instance, and some demands for more active British support of its commercial interests there.[16] Nor was China unusual in that regard. Robinson and Gallagher have argued that such increased competition in Africa ultimately undermined Britain's policy of "free trade imperialism" since both trade and investment now required more direct diplomatic support.[17]

In the case of foreign investment, the Foreign Office does seem to have taken a somewhat more active stance, beginning in the mid-1850s. In a rare departure, it supported the floatation of loans to the Ottoman Empire during the Crimean War. At about the same time, when political chaos threatened British bondholders in Mexico, the Foreign Office directly imposed a diplomatic solution. After that collapsed, British officials tried unsuccessfully to force payments on the defaulted debt. Finally, in 1861, Great Britain intervened militarily alongside the French and Spanish.[18] In Venezuela, where circumstances were roughly similar, the Foreign Office declined to act militarily but did offer diplomatic support to bondholders. Summarizing these developments, Edwin Borchard claims that "we can observe a progression of a policy over a relatively short span of years."[19]

This progression should not be exaggerated. The British government still displayed considerable restraint in interfering with foreign commercial transactions. When the government did intervene, its goal was typically either to offset the more active policies of other states or to combat local fraud or civil disorder. It consistently sought to withdraw from direct assistance as soon as possible.[20] The work of D. C. M. Platt and his students is particularly useful in clarifying these limits in British commercial diplomacy. In Venezuela, for instance, the Foreign Office asserted its position in 1866 only after local officials had sequestered funds already paid to the bondholders' local agent. British policy may have been active, but it was well within traditional guidelines opposed to fraud and misrepresentation. Moreover with Maximillian's brief reign in Mexico still fresh in mind, the Foreign Office was especially reluctant to intervene militarily in Venezuela. In all these episodes there was an important continuity in British policy. The aim was not to win special concessions for British merchants and investors but rather to secure "fair field and no favor." This formula, combined with Britain's industrial and financial prowess, ensured considerable economic success.

Besides the commitment to laissez faire principles, the British government had another compelling reason for restraint: the very scale of her overseas commerce and investment. Because London was such an important financial center and because British nationals had an opportunity to invest widely without state direction, the Foreign Office was exposed to a vast range of commercial conflicts and risks, including bad debts.

The Foreign Office managed to draw a careful line around its responsibilities. It was willing to assert the rights of British nationals in clear-cut cases of fraud or civil disorder. In this important sense it provided a set of minimalist property rights and a global framework of contracting—one consistent with traditional interpretations of international law. At the same time the government avoided any prior commitments to defend its nationals abroad. It stood ready to defend them (along predictable lines) but at the discretion of the Foreign Office. Palmerston had made these policies clear in his celebrated diplomatic circular of 1848: "Respecting the Debts due by Foreign States to British Subjects."[21] One aim of the circular was to reiterate the distinction between commercial risks, which the private investor must bear, and the larger political questions that necessarily involved the Foreign Office. Equally important, the circular underscored the latitude and discretion of foreign policy officials, not their obligations to bondholders. For the British government, the decision to intervene in cases of default was, in Palmerston's words, "entirely a question of discretion and by no means a question of international right ...."[22] This policy, too, conformed to the traditional international legal view that governments could choose whether or not to assert the rights of their citizens abroad.

Given the scale of British investments, these policies were prudent indeed. To provide diplomatic backing or military support indiscriminately would send disturbing signals to other British investors. If, for example, a dispute concerned an investment that had failed for essentially commercial reasons, then a bailout by the British government would stimulate more such risk taking, followed by more bailouts. The logic is straightforward: other investors would have less reason to avoid high-risk investments in the future. Successful government intervention would diminish the risks of investments abroad, lull potential investors into a sense of security, lower the need for careful private scrutiny of loans and investments, and ultimately foster new disputes when these poorly conceived investments turned sour.

The British government clearly understood this problem of moral hazard. As Palmerston had observed, "The British Government has considered that the losses of imprudent men who have placed mistaken confidence in the good faith of foreign Governments would prove a salutary warning to others."[23] Palmerston was simply confirming a basic principle of British policy, one that can be traced back to Castlereagh.

This long-standing policy was tested by rising foreign competition in the waning decades of the nineteenth century. The Foreign Office responded by assuming somewhat wider responsibilities for commercial interests in Persia, Turkey, West Africa, and Japan.[24] This more active policy was rooted, most immediately, in strategic concerns about the path to India. That route was threatened by the collapse of local governance in the Near East and Africa and, in a closely related development, by the seizure of new colonies by European rivals.

But if British policy evolved during the latter decades of the nineteenth century, its fundamental tenets remained the same. As far as foreign investors were concerned, intervention and direct support were not ruled out, but they were usually designed to stop discriminatory competition or some deliberate maltreatment by the host government. When strategic issues were paramount, foreign investors might receive encouragement and some protection, but even then the British government was typically restrained.

It is clear that the Foreign Office sought to circumscribe its involvement in foreign financial problems. The question for us is how security considerations helped reshape these boundaries. One way to explore this question is to consider regions of strategic significance, comparing British responses to debt problems there to responses in other, less vital areas. When areas were strategically significant, was British policy more active in support of bondholders? Conversely, were bondholders' interests more likely to be subordinated to broader policy concerns?

In addition to these regional comparisons, we can examine specific cases in which the Foreign Office faced difficult choices involving both local financial problems and broader diplomatic interests. How important were the interests of bondholders, and how were they incorporated into overall British policy?

To answer these questions, it is useful to examine two "hard cases," the Ottoman Empire and Venezuela. These are certainly not the only cases that could be considered, but they are historically prominent and do pose real problems of interpretation. In both cases, Britain faced serious problems with its investments and, in one (Venezuela) ultimately used force to assert its interests. The deployment of gunboats off Venezuela's coast (1902–3) is often cited as a crucial moment in that country's history. Its resonance was far wider since it led Latin American jurists to assert that no government should use force to collect foreign debts. The intervention is still cited as a clear case of British military power used to protect foreign bondholders. In the Ottoman Empire, British involvement was less direct but did involve competition with major powers over a region of obvious strategic significance.

Each of these cases is complex, with contextual details that deserve careful treatment. The aim here is not to discuss these cases at length but rather to sketch their overall outlines and to examine interaction between security issues and foreign debt. The goal is less to illuminate the specific cases than to understand the more general issues.

If these cases involve both economics and security, it is important to note the limits of that intersection. British lending was almost entirely separate from the overriding security issues of the nineteenth century: Great Power politics and the European balance of power. British capital was not specifically directed toward allies and was not used to cement relationships. Indeed, there were no institutional mechanisms to do so. Likewise major debt problems were almost wholly peripheral to European alliance politics. (The exception, which we will discuss, was the Ottoman Empire.) In general, then, debt issues were independent of the most important security concern: the defense of home territory, its population, and basic political structure. This basic independence between debt problems and core security concerns also holds for the debt crisis of the 1980s.

Going beyond these core security issues, Britain's greatest diplomatic concern was to secure the route to India, the centerpiece of its empire. That preoccupation played a critical role in British policy all along the two routes to the East: through the eastern Mediterranean and around West Africa and the Cape. Debt problems were, of course, recurrent in the eastern Mediterranean—in Greece, Turkey, and Egypt. If security concerns were overriding in these cases, then they should be handled somewhat differently from, say, Latin American debt, where security issues were far less important. In the eastern Mediterranean, one might expect either (1) significant efforts to subordinate the claims of private investors when they interfered with larger policy objectives or (2) more activist diplomatic policies, including the imposition of political and financial controls that could reconcile private commercial interests and security objectives.

In fact British policies were somewhat more active in the eastern Mediterranean, but not markedly so. They were still subject to the limitations discussed earlier: a reluctance to support private claimants except in clear-cut cases of fraud and abuse, an unwillingness to channel or guarantee private capital flows or to substitute public ones, and a grave concern about long-term involvement, even in important regions, if local governments were stable. These self-imposed limitations did not mean that Britain was unwilling to use force, especially naval force. But it did mean that the Foreign Office was attentive to the costs and anxious to avoid long-term commitments.

In Latin America during the nineteenth century, the British used their navy repeatedly (Platt cites some 40 cases[25]), but always with sharp limits upon its scope. Typically, naval force was threatened or deployed in port cities to secure British citizens in the face of rioting or local rebellion. The British always sought to avoid direct, long-term involvement, and did so successfully, while at the same time excluding other European powers from a larger political role in the region. It was much more difficult to pursue these policies with success in the Near East. The difference is attributable to the fundamental and irreversible political decay of the Ottoman Empire—a decay that led first to the accumulation of debt and then to the inability to repay it.

The Ottoman Empire was ineluctably drawn into nineteenth-century European politics because its location was strategically important and because its financial decline created opportunities for rival powers to acquire concessions and financial control. The empire stood between Russia and the Mediterranean and between western Europe and the Middle East. For Britain, it lay astride the land route to India. After 1869, when the Suez

Canal was opened, it stood alongside the water route as well. This strategic position ensured Britain's keen interest. The Foreign Office was concerned about the Porte's political stability and anxious that no rival power should become dominant in the region. These concerns became increasingly important during the Crimean War (1853–56) and after, as Ottoman political control became less effective and its financial condition deteriorated. Debt burdens were an integral part of this crisis, drawing major European powers deeply into Ottoman imperial affairs.

As the Ottoman fiscal system weakened, public borrowing rose markedly. The first Ottoman foreign loan was made in 1854, and others quickly followed. Domestic and foreign borrowing grew dramatically over the next two decades. By 1875, the nominal public debt reached £200 million. Debt service had reached unsustainable levels, consuming half the national revenues.[26] To keep up payments, the empire needed still more loans. Those became unattainable after the European financial crisis of 1873.[27] As conditions worsened, the old empire fell still further behind in its debt service, meeting only half its interest obligations.

This debt crisis was only part of a larger political crisis in Ottoman-controlled territories. Peasants were already suffering under onerous land tenure arrangements. After midcentury they also faced rising taxes and greater military conscription. These problems came to a head when severe drought (1873) and floods (1874) produced intermittent famine and widespread discontent.[28] The ensuing peasant revolts, especially those in the Balkans, had international ramifications. They led to some loss of territories and to a larger regional role for both Russia and Britain. At the Congress of Berlin (1878), Britain took control of Cyprus and later sought to play a major role in Ottoman administrative reforms.

At about the same time, after debt payments had fallen seriously into arrears, a council of European creditors took control of the empire's external finances. The empire was paying only half the interest due on its loans, and in 1881 it agreed to allow foreign bondholders to collect tax revenues to service the debts. The result was the establishment of the Ottoman Public Debt Administration.

The Debt Administration was an event of political and economic significance. Donald Quataert, who has written of popular resistance to Ottoman rule, calls the new Debt Administration "the landmark event of late Ottoman history. Its creation marked one of the major Ottoman concessions of sovereignty in the nineteenth century and quieted European fears of possible Ottoman debt repudiation in the future."[29] The most important sources of revenue were placed directly under its control, everything from timber and tobacco to salt and silk. These ceded revenues, which were the largest and most readily available, were then distributed to European bond holders.

The Administrative Council was composed of private bondholders from Britain, the Netherlands, France, Germany, Austro-Hungary, and Italy. According to D. C. M. Platt, these representatives were appointed without intervention by the European powers and, in Britain's case, without especially close links to governmental power.[30] Platt's central point is that the British government distinguished carefully among its national bondholders, adhering to its general rule that investors had to bear their own risks.

Even though foreign bondholders had become directly involved in Ottoman finance, the British government sought to limit its own obligations to them. The Foreign Office did take some responsibility for loans made in 1854 and 1862 and was entirely responsible for a loan made in 1855, which it had explicitly guaranteed. Although such a guarantee was quite rare, it had been deemed essential to support Ottoman finances during the Crimean War. Where there was no guarantee, and no direct involvement in the flotation of the loan, the Foreign Office allowed investors to protect their own interests without formal assistance.[31]

The Debt Commission was successful in restoring payments, which so reassured European bondholders that they resumed lending and investing. Direct foreign investment in the empire, which had been virtually constant from the 1860s to the 1880s, tripled between 1890 and 1914.[32] New lending also resumed.

This new investment posed serious diplomatic problems for Great Britain. Once the largest investor in the empire, it had been overtaken by France and, much more significantly, by Germany. The allocation of economic concessions to these rival powers enhanced their local political power. Because of the empire's strategic location, this power shift posed problems for Britain. The Foreign Office responded with more active promotion of British commercial interests than in earlier, less competitive times or in less important locations. According to diplomatic historian David McLean, "The principal concern of British officials was to stop the German Baghdad Railway from reaching the Persian Gulf where Britain's trading supremacy, her political predominance, and the security of the Indian Empire would all be jeopardized."[33] At this stage, in other words, overriding security interests were said to shape economic diplomacy.

In this same vein, the Foreign Office was concerned about new foreign loans to the Turkish government, which were essential for administrative reforms. Unless those loans were well secured, they would likely fall into default and create political chaos. Unless the British had a major role, these financial problems would invite still greater influence by rival powers. For these reasons, argues McLean, the Foreign Office strongly supported British financial interests when they founded the National Bank of Turkey (on their own initiative) just before World War I. As one British official observed, "Without a British bank we cannot help Turkey financially, and those powers who do help her will have greater influence."[34] Rather than simply competing with French financial interests, the National Bank was seen as a useful instrument of alliance.

The Foreign Office went further than this verbal support. It helped find personnel for the new Bank and gave it preferential treatment among British firms. These actions reinforce McLean's argument that British policy actively sought to use commercial interests for political goals.

This is an important argument, but it fails to recognize the sharp limits on British policy, even in this area of acknowledged strategic importance. First of all, the Bank itself was created by private initiative, relying on the individual efforts of British financiers. Second, as McLean himself notes, this case is highly unusual, contravening the Foreign Office's usual neutrality among British firms.[35] Third, and most important, the Foreign Office could do little when the Bank's leader, Sir Ernest Cassel, decided for commercial reasons to abandon the venture. The British government had few effective tools and, equally important, no desire to incur financial responsibilities. Messages by the foreign secretary, Sir Edward Grey, and his under secretary are emphatic on that point. As Grey wrote, "It is very undesirable that the National Bank should withdraw but the future of Turkey is so unpromising that we cannot urge them to stay on without incurring undesirable responsibility."[36] Given the general principles of British policy, that argument was sufficient.

The events in Turkey are not unique. Indeed, the outlines of British involvement in Persia are similar. By the end of the nineteenth century the Foreign Office was sometimes willing to manipulate private financial ties for larger political purposes. But they still could do little to influence capital flows directly, even in strategically important cases. Nor were they willing to underwrite private losses in commercially unsound ventures. The Turkish case shows something more. It suggests that strategic interests, even in areas of great importance, could not overturn basic relationships between British investors and their government.

Still, there were tensions in British policy in areas of strategic significance. That was clear in Greece, which suspended debt service in 1893.[37] W. H. Wynne sees the underlying causes of default as similar to those in

Turkey: "excessive borrowing applied mainly to military expenditure and the funding of floating debt, an inefficient tax system, and a lack of budgetary control."[38] The debt problems were compounded by deteriorating relations between Greece and Turkey, which ended only after Turkish armies had overrun Thessaly and advanced on Athens. It was the resolution of this conflict, not the earlier default, that drew the Great Powers into Greek finances.

In 1897, the Greek foreign minister sought the mediation of six European powers, including Britain, France, and Germany, and formally placed in their hands the safeguarding of Greek interests. The immediate financial issue was Turkey's demand for a war indemnity, fully backed by their ally, Germany, and by the continued presence of occupation troops. Unfortunately, an impoverished and administratively weak Greece had no chance of raising sufficient tax revenues or borrowing on its own resources. So the ultimate question was whether Turkey would permit an indemnity based on Greece's capacity to pay or, alternatively, whether the Great Powers would impose outright financial controls or, less intrusively, guarantee a commercial loan. A related issue was how old creditors, holding defaulted bonds, were to be satisfied.

The French and German governments spoke openly about imposing international financial controls.[39] Only the British, under Lord Salisbury, objected to such controls. Their alternative was for Britain, France and Russia to guarantee a loan. Salisbury also wanted to avoid official commitments to outstanding creditors. Again, the British position was consistent, even in this region of strategic significance. Salisbury was willing to recognize outstanding claims "so far as they were justified by the circumstances of the time," but even so, he did not admit "the duty of seeing them righted partook in any degree of an international control."[40] John Levandis, writing on these negotiations, has called the British position "firm and uncompromising."[41] So, too, was the German position, which favored international controls. The predictable result was an impasse, which was finally broken by the Greek government, which agreed to international controls and pledged sufficient revenues to satisfy all creditors, new and old. It was only after the Greek government's initiative that Salisbury removed his dissent.[42]

Britain's policy of restraint—in Greece, in Turkey, and elsewhere—was based on prudential calculation, not on military weakness. Its fleet endowed it with dominant naval power and the capacity to project force around the world. When necessary, Britain was willing to use that force, especially when there was little risk of sustained involvement. Indeed, it used naval force with some regularity in Latin America, typically when riots broke out in port cities and threatened British commercial interests. Such interventions were limited—in time, in scope, and in area. But that did not always limit their political repercussions. That was surely the case in Venezuela, where gunboats raised a blockade just after the turn of the century.

The background of this dispute lies in a long-standing boundary dispute, a military revolt, and a military assault on foreign businessmen in Venezuela. The boundary dispute began in the 1890s, where eastern Venezuela and British Guiana meet. The land itself was jungle, but underneath lay gold. As the dispute escalated, Venezuela appealed to the United States for aid. The United States in turn pressed Britain to submit the dispute to international arbitration. The decision, issued in 1899, hardly satisfied Venezuela.

While this dispute was still simmering, an Andean general, Cipriano Castro, seized power in Caracas. His rule was brutal and capricious, not least to foreigners. According Edwin Lieuwen, "His regime was characterized by administrative tyranny, financial irresponsibility, almost constant domestic revolt, and frequent foreign invention."[43]

The foreigners involved were not merely Britons and Americans. They included Italians, Dutch, French, and Germans. Indeed, the German commercial presence in Venezuela was growing and had strong backing from Berlin.[44] Germany's rising stature in world trade and production had not yet led to a similar position in international banking and finance. Those functions remained firmly in London's hands. Indeed, most German banks, including those operating in Venezuela, still relied on London to handle many overseas accounts.[45]

Despite this economic interdependence, German firms and the imperial government might well have benefited from rising conflict between Britain and Venezuela. It could have opened the door for closer diplomatic relations, more extensive trade, and perhaps a German naval presence. As it turned out, however, German investors confronted much the same difficulties as the British and were denied all compensation for damages from years of local revolt. Holger Herwig argues that these commercial issues were the root cause of worsening relations between Berlin and Caracas.[46]

German merchants, like the British, began to demand military protection. The German Foreign Office, like the British, was reluctant to provide it, fearing that the costs would be too high.[47] The pressure escalated as the London Council of Foreign Bondholders urged Prime Minister Balfour to seize Venezuelan customs houses for the benefit of all European bondholders.[48] Ultimately, the British, Germans, and Italians joined together in a short-lived blockade, one that did not specially emphasize defaulted debt. Castro responded by arresting all foreigners and sequestering their property. This aggressive response was soon abandoned when the United States refused to defend Castro, much to his surprise. His policy of confronting the European powers had always assumed that the United States support his position by vigorously asserting the Monroe Doctrine.[49] Instead, the United States offered its services as mediator, encouraging a withdrawal of the blockade in return for Venezuela's promise to pay compensation.[50]

Because the European intervention was publicized by Luis Drago in his effort to reshape international law, it is easy to exaggerate the actual events. The blockade itself was brief (two months) and involved little more than the bombarding of two obsolete forts.[51] The British government, in victory, simply confined its claims to traditional international property rights, as recognized in international law. Assistance was given to nationals who were unlawfully imprisoned and commercial claimants who had already sought damages in local courts. Bondholders' claims were incorporated as part of an overall settlement on British property. Moreover the Foreign Office made considerable efforts to distinguish among classes of claims and to evaluate their authenticity. Balfour himself argued in parliamentary debate that "the real crux of this difficult has been the outrageous manner in which the Venezuelan government, not once nor twice, but time after time, have invaded the rights of British seamen and British shipowners, have insulted our nationality, have treated English sailors and English captains as no nation in the world treats us."[52]

Balfour's description has been confirmed by subsequent historians and helps explain why Britain resorted to a blockade in this case but no military threats in previous instances of default.[53] (According to Peter Lindert's figures, Venezuela had defaulted on privately held bonds in 1834, 1847, 1864, 1878, and 1892.[54]) The issue in 1902 was not simply default but one of repeated provocations and unilateral acts by Cipriano Castro. Taken together, they showed a fundamental unwillingness to recognize international obligations, as those were traditionally understood by European powers and ratified in international law.

Castro certainly had not caused Venezuela's financial disarray. He had inherited it, as he had inherited the border dispute with Britain. But these problems rapidly worsened under his mercurial and dictatorial rule. Against this background the precipitating cause of European intervention was Castro's decision to reject all European claims for damages associated with civil turmoil and local plunder. In January 1902 Castro created a three-man "Junta for the Examination and Qualification of Credits," which started business by summarily rejecting some 80 percent of all outstanding European claims for damages. In addition Castro himself flatly rejected any claims for damages incurred before May 1899, when he had assumed power. He dismissed, in other words, any responsibilities as a successor government.

The European powers responded predictably, rejecting the commission's legitimacy. The United States and Germany sent warships but did not immediately commit them to action.[55] "The slightest effort by Castro to meet Venezuela's financial obligations would probably have calmed the situation in 1902," in Herwig's judgment. "Unfortunately, the President grew confident in his self-assumed role as defender of the Americas against Europe and probably counted on the United States to enforce the letter for the Monroe Doctrine against Berlin and London."[56] Britain's decision to use force in this case, then, is consistent with Palmerstonian policies and general restraints on the use of force to protect bondholders.

Even though the history of Venezuela's blockade is far different from the myths that surround it, the use of force here was important. The blockade shows that British efforts to restore local order could directly benefit bondholders, whose rights were already well established in international law. It indicated, if there was any doubt, that Britain and other European powers were willing to intervene well beyond the areas of immediate interest, well beyond security perimeters. This was one use of military force that had little grounding in broader security concerns. Precisely for that reason, and because investors had been mistreated, many argue that British policy was narrowly interested in bondholders' demands. It was not. The effect was more subtle and indirect: sustaining traditional international law, even with its limitations on self-help, was still the best assurance for property and contractual rights.

7.2 American Security Policy and the Modern International Economy

The connection between security policies and economic interests in post-America, like that in Victorian Britain, is among the most difficult and contested issues in diplomatic history. It is central to the discourse over twentieth-century U.S. diplomacy, from the recent debate over American policy in interwar Europe[57] and the long-standing debate over American stakes in the Middle East.[58] Nowhere has the dispute been sharper or more fully documented than for the early Cold War. The late 1940s were, after all, the formative moment for America's global role, one that entailed the reconstruction of war-torn Europe and Japan and the simultaneous formation of an Atlantic alliance to contain Soviet power. The debate over this period ought to be vigorous since it was then that fundamental U.S. policies were established for both national security and the international economy. The foundation was laid for key alliance relationships and multilateral institutions. Those same organizations remain central today.

For theorists of international politics, these crucial events evoke a perennial search for the most parsimonious explanation, one that claims to show the monocausal dominance of security motives or economic interests in U.S. postwar policy. Was it the fear of Soviet expansion that shaped U.S. policy, including international economic policies?[59] Or was international economic policy framed largely in its own terms, and for its own goals?[60] Were rising public concerns about Soviet expansion manipulated to forge support for key economic policies, most notably trade and aid policies designed to foster a liberal world order for commerce and investment?[61]

This search for parsimony is important, but it comes at a cost. The cost is not simply one of descriptive detail. That is always true, and not always a cost. The real problem with these monocausal approaches is that they may well obscure the inner connection between security and economy, as that connection is understood by the policymakers themselves.

Consider America's basic policies for postwar reconstruction, from the Bretton Woods conference of 1944 to the formation of NATO in 1949. The architects of these policies had lived through both world war and world depression, and they saw the two as deeply linked. The Axis powers were, after all, strong centralized states with managed economies and closed regional trade.[62] As Charles Kindleberger notes, "The most efficient system of foreign-exchange control the world has experienced was established probably by accident by the Nazis in the 1930s, as they tried to go on trading without foreign-exchange reserves, and developed a barter system into bilateral clearing."[63] Similarly, Imperial Japan's trade centered on its own newly captured territories, while throughout Europe virtually all industrial powers raised their tariffs substantially. France, Britain, and the Netherland further contributed to the fragmentation of trade patterns by strengthening commercial ties to their colonies.

Taken together, these beggar-thy-neighbor policies had a serious impact on world income and employment. They left a lasting impression on the political leaders and advisors who were charged with rebuilding the postwar world. In Washington, policymakers saw this regional closure, to which the United States had contributed with its own Smoot-Hawley tariff, as both deepening the depression and worsening conflicts among states. Likewise, they recognized that competitive depreciations (in which the United States had also been involved) were essentially designed to export unemployment. As such, they were bound to complicate other kinds of cooperation and worsen interstate relations.

These shared perceptions of the interwar period colored the plans for reconstruction after World War II. The new arrangements for exchange rates and trade must be understood in response to this broad view linking closed economies, depression, and war. The proposed multilateral arrangements sought to open national economies progressively to trade and capital flows, while ensuring uniform treatment for trading partners. The aim was to establish consensual limits on protectionist policies, to channel the remaining protection into less destructive forms (tariffs, not quotas), and to work for their gradual diminution. Still, these were not simple echoes of mid-Victorian free-trade policy.[64] They recognized that governments now had increased responsibility to sustain employment, to protect industries from rapidly changing trade patterns, and, when necessary, to protect currency rates by establishing temporary exchange controls.

Even with these reservations, however, America's commitment to multilateral solutions less than complete. Negotiations over the comprehensive new International Trade Organization (ITO) produced only an unsatisfactory compromise, including concessions to Latin America over the legal status of foreign investments. The ITO, as it finally emerged from bargaining in Havana, could not win Senate approval and was quietly withdrawn.[65] The Bretton Woods organizations, which had been approved and were now in place, fell far short of their initial goals. Poorly funded, they contributed little to the overriding task of European reconstruction. Financial aid for that effort was, in the end, appropriated directly by the United States and channeled through its own European Recovery Program.

These policies may have used economic instruments and sought the economic goals, chiefly reconstruction and liberalization, but their security implications were never far from the surface. After all, the countries at issue were not only to be rebuilt but also to be protected from Soviet expansion and intrigue. The Marshall Plan clearly illustrates the close connection that policymakers saw between international economics and security.[66] As Secretary of State George Marshall himself concluded in the speech announcing his ambitious plan for Europe, "The United States should do whatever it is able to do to assist in the return of normal economic health in the world, without which there can be no political stability and no assured peace."[67]

But if security and economic considerations were intertwined in the creation of a postwar order, the very success of that order meant that these issues could now be considered separately, handled by bureaucracies with narrower scope and specific expertise. Even though America sought to construct a world order in which economic growth reinforced military containment, and vice versa, the detailed policy issues no longer had to be treated in tandem. The basic policies were now in place, the basic achievements in view, so that most policy issues could be considered on terms that were more circumscribed and self-contained.

This bureaucratic rationalization and compartmentalization has important implications for the treatment of security and economic issues. Negotiations between the European Community and the United States over trade barriers, for example, need not affect allied discussions over NATO force structure or burden sharing. Even a close substantive relationship between policy issues may not breach this compartmentalization, once it has been encapsulated in different domestic bureaucracies and different international institutions. Note, for example, that trade negotiations are now treated completely independently from international financial issues. This separation has persisted even though fluctuations in exchange rates can dwarf the impact of tariff changes on relative prices. Likewise bilateral trade disputes, such as the one between Brazil and the United States over computer software, have been remarkably insulated from debt negotiations, despite the obvious substantive connections. Unless there is a high-level decision to link such issues in specific negotiations, they will typically be segregated and encompassed by distinct bureaucracies and political networks, each with its own focus and expertise, each able to negotiate with counterparts abroad.

7.3   Security Issues and Debt Problems in the 1970s and 1980s

In the case of debt renegotiations and security issues, this de-linkage has been almost complete. Even though dozens of countries, including virtually all of Africa and Latin America, have required substantial debt restructuring, only rarely have security issues intruded on the formulation of U.S. debt policy. The absence of security issues is all the more striking because it comes at a time when the United States has conducted vigorous foreign policy initiatives in regions beset with debt problems and sluggish economic growth. In Central America, southern Africa and the Horn of Africa, the United States has vigorously contested the role of Soviet aid and Cuban troops. These policy initiatives have been coupled with support for more financial aid, including substantially increased assistance for sub-Saharan Africa.[68] On the other hand, the obvious importance of these security issues to the Reagan administration has produced little spillover into larger debt questions, beyond some special relief for African aid recipients.

In fact, reviewing the long list of troubled debtors in the 1970s and 1980s, only a few suggest any significant diplomatic and security concerns:

Turkey, whose economic problems were significant militarily because it is a member of NATO and vital to its southern flank.

Iran, whose foreign assets were frozen during a time escalating tensions between the United States and the fundamental Islamic government.

Nicaragua, which rescheduled foreign debts on favorable terms after the Sandinista victory.

Mexico, whose economic difficulties have been at the center of the debt crisis since it announced the need to reschedule in 1982.

I am not claiming that security and diplomatic considerations were dominant or even important in all these cases, only that these few cases require closer consideration.[69]

The Nicaraguan case, for instance, is suggestive because its bank creditors concluded an unusually forthcoming rescheduling agreement at a time when the Carter administration was seeking accommodation with the new government in Managua. Is there a connection?

First, it is clear that Nicaragua did win terms that were considerably less onerous than those of other countries'. Although the banks did insist on commercial interest rates, they made important concessions regarding the repayment period for principal and, most important, permitted most of the country's overdue interest to be capitalized and deferred. Moreover they did not insist on an IMF stabilization agreement as a condition for the debt rescheduling. The 12-year repayment period was among longest negotiated up to that point. The deferral of interest payments and the absence of an IMF agreement were virtually unique—then and now—and the banks took pains to indicate that it was not to be repeated elsewhere.[70]

The important point here, however, is not that the terms were less burdensome than usual but whether those terms were influenced by U.S. policy. The Carter administration, it should be remembered, had successfully sponsored an economic aid package for the new Sandinista regime and had withheld support from counterrevolutionary forces.[71] So there is at least an initial parallel between the banks' weak terms for debt restructuring and the U.S. government's conciliatory stance during the first year of Sandinista rule.

The apparent connection, however, is misleading. According to senior U.S. officials dealing with Nicaragua, the U.S. government had virtually no impact on the negotiations. There was little direct contact between the banks and the U.S. government, and no serious attempt to influence the negotiations. One senior banker on the creditors' committee did hold brief discussions with White House staff, who urged the banks to "remain flexible." But there was little contact beyond that. This same official was clear: the banks drove the best deal they could under the circumstances, and the U.S. government had little impact on the terms.[72] The banks, in this view, understood the weakness of Nicaragua's economy and recognized the political difficulties of repaying debts that Somoza had personally appropriated.[73] As one London banker summarized the deal, "Everyone went along, although they were dragged rather reluctantly. But when you consider the alternatives, it wasn't so bad. It was as close to a commercial transaction as we could get, the least of many evils."[74]

The Iranian case, where both commercial debts and national security issues were central, is much more complicated. Here, too, the debt problems involved a revolutionary regime, saddled with the loans of a predecessor. The U.S. government's role, in the end, was much more direct than in Nicaragua. In the midst of escalating tensions, with American diplomats recently seized and held hostage in Teheran, Washington decided to freeze some $12 billion in Iranian assets. Those assets included not only accounts in American banks but also accounts in their overseas branches and subsidiaries.[75] Robert Carswell, who served as the deputy secretary of the Treasury and helped initiate the freeze, has stressed its unprecedented scale and overall success:

This was by far the largest blocking of assets in U.S. history, and by far the most successful. It was controversial with our Western allies, potentially threatening to the Saudis and other foreign investors in the United States, and raised novel and often difficult questions of law and policy.[76]

Major bank creditors were the immediate beneficiaries of the freeze since they could use the blocked credits to liquidate outstanding loans. Iran, unlike most debtors, actually held substantial foreign deposits, which could be used to repay outstanding claims (termed a "setoff"). Given the banks' exposures, and the substantial Iranian assets available, these setoffs were financially significant. Iran's accounts in offshore U.S. banks, for instance, amounted to around $5.6 billion. As part of the final settlement in January 1981, $3.7 billion of that went to repay syndicated loans and another $1.4 billion went to nonsyndicated loans.[77]

Why was the asset freeze undertaken? What were the major effects, aside from the repayment of these bank loans? Carswell himself does not answer these questions directly, although he does stress the importance of the freeze in securing release of the hostages as well as the costs imposed on Iran in financing its war with Iraq.

Perhaps the answer lies partly in the Iranian declarations that prompted the freeze. On November 13, 1979, at 4 a.m. (Washington time), the acting foreign and finance minister of Iran, Abolhassan Bani-Sadr, announced that he intended to withdraw all Iranian funds from U.S. financial institutions. It was yet another attack on the "Great Satan" in a rapidly escalating war of epithets. The Treasury was ready. It had been studying such contingencies for several months as Iran's political instability had steadily worsened.[78] Within four hours of Bani-Sadr's announcement, the secretaries of state and treasury had been briefed on the threat, the president had been brought into the discussions, congressional leaders had been telephoned, and the president had signed the necessary executive order. By 10 a.m. the first regulations for implementing the freeze had actually been promulgated.[79]

The administration justified this swift action by referring to its fears of financial disruption, involving either an attack upon the dollar or debt repudiation. The potential leverage in hostage negotiations was not mentioned and was probably not considered until much later. In retrospect, Iran's ability to carry out its financial threats was weak. Its deposits easily exceeded its debts and, in any case, its assets were mostly in the form of time deposits that could not be withdrawn quickly. Still, Iran's threat was taken seriously at the time and was at least one provocation that U.S. policymakers could meet effectively. This last consideration—the need to take some decisive action in the face of repeated assaults—was undoubtedly an important motive for the White House.

As Benjamin J. Cohen notes, the ability to use frozen assets to repay bank loans was important politically as well as financially. Normally, U.S. banks would oppose the extraterritorial application of U.S. law. It impedes their ability to act abroad and adds to operating costs in competitive financial markets. They did not oppose extraterritoriality in this case because it benefited them quite directly.[80] In the end, the presence of these transnational financial relationships gave the United States an important source of diplomatic leverage, one that proved useful in securing the hostages' release.

This manipulation of international banking relationships to advance diplomatic goals is, however, quite rare. In Iran's case it depended upon a unique configuration of the country's net assets abroad and the paucity of other U.S. policy instruments. I have found no similar cases.

The case of Turkey, which had to reschedule its bank debts and official loans in 1979–80, is much more straightforward. The country was an important security partner in economic trouble, and the U.S. provided financial aid as part of the overall debt-restructuring agreement. The sums to be rescheduled were large: some $6.5 billion in short- and long-term debts, ranging from private loans to guaranteed suppliers credits. The terms were not markedly different from other reschedulings: the interest rates were high (1.75 percent above the London interbank rate) and covered only the principal falling due in the early 1980s. As usual, an IMF stabilization program was an essential part of the deal.

The Turkish case is unusual, however, because the Fund's conventional policy recommendations—realistic exchange and interest rates, tight control over credit, fewer economic subsidies—actually conformed to an aggressive program of economic restructuring undertaken by Turgut Özal. That program included a liberalization of foreign currency arrangements, export incentives, import liberalization, and encouragement of foreign investment. This was not simply a program that met IMF guidelines, it amounted to a fundamental reversal of a half-century of Turkish economic policy and statecraft, founded on protection, import substitution, and strong, inward-looking government direction of the economy.[81]

IMF naturally considers Turkey's recovery a kind of showcase. As a recent Fund study explains:

Following a severe balance of payments crisis, sustainable economic growth can be attained with a reasonable period of time through an adjustment effort that combines high export performance and revival of domestic financial intermediation, supported by adequate capital inflows from abroad—in a stable social and political environment.[82]

Yet even the IMF recognizes the critical role played by large-scale external aid. The report goes on to say that "the Turkish experience suggests that the effectiveness of these policies can benefit greatly from prompt and sizable external financial assistance especially during the initial period of the adjustment." It also says, in effect, that such external resources must come from public resources since foreign investment can only be expected at later stages of recovery.[83]

Clearly, what prompted this essential aid in Turkey's case was its critical role on NATO's southern flank. The issue had been discussed in January 1979 by Western leaders in their summit meeting in Guadaloupe. The meeting, limited to the leaders of France, Britain, Germany, and the United States, was mainly devoted to the problems of theater nuclear forces in Europe. But the heads of state agreed on several other initiatives, including a financial rescue operation for Turkey.[84]

That rescue was arranged through an OECD consortium and by private creditors. The OECD agreement, concluded in July 1980, soon after Turkey had signed an agreement with the IMF, provided $1 billion in economic assistance. In addition some $2.7 billion in short-term debts to foreign banks and another $2.5 billion in official debt were restructured under OECD auspices. Commercial banks extended a new syndicated loan of $400 million.[85] These efforts were not initially successful, according to the IMF, mainly because of "inadequate restraint on domestic demand and severe limitations on supply."[86] These problems were exacerbated by the doubling of oil import prices and a soft market for Turkish exports.

Over the next five years, however, major donors continued to support the Turkish economy. Turkey received some $1.5 billion in concessional loans for balance-of-payments purposes by the OECD and the Saudi Arabian Monetary Agency. Over the same five-year period, it received another $5.1 billion from the IMF, the World Bank, and bilateral sources. The World Bank, for instance, contributed $1.6 billion in Structural Adjustment Loans (SALs) to support Turkey's continued restructuring.[87] The result, in the IMF's view, was enough external assistance to ensure "a minimum level of resource inputs for viable export-led growth."[88]

The Turkish case provides the only clear-cut example of concessional debt relief for national security purposes during the debt crisis of the 1980s. The Mexican case, at the heart of the debt problem since 1982, indicates that the United States is also willing to mobilize debt relief for broader policy goals. But that case, too, is unique because of Mexico's proximity and its primacy in U.S. relations with Latin America.

Given Mexico's strategic and diplomatic significance, the U.S. government has been willing to do far more in debt restructuring and temporary financing than with other major debtors. Consider, for example, Mexico's financial crisis in 1976, precipitated by the disastrous economic policies of President Luis Echeverría Álvarez. Now that we are used to $100 billion debts in Mexico and Brazil, these early debt figures seem quite small: foreign debts of $17.5 billion, two-thirds of it to U.S. commercial banks. Still, their impact on Mexico's external finances was serious, consuming about 25 percent of export earnings for debt service.[89] The problems were exacerbated by massive capital flight from an overvalued peso. There was steep inflation, a deteriorating trade balance and, as a result, heavy reliance on foreign borrowing. Although Mexico had discovered major oil reserves in the 1973, they were not yet producing important export revenues. At best, they served to encourage further foreign borrowing. A series of drastic devaluations during August and September only fed the growing panic. Small depositors joined major industrialists in converting their savings from pesos to U.S. dollars.

When the problems finally came to a head, the U.S. government played a central role in the restructuring. It pieced together a series of ad hoc financial arrangements to provide short-term financing. The aim was to preserve order in currency markets and to serve as a bridge until IMF financing was made in place for economic stabilization. In April 1976, the U.S. Federal Reserve provided some $360 million in short-term currency "swaps." Later that summer the Federal Reserve and Treasury offered additional support. The IMF provided $1.2 billion in November, and a consortium of commercial banks (led by Bank of America) provided another $800 million, largely in anticipation of the new oil revenues.[90]

The scale was much smaller than the 1982 financial crisis, but the basic policy instruments were much the same, including the rare use of currency swaps. Both crises reached the presidential level and the involved a commitment of U.S. resources that was unique in dealing with LDC debt. Indeed, according to one White House official, the U.S. government was more willing to extend credits (especially short-term credits) than for any other debtor and more willing to try arm-twisting with commercial creditors.[91] Other Latin American debtors are well aware of America's special commitment to Mexico's external finance and often try to pattern their own settlements on Mexican terms.

These commitments were clearly evident during the 1982 Mexican debt rescheduling, which marked the beginning of the modern debt crisis. The story is familiar and need not be repeated here.[92] But the terms of U.S. assistance are important and unprecedented, and so is the speed with which the government package was assembled. The crisis began with a telephone call by Mexico's finance minister to the U.S. Treasury on Thursday evening, August 12. The basic elements of the multibillion dollar package were assembled in secret over the following weekend. By 11:30 Sunday night, the U.S. Treasury had agreed to provide nearly $3 billion to stave off a Mexican default.[93] The Federal Reserve, which had already extended

Mexico $700 million in swaps earlier that month, moved aggressively to assemble financing from other central banks.

The package assembled in Washington that August weekend came from a number of sources, some of them with little direct interest in Mexico. What they had in common was the capacity to supply significant funds quickly and to secure them with Mexican exports or other assets. Some $1 billion went to increase imports of Mexican farm products; roughly the same amount went to buy Mexican oil for the U.S. Strategic Petroleum Reserve. The Department of Agriculture paid for the food purchases (through the Commodity Credit Corporation); the Department of Defense paid for the petroleum reserve. The Treasury contributed another $1 billion from the Exchange Stabilization Fund.[94] The whole program was pieced together by the Treasury and the Federal Reserve. The Fed later worked closely with the IMF to ensure private bank participation in the rescheduling package.

For the United States to provide this kind of emergency financing is rare, but not unique. The United States also provided Brazil with $1.2 billion in crucial bridge loans during 1982, indicating a general willingness to hold off financial emergencies arising from LDC debts. What was unique to Mexico was not the general U.S. commitment, but rather its scale and rapidity, and the scope of bureaucratic involvement. Taken together, they indicate the diplomatic and financial importance of the bilateral relationship.

Few relationships merit such attention, and, as we have seen, few debt negotiations are seriously affected by broader diplomatic and military issues. Except for Turkey (and perhaps the Philippines), our important allies are not troubled by debt problems. One reason, of course, is that our most important alliance is with the developed economies of Europe. Among less developed countries, our security commitments have increasingly focused on military aid and arms transfers rather than broader developmental questions. The United States had not abandoned those development issues—indeed, throughout the Reagan administration we have spoken out forcefully on privatization and liberalization—but the United States has slowly reduced its bilateral aid instruments. Except for rare cases like Mexico and Turkey, it is difficult to mobilize substantial resources to assist debtors.

Finally, the United States has few instruments to control debt negotiations by private bankers. Their role, after all, is central to most debt restructuring outside Africa. The U.S. government is not entirely without instruments: the Federal Reserve can use its powers of persuasion; the controller of the currency can facilitate or impede the provision of new loans by its classification of old ones. But the U.S. government played almost no role in the initial private lending, and it has refused to bear the costs of the resulting debt problems. Even the German government, which has close relationships with its leading banks, refused to guarantee retroactively any loans to Eastern Europe. The banks argued that those loans helped support the government's own policy of Ostpolitik. Perhaps so, the government responded, but we will not underwrite your commercial lending risks.[95] This independence is usually prized by the banks themselves, who reject government interference with their lending. Even loan guarantee programs allow banks to evaluate the credit risks and choose among individual borrowers. A senior vice-president at Citicorp put the matter in sharp focus in 1979:

We don't look to the U.S. government for any guidance or help. If anyone from the Treasury phoned asking us to lend to a specific borrower, I'd hang up on him. If I began to hear that the State Department was happy with our lending, I'd start to worry that maybe we're making the wrong decisions.... If the [National Bank Examiners'] ranking of a particular country isn't justified by our own research, we follow our own analysis.[96]

There have been a lot of bad loans written down since 1979, and the U.S. government has played a more active role in debt rescheduling and loan classification, but the point still holds: public institutions did not play an important role in the initial recycling and have been unwilling to bear the costs that followed.

7.4 Conclusions

After this examination of British and American lending, we can reconsider our initial questions. First, though there are vast differences in the policy instruments available to these two governments, neither did much to channel private investments abroad. On rare occasions, the British government did issue guarantees, as it did in some loans to the Ottoman Empire during the Crimean War. The U.S. government has larger and more active facilities to guarantee credits, principally to encourage trade. These guarantees, along with foreign aid loans, mean that creditor states like the United States must now conduct their own negotiations with debtor states, alongside negotiations between debtors and private creditors. This direct public stake in debt restructuring is important. But it should be understood that these guarantees are not really tools to redirect capital investments abroad; they are efforts to increase exports. Because governments have played little direct role in channeling or encouraging capital exports to specific countries, there has been little room to claim that they bear responsibility for bad debts. Here the parallel with nineteenth-century lending is very close.

Second, in both centuries, private creditors sometimes sought support from their home governments. Yet only rarely did they receive significant help. When they did, it was typically because the creditors had previously received explicit guarantees or because security considerations applied.

There are some differences, of course, between the British and American experiences in this regard. British policy, which followed Lord Palmerston's careful guidelines, drew sharp distinctions between private commercial risks and public obligations. In general, Foreign Office support for bondholders was restrained, except in cases of fraud or the breakdown of public order. As the permanent under secretary of the Foreign Office wrote in 1871:

Her Majesty's Government are in no way party to private loan transactions with foreign States. Contracts of this nature rest only between the Power borrowing and the capitalists who enter into them as speculative enterprises .... Further, it is scarcely necessary to point out the endless troubles which certainly would arise if the active intervention of England were exerted to redress the grievances of bondholders. Independently of the expense which would necessarily be incurred, and the risk of international complications, forcible measures, if adopted towards small States, which for the most part are the ones complained of, would subject this country to grievous imputations.[97]

American policy has not followed Palmerston's strict injunctions, but it too has been restrained. There has been no retroactive guarantee of LDC debts, no voluntary public assumption of bad loans. Subject to these limitations, American policy has been somewhat more interventionist than the British. Public loans have been advanced to major debtors such as Mexico to facilitate rescheduling and additional aid has been given to severely impoverished regions, such as sub-Saharan Africa, that are saddled with heavy debts from public authorities. The very availability of public instruments, both bilateral and multilateral, is part of the reason. These instruments are part of a more active use of financial tools in diplomacy. These tools have been combined with a willingness to address macroeconomic issues in debtor countries. Moreover these financial tools often mean that the U.S. government is itself a creditor, with debts to be rescheduled alongside other aid donors. (This is done through the informal institution of the Paris Club.) These public reschedulings have often helped to establish terms for private debt restructuring.

But the mere availability of policy tools, and the increased understanding of macroeconomic policy, is only part of the reason for increased state intervention. Another crucial reason is that postwar American lending has been mainly bank lending. Default on the largest foreign loans thus threatens the capital structure and solvency of major financial institutions. Under the circumstances the Federal Reserve and the U.S. Treasury have had an indirect interest in LDC debt repayment.

British loans, by contrast, were overwhelmingly bonds and were widely distributed to the investing public. Unless an issuing house held large quantities for its own account, which sometimes happened, a default would leave financial institutions largely unscathed. When such institutions were involved, as in the Barings crisis of 1890, the Bank of England acted promptly. This type of intervention, it should be noted, does not involve security issues and, indeed, is not focused on the debtor's problems but on the private creditor's.

In the end, both Victorian Britain and postwar American governments shared a deep desire to ensulate themselves from the decisions of private investors, to ensure that foreign policy was not shaped by choices in capital markets. Security considerations could always intrude, and occasionally did, but the basic policy was to require that private investors secure their own interests in commercial transactions. To do otherwise was to embrace the dangers of moral hazard and to open the gates to private claimants.

Notes

1. Pioneering work on these connections was conducted by Robert Gilpin. Gilpin argues that, in both postwar America and Victorian Britain, the hegemonic power provided a "political umbrella" for this international economic expansion. Robert Gilpin, *U.S. Power and the Multinational Corporation* (New York: Basic Books, 1975). See also Stephen D. Krasner, "State Power and the Structure of International Trade," *World Politics* 28, 3 (April 1976), pp. 317–47.

2. Such extensive international economic interests are typical of major powers, but they are not uniformly present in all such powers. For decades, the Soviet Union has had relatively modest commercial ties beyond Eastern Europe and few foreign investments anywhere. The basic organization of a planned socialist economy, together with the Soviets' large internal market, work to limit their international economic ties. Direct foreign investment, though not unknown, is extremely small, given the size of the Soviet economy.

It should not be assumed, however, that only communist states have weak international economic links. The rapidly industrializing German Empire of the late nineteenth century had relatively modest foreign investments until the turn of the century. Indeed, the Imperial government played an important role in trying to stimulate such investments in support of its diplomatic aims.

The more general assertion that major powers are not usually interdependent economically plays a central role in Kenneth Waltz' theory of international politics.

See his "The Myth of National Interdependence," in Charles P. Kindleberger, ed., *The International Corporation: A Symposium* (Cambridge, MA: MIT Press, 1970), pp. 205–23; *Theory of International Politics* (Reading, MA: Addison-Wesley, 1979): and "Reflections on Theory of International Politics: A Response to My Critics," in Robert O. Keohane, ed., *Neorealism and Its Critics* (New York: Columbia University Press, 1986), pp. 322–45.

3. For a counterargument, drawn largely from labor economics, see the recent work of Samuel Bowles and Herbert Gintis.

4. For a concise discussion, see Robert J. Art and Robert Jervis, "The Meaning of Anarchy," in Robert J. Art and Robert Jervis, eds., *International Politics* (2d ed.; Boston: Little, Brown, 1985), pp. 2–7, and the articles that follow. For analysis of how the assumption of anarchy affects models of international economic cooperation, see Kenneth A. Oye, ed., *Cooperation under Anarchy* (Princeton, NJ: Princeton University Press, 1985).

5. On the parties' general willingness to incur enforcement costs, see L. G. Telser, "A Theory of Self-Enforcing Agreements," *Journal of Business* 53 (January 1980), pp. 27–44.

6. For a general argument on the uses of collateral and hostages to make contracts credible, see Oliver Williamson, *The Economic Institutions of Capitalism* (New York: Free Press, 1985). Williamson himself is quite clear on the difficulties of using collateral and hostages without third parties (e.g., escrow arrangements). The fundamental problem of opportunism in international contracts cannot be solved easily, either in theory or in practice.

7. Charles Lipson, "Bankers' Dilemmas: Private Cooperation in Rescheduling Sovereign Debts," in Kenneth Oye, ed., *Cooperation Under Anarchy* (Princeton, NJ: Princeton University Press, 1985).

8. Sovereign borrowers may actually wish to pledge such collateral because it lowers the risks and therefore the costs of new credit. But the lenders' home government may not be a willing partner to the transaction since the government would, in effect, be pledging to seize the customs revenues of another country— with all the attendant costs and uncertainties.
   In 1879, in order to lower the costs of foreign borrowing, Venezuela specifically asked the British government to pledge that it would intervene on behalf of bondholders in case of default. Salisbury refused the request. D. C. M. Platt, "British Bondholders in Nineteenth Century Latin America—Injury and Remedy," *Inter-American Economic Affairs* 14 (Winter 1960), pp. 36–37.

9. This is a major theme in Herbert Feis, Europe, *The World's Banker, 1870–1914* (1964 reprint; New Haven, CT: Yale University Press, for the Council on Foreign Relations, 1930).

10. For a breakdown of these investments by categories, see, Irving Stone, "British Long-Term Investment in Latin America, 1865–1913," *Business History Review* 42 (Autumn 1968), pp. 323–24, tables 7 and 8.

11. F. C. Floud, "Britain 1860–1914: A Survey," in Floud and Donald McCloskey, eds., *The Economic History of Britain since 1700: 1860 to the 1970s*, Vol. 2 (Cambridge, UK: Cambridge University Press, 1981), p. 3.

12. Britain's capital exports were not the result of a surplus in merchandise trade. Merchandise imports exceeded exports in every year from 1816 onward. But these deficits were more than offset by earnings from shipping and from other foreign-trade services. See S. B. Saul, *Studies in British Overseas Trade, 1870– 1914* (Liverpool, U.K.: Liverpool University Press, 1960), p. 10; A. Imlah, "The British Balance of Payments and Export of Capital, 1816–1913," *Economic History Review*, 2d series, 5 (1952), pp. 234ff. For Britain's increasing sophistication in financing export trade and its relationship to new investments, see Ralph Davis, *The Industrial Revolution and British Overseas Trade* (Leicester, UK: Leicester University Press, 1979), pp. 57–61.

13. Edwin M. Borchard, *The Diplomatic Protection of Citizens Abroad, or, The Law of International Claims* (New York: Banks Law Publishing, 1915), p. 315n. Borchard mentions Canning, Aberdeen, Palmerston, Russell, Derby, Granville, and Salisbury as favoring policies that limited the Foreign Office's commitments to aid foreign investors in commercial disputes.

14. The lack of government regulation also reduced the cost of financial intermediation. These lower costs in turn contributed to the rise of entrepôt functions in Britain and to the growth of an international financial market there. Paul Kennedy, "Strategy versus Finance in Twentieth-Century Britain," in Kennedy, *Strategy and Diplomacy, 1870–1945* (London: George Allen & Unwin, 1983), p. 93.

15. M. Edelstein, "Foreign Investment and Empire, 1860–1914," in R. C. Floud and Donald McCloskey, eds., *The Economic History of Britain since 1700: 1860 to the 1970s*, Vol. 2 (Cambridge, UK: Cambridge University Press, 1981), p. 71.

16. David McLean, "Commerce, Finance, and British Diplomatic Support in China, 1885–86," *Economic History Review*, 2d series, 26 (August 1973), p. 465.

17. Ronald Robinson and John Gallagher with Alice Denny, Africa and the Victorians (Garden City, NY: Anchor/Doubleday, 1968 [1961]); John Gallagher and Ronald Robinson, "The Imperialism of Free Trade," *Economic History Review*, 2d series (1953), pp. 1–25.

18. For a succinct and subtle argument about the Great Power politics that underlay British policy in Mexico, see Kenneth Bourne, *The Foreign Policy of Victorian England, 1830– 1902* (Oxford, UK: Oxford University Press, 1970), pp. 89–90.

19. Edwin M. Borchard, *The Diplomatic Protection of Citizens Abroad, or, The Law of International Claims* (New York: Banks Law Publishing, 1915), pp. 240–42.

20. The work of D. C. M. Platt and his students is particularly useful in clarifying these limits in British commercial diplomacy.

21. "Circular addressed by Viscount Palmerston to Her Majesty's Representatives in Foreign States, respecting the Debts due by Foreign States to British Subjects,"

January 1848 [Printed as P.P. 1849 (1049), LVI]. Reprinted in D. C. M. Platt, *Finance, Trade and Politics in British Foreign Policy, 1815–1914* (Oxford, UK: Oxford University Press, 1968), pp. 398–99.

22. "Circular addressed by Viscount Palmerston to Her Majesty's Representatives in Foreign States, respecting the Debts due by Foreign States to British Subjects," January 1848 [Printed as P.P. 1849 (1049), LVI]. Reprinted in D. C. M. Platt, *Finance, Trade and Politics in British Foreign Policy, 1815–1914* (Oxford, UK: Oxford University Press, 1968), pp. 398.

23. "Circular addressed by Viscount Palmerston to Her Majesty's Representatives in Foreign States, respecting the Debts due by Foreign States to British Subjects," January 1848 [Printed as P.P. 1849 (1049), LVI]. Reprinted in D. C. M. Platt, *Finance, Trade and Politics in British Foreign Policy, 1815–1914* (Oxford, UK: Oxford University Press, 1968), pp. 398–99.

24. John Gallagher and Ronald Robinson, "The Imperialism of Free Trade," *Economic History Review*, 2d series, 6 (1953); Robinson and Gallagher with Alice Denny, *Africa and the Victorians* (New York: St. Martin's, 1961), ch. 1.

25. D. C. M. Platt, *Finance, Trade and Politics in British Foreign Policy, 1815–1914* (Oxford, UK: Oxford University Press, 1968), pp. 330.

26. Malcolm Edward Yapp, "Turkey and Ancient Anatolia," *Encyclopaedia Britannica*, 28 (1987), pp. 930–31.

27. This larger financial crisis was itself rooted European great power politics since it stemmed from the reparations for the Franco-Prussian war. See Charles P. Kindleberger, *Manias, Panics, and Crashes* (New York: Basic Books, 1978), pp. 132–33.

28. Malcolm Edward Yapp, "Turkey and Ancient Anatolia," Encyclopaedia Britannica, 28 (1987), pp. 930–31.

29. Donald Quataert, *Social Disintegration and Popular Resistance in the Ottoman Empire, 1881–1908: Reactions to European Economic Penetration* (New York: New York University Press, 1983), p. 10.

30. D. C. M. Platt, *Finance, Trade and Politics in British Foreign Policy, 1815–1914* (Oxford, UK: Oxford University Press, 1968), pp. 206.

31. D. C. M. Platt, *Finance, Trade and Politics in British Foreign Policy, 1815–1914* (Oxford, UK: Oxford University Press, 1968), pp. 197–207.

32. Şevek Pamuk, "Foreign Trade, Foreign Capital and the Peripheralization of the Ottoman Empire, 1830–1913," Ph.D. dissertation, University of California, Berkeley, pp. 115–17, cited in Donald Quataert, *Social Disintegration and Popular Resistance in the Ottoman Empire, 1881–1908: Reactions to European Economic Penetration* (New York: New York University Press, 1983), p. 7.

33. David McLean, "Finance and 'Informal Empire' before the First World War," *Economic History Review*, 2d series, 29 (May 1976), p. 293.

34. Minute by Parker on Lowther to Grey, 20 June 1913, F.O. 371/1826, as cited in David McLean, "Finance and 'Informal Empire' before the First World War," *Economic History Review*, 2d series, 29 (May, 1976), p. 294.

35. David McLean, "Finance and 'Informal Empire' before the First World War," *Economic History Review*, 2d series, 29 (May 1976), p. 296. Although McLean notes that this case is unusual, he observes that it is not unique.

36. Minute by Grey on memorandum by Parker, 14 June 1913, F.O. 371/1826, as cited in David McLean, "Finance and 'Informal Empire' before the First World War," *Economic History Review*, 2d series, 29 (May 1976), p. 297.

37. John A. Levandis, *The Greek Foreign Debt and the Great Powers, 1821–1898* (New York: Columbia University Press, 1944), pp. 75ff.

38. W. H. Wynne, "Causes of Insolvency," in Edwin Borchard, *State Insolvency and Foreign Bondholders: General Principles*, Vol. 1 (New Haven, CT: Yale University Press, 1951), p. 148.

39. John A. Levandis, *The Greek Foreign Debt and the Great Powers, 1821–1898* (New York: Columbia University Press, 1944), p. 93.

40. Salisbury's quote is from John A. Levandis, *The Greek Foreign Debt and the Great Powers, 1821–1898* (New York: Columbia University Press, 1944), p. 96.

41. John A. Levandis, *The Greek Foreign Debt and the Great Powers, 1821–1898* (New York: Columbia University Press, 1944), p. 96.

42. John A. Levandis, *The Greek Foreign Debt and the Great Powers, 1821–1898* (New York: Columbia University Press, 1944), p. 97.

43. Edwin Lieuwen, "Venezuela," in *Encyclopaedia Britannica* 29 (1987), p. 495.

44. Holger H. Herwig examines this growing presence in *Germany's Vision of Empire in Venezuela, 1871–1914* (Princeton, NJ: Princeton University Press, 1986).

45. Holger H. Herwig, *Germany's Vision of Empire in Venezuela, 1871–1914* (Princeton, NJ: Princeton University Press, 1986), p. 27. Herwig notes that some German financial houses in Venezuela also relied on French *haute banques* such as de Neuflize & Cie. for their international transactions.

46. Holger H. Herwig, *Germany's Vision of Empire in Venezuela, 1871–1914* (Princeton, NJ: Princeton University Press, 1986), p. 83.

47. Holger H. Herwig, *Germany's Vision of Empire in Venezuela, 1871–1914* (Princeton, NJ: Princeton University Press, 1986), pp. 94–97.

48. Not all merchants and financiers sought intervention. Herwig notes that the largest German merchant house in Venezuela, G. H. and L. F. Blohm of Hamburg, was counseling restraint and arbitration in December 1902. But Blohm's was clearly a minority opinion. Herwig, *Germany's Vision of Empire in Venezuela, 1871–1914* (Princeton, NJ: Princeton University Press, 1986), pp. 99–100.

49. Castro's hopes for U.S. backing were not without foundation and, indeed, the resident British minister, W. H. D. Haggard, had written to Salisbury of the United States' new emphasis on the Monroe Doctrine (and on Germany's seeming indifference to it).

Although my explanation stresses broader diplomatic issues and standard British policies, Haggard's own role may have contributed to the decision to use force in Venezuela. As in most individual policy choices, idiosyncracies and contingent factors are important. Haggard himself continually stressed the efficacy of using force against Venezuela. Miriam Hood, in her history of turn-of-the-century Venezuela, concludes that Haggard was strongly antipathetic toward Venezuela and that his attitude was "a contributing factor resulting in the Anglo-German blockade." Miriam Hood, *Gunboat Diplomacy, 1895–1905: Great Power Pressure in Venezuela* (London: George Allen & Unwin, 1975), p. 141.

50. Holger H. Herwig, *Germany's Vision of Empire in Venezuela, 1871–1914* (Princeton, NJ: Princeton University Press, 1986), pp. 101–2.

51. D. C. M. Platt, "The Allied Coercion of Venezuela, 1902–3—A Reassessment," *Inter-American Economic Affairs* 15 (Spring 1962), pp. 3, 10.

52. D. C. M. Platt, "The Allied Coercion of Venezuela, 1902–3—A Reassessment," *Inter-American Economic Affairs* 15 (Spring 1962), p. 21. According to Holger Herwig, German leaders made similar—and quite credible—claims. See Herwig, pp. 108–9.

53. Balfour also faced some pressures against using naval force in Venezuela beyond the usual prudential reasons. Popular anti-German feeling was rising and, indeed, led to a storm of protest when the Anglo-Italian-German blockade was announced. The dominant issue in Parliament was not whether force was appropriate in this case, but whether it was appropriate to act in concert with Germany. Ruddock F. Mackay, *Balfour: Intellectual Statesman* (Oxford, U.K.: Oxford University Press, 1985), pp. 129, 135–37; Max Egremont, *Balfour: A Life of Arthur James Balfour* (London: Collins, 1980), p. 164.

54. Peter H. Lindert and Peter J. Morton, "How Sovereign Debt Has Worked," in Jeffrey D. Sachs, ed., *Developing Country Debt and Economic Performance: The International Financial System* (Chicago, IL: University of Chicago Press, forthcoming), app. table B.1; W. H. Wynne, "Causes of Insolvency," in Edwin Borchard, ed., *State Insolvency and Foreign Bondholders: General Principles*, Vol. 1 (New Haven, CT: Yale University Press, 1951), p. 147.

55. Holger H. Herwig, *Germany's Vision of Empire in Venezuela, 1871–1914* (Princeton, NJ: Princeton University Press, 1986), p. 92.

56. Holger H. Herwig, *Germany's Vision of Empire in Venezuela, 1871–1914* (Princeton, NJ: Princeton University Press, 1986), pp. 94–95.

57. Frank Costigliola, *Awkward Dominion: American Political, Economic, and Cultural Relations with Europe, 1919–1933* (Ithaca, NY: Cornell University Press, 1984); Stephen Schuker, *The End of French Predominance in Europe: The Financial Crisis of*

1924 and the Adoption of the Dawes Plan (Chapel Hill, NC: University of North Carolina Press, 1976), and the very useful review essay by Jon Jacobson, "Is there a New International History of the 1920s?" *American Historical Review* 88 (June 1983), pp. 617–45.

58. On America's early search for a policy, see David S. Painter, *Oil and the American Century: The Political Economy of U.S. Foreign Oil Policy, 1941–1954* (Baltimore, MD: Johns Hopkins University Press, 1986); Irvine H. Anderson, *Aramco, the United States and Saudi Arabia* (Princeton, NJ: Princeton University Press, 1981); also Michael B. Stoff, *Oil, War, and American Security* (New Haven, CT: Yale University Press, 1980). For a longer-term diplomatic history, see Benjamin Shwadran, *The Middle East, Oil and the Great Powers* (3d ed.; New York: Wiley, 1973).

59. For a recent, postrevisionist argument to that effect, see Robert A. Pollard, *Economic Security and the Origins of the Cold War* (New York: Columbia University Press, 1985).

60. The argument that economic issues were of overriding importance is made quite explicitly in Imanuel Wexler, *The Marshall Plan Revisited: The European Recovery Program in Economic Perspective* (Westport, CT: Greenwood Press, 1983). For a novel and closely argued revisionist interpretation, also focused exclusively on economic issues, see Alan S. Milward, *The Reconstruction of Western Europe, 1945–51* (Berkeley: University of California Press, 1984).

61. Joyce and Gabriel Kolko, *The Limits of Power: The World and United States Foreign Policy, 1945–1954* (New York: Harper and Row, 1972).

62. On the Nazi's regional trade system, see Albert O. Hirschman, *National Power and the Structure of Foreign Trade* (1945; reprinted: University of California Press, 1980).

63. Charles P. Kindleberger, *Power and Money: The Politics of International Economics and the Economics of International Politics* (New York: Basic Books, 1970), pp. 171–172. Kindleberger goes on to observe that the Nazi's exchange controls were not especially effective.

64. This point is nicely made by John Ruggie, who distinguishes between the laissez faire liberalism of midnineteenth century British trade policy and America's recognition that domestic social programs (including employment policies) should not be strictly subordinate to multilateral trade liberalization. As Ruggie states, "The principles of multilateralism and tariff reductions were affirmed, but so were safeguards, exemptions, exceptions, and restrictions—all designed to protect the balance of payments and a variety of domestic social policies." Ruggie calls this compromise "embedded liberalism." The idea is grounded in Karl Polanyi's argument that economic arrangements are typically embedded in a domestic social context and that Victorian Britain's isolation of economic motives was atypical and could not be long sustained. Ruggie, "International Regimes, Transactions, and Change: Embedded Liberalism in the Postwar Economic Order," in Stephen D.

Krasner, ed., *International Regimes* (Ithaca, NY: Cornell University Press, 1983), p. 212.

65. William Diebold, Jr., *The End of the ITO* (Princeton, NJ: Princeton University Essays in International Finance, no. 16, October 1952); Richard N. Gardner, *Sterling-Dollar Diplomacy: Anglo-American Collaboration in the Reconstruction of Multilateral Trade* (Oxford, UK: Oxford University Press, 1956), ch. 17.

66. This was particularly clear in the case of Germany, which was increasingly seen as the crucial boundary between Soviet and American security spheres and, simultaneously, the crucial element of European economic reconstruction. On Germany's central place in thinking about the Marshall Plan, see John Gimbel, *The Origins of the Marshall Plan* (Stanford, CA: Stanford University Press, 1976).

67. Address of Secretary of State George C. Marshall at Harvard University, June 5, 1947, in Forrest C. Pogue, *George C. Marshall: Statesman 1945–1959* (New York: Viking, 1987), p. 527.

68. Carol Lancaster and John Williamson, eds., *African Debt and Financing*, Special Reports no. 5 (Washington, DC: Institute for International Economics, 1986).

69. Casting a somewhat wider net, we might consider debt problems in Poland and Argentina, both of which are plausibly linked to security issues. In Poland, the debt rescheduling was closely linked to economic and political crisis in the early 1980s. But the United States played little role in the overall settlement, except to sanction Poland. The Federal Republic was somewhat more active, but they too did little to rescue their own banks and provided no emergency financing. What the Polish case did clearly show was the fallacy in the commercial banks' own views of security relationships: the Russians did not bail the Poles out of bankruptcy. Until then, many banks had relied on the so-called "Umbrella Theory," referring to a hoped-for Russian umbrella over Eastern Europe's external finances. The Russians managed to maintain their political hegemony without paying for the umbrella.

The Argentine case involves military issues quite directly since its war with Britain led banks to suspend virtually all new bank lending to Latin America and so helped begin the continuing debt crisis of the 1980s. The specific debt negotiations with Argentina were not affected by other security concerns.

70. John Dizard, "Why Bankers Fear the Nicaraguan Solution," *Institutional Investor, International Edition* (November 1980), p. 53. Steve Downer, "Nicaragua: The Recovery Is Only Just Beginning," *Euromoney* (December 1980), pp. 125–29. The Dizard article offers a detailed account of the negotiations between Nicaragua and the banks.

71. On the Carter administration's policies, see Robert Pastor, *Condemned to Repetition: The United States and Nicaragua* (Princeton, NJ: Princeton University Press, 1987), chrs. 10–11.

72. Personal interviews.

73. On Somoza's uses for the borrowed money, see "Where did Somoza's Borrowed Millions Go?" *Euromoney* (September 1979), p. 25.

74. "The Nicaraguan Precedent," *Institutional Investor, International Edition* (December 1980), p. 110.

75. The freeze came less than two weeks after the hostages had been seized in November 1979. For a discussion by the key U.S. officials responsible for the freeze, see Robert Carswell and Richard J. Davis, "The Economic and Financial Pressures: Freeze and Sanctions," in Warren Christopher et al. *American Hostages in Iran: The Conduct of a Crisis* (New Haven, CT: Yale University Press, 1985), and Carswell, "Economic Sanctions and the Iran Experience," *Foreign Affairs* 60 (Winter 1981–82), pp. 247–65.

76. Robert Carswell, "Economic Sanctions and the Iran Experience," *Foreign Affairs* 60 (Winter 1981–82), p. 248.

77. Robert Carswell, "Economic Sanctions and the Iran Experience," *Foreign Affairs* 60 (Winter 1981–82), p. 256.

78. U.S., House, Committee on Banking, Finance and Urban Affairs, *Iran: The Financial Aspects of the Hostage Settlement Agreement*, July 1981, pp. 6, 51, as cited in Cohen, *In Whose Interest*, p. 158.

79. For a very clear account of these events, see Benjamin J. Cohen, *In Whose Interest? International Banking and American Foreign Policy* (New Haven, CT: Yale University Press, 1986), ch. 6.

80. Benjamin J. Cohen, *In Whose Interest? International Banking and American Foreign Policy* (New Haven, CT: Yale University Press, 1986), p. 161.

81. David Barchard, *Turkey and the West* (London: Routledge & Kegan Paul for the Royal Institute of International Affairs, 1985), ch. 3.

82. George Kopits, *Structural Reform, Stabilization, and Growth in Turkey*, IMF Occasional Paper 52, May 1987, p. 28.

83. George Kopits, *Structural Reform, Stabilization, and Growth in Turkey*, IMF Occasional Paper 52, May 1987, p. 28.

84. Robert D. Putnam and Nicholas Bayne, *Hanging Together: The Seven-Power Summits* (Cambridge, MA: Harvard University Press, 1984), p. 111.

85. George Kopits, *Structural Reform, Stabilization, and Growth in Turkey*, IMF Occasional Paper 52, May 1987, pp. 3–4.

86. George Kopits, *Structural Reform, Stabilization, and Growth in Turkey*, IMF Occasional Paper 52, May 1987, p. 4.

87. George Kopits, *Structural Reform, Stabilization, and Growth in Turkey*, IMF Occasional Paper 52, May 1987, pp. 7–8.

88. George Kopits, *Structural Reform, Stabilization, and Growth in Turkey*, IMF Occasional Paper 52, May 1987, p. 27.

89. George W. Grayson, *The United States and Mexico: Patterns of Influence* (New York: Praeger, 1984), p. 50.

90. George W. Grayson, *The United States and Mexico: Patterns of Influence* (New York: Praeger, 1984), pp. 50–52.

91. Anonymous interview. In one important sense, however, the difficulties of Mexican rescheduling are especially severe. Because of Mexico's proximity and its extensive trade with the southwestern United States, its creditors include many smaller banks that lack extensive international portfolios. Gaining their adherence to debt-rescheduling packages has been especially difficult. The task has been complicated further because many of these institutions are saddled with heavy losses from domestic energy loans and so have little flexibility in contributing to the Mexican debt packages.

92. For a thorough chronology, see Joseph Kraft, *The Mexican Rescue* (New York: Group of Thirty, 1984).

93. Don Oberdorfer, "Mexico Crisis Altered U.S. Foreign Loan Views," *Washington Post*, January 30, 1983, pp. A1, A10.

94. Susan Kaufman Purcell, "War and Debt in South America," *Foreign Affairs: America and the World 1982* 61 (1983), p. 669.

95. Anonymous interviews with German bankers.

96. Quoted in Philip A. Wellons, *Passing the Buck: Banks, Governments, and Third World Debt* (Boston, MA: Harvard Business School Press, 1987). The Citicorp officer who was quoted had extensive responsibilities for international lending and was interviewed for a Harvard Business School case study. He requested anonymity for published quotation, but his views mirrored those of bank chairman Walter Wriston. The bank's viewpoint on the then-emerging debt crisis are presented in "World Money and Credit: The Crisis and Its Causes" (Boston, MA: Harvard Business School Case Services, 1983), No. 9-983-003, especially pp. 91ff (Case No. 381-146).

97. Under Secretary Edmund Hammond to Mr. Hyde Clark, on the direction of Earl Granville. Reprinted in D. C. M. Platt, *Finance, Trade and Politics in British Foreign Policy, 1815–1914* (Oxford, UK: Oxford University Press, 1968), pp. 400–401.

8   Response to Debt Crisis: What Is Different about the 1980s?

Peter H. Lindert

When the past serves as a background for the present, contrasts are usually as revealing as similarities. Earlier history illuminates the lingering international debt crisis in both ways. In the optimistic phase of heavy international lending from 1974 through 1981, the present wave resembled earlier experiences more closely than most participants realized. The onset of crisis in 1982 again looked hauntingly familiar to those who have read the history of debt crises. It is the official response to crisis since 1982 that stands in stark contrast to the past. The 1980s offer a unique opportunity to determine the effects of a new policy response to an old problem.

The results to date suggest that the 1980s have rewritten the official rules of international debt. Officials in creditor countries and international agencies have now intervened globally, apparently out of concern over the unprecedented exposure of major banks, especially in the United States. The 1980s introduced a new pair of policies, one for large debtor countries, whose debts threaten major-bank solvency, and another for smaller debtors. Large debtors, particularly those with middle income levels, are made to pay high near-market interest rates to official as well as private creditors. Small debtors, especially those with lower income per capita, borrow at interest rates that are concessionary from the start.

To the extent that the new regime of the 1980s has prevented outright default, it has helped insure creditors against massively negative rates of return. It is still too early to tell whether this generation of creditors can match the interest premia earned by their predecessors in the age in international bond lending. Although some debtors have been making genuine repayment transfers in the 1980s, these have not been sufficient to keep up with the rise in the real interest rates the creditors could have earned by lending to the United States instead of re-lending to developing countries. It is natural to ask why the debtors repay at all in 1980s, but the experience to date finds that most of them are not repaying. Out of 97 debtor countries, only five countries near the United States account for fully half of all net resource transfers from debtors to private creditors, and only three of these debtors (Ecuador, Venezuela, and Mexico) have yielded large transfers to all their creditors.

The global official intervention since 1982 does not fit the "illiquidity" model in which officials provide needed temporary liquidity, which eliminates the need for itself after a brief crisis period. Rather debtor countries have, in virtually all cases, continued to renegotiate and reschedule, with no visible positive effects on their own recovery. Debtor countries have shown slower growth, slightly lower investment shares and accelerating inflation, relative to other countries and to their own past trends. Nor has private foreign lending to developing countries revived.

There can be no mistaking the tentative nature of any historical judgments on a decade still in progress. The phrase "So far it appears that ..." must stand as an unwritten prefix to every sentence that follows. The other main disclaimer to enter at the outset is that this chapter cannot be a comprehensive treatment of all the differences and similarities such a broad comparative history might illuminate. Rather, it concentrates on selected issues, to complement other studies in this volume and elsewhere.[1]

Historical contrasts and similarities reveal themselves best if we follow the cycle of lending optimism and repayments crisis, comparing different historical eras for each phase of the cycle. Section 8.1 selects three aspects of the prelude to crisis, namely, the terms on which countries borrowed abroad before announcing the imminent danger of arrears, the amounts they borrowed, and whether or not governments were expected to intervene in any later repayments crisis. Section 8.2 follows the changing responses of creditor-country governments and international agencies to announced crises, noting a curious international pattern of the 1980s. Section 8.3 examines the returns that private creditors ended up receiving in different historical settings, sometimes with and sometimes without official help. Section 8.4 asks which debtor countries have been repaying in the 1980s. Section 8.5 weighs the economic recovery of debtor countries in the 1980s.

8.1 Comparing the Preludes to Crisis

Thanks to recent scholarship, we know that two key proximate causes of a debt crisis are an acceleration of lending and unforeseen economic shocks. The acceleration of lending in the period 1974–82 was faster and briefer than previous waves of international lending. Were the subsequent economic shocks also outstanding in historical perspective? Figures 8.1 and 8.2 say no.

Like most debt crises, that of the 1980s occurred in a context of terms-of-trade shock. According to figure 8.1, the terms of trade turned less severely against debtors that they did in the 1930s, to judge from a simple comparison of the terms-of-trade movements for non-oil debtors (or all debtors) in the period 1973–85 with those for Latin America in the period 1925–40. Latin America's terms of trade dropped 37 percent from 1928 to 1931, and did not recover substantially until 1934. In the 1980s developing countries faced less of a terms-of-trade challenge. Oil exporters achieved such gains in the second oil shock that the terms of trade for all developing countries in the aggregate rose twice in the 1970s and were essentially stable over the period 1980–85. National experiences differed widely from this grand average, of course. The worst national trends within the 1980s, such as the drops in El Salvador's and Brazil's terms of trade, were as bad as the average Latin American drop of 1928–31. But when one compares national experiences for the same country, it turns out for virtually all countries (including El Salvador and Brazil) that 1928–31 was worse than any experience from the 1980s. And, at the aggregate level, figure 8.1 shows that the non-oil-exporting developing countries of the 1980s did not experience anything like the drop felt by Latin America in the 1930s.

A second kind of shock common to many debt crises is an unexpected jump in real interest rates in world lending markets, which adds to the real burden on debtors. Figure 8.2 compares the movements of ex-post real interest rates in the periods 1922–40 and 1974–86. At face value, the two periods 1928–31 and 1979–82 seem comparable and could be jointly listed as historically extreme cases of a jump in real interest rates. It would appear that the more recent jump lasted longer, inasmuch as the real interest rate stayed at or above 6 percent for five years in the 1980s, in contrast to its quicker retreat in the 1930s. On the other hand, the choice of one-year interest rates in figure 8.2 tends to hide some of the severity of the 1930s and to overstate it in the 1980s, from the point of view of debtors faced with longer-term obligations. In the 1930s the gap between long and short interest rates widened, while during the second oil shock of 1979–81 it was the one-year and shorter interest rates that jumped most. So a debtor more concerned about long-term debt service would have been relatively more burdened in the 1930s vis-à-vis the 1980s than figure 8.2 can show. On balance, the real interest rate surprise from 1979 on was only as serious *as* that from 1928 on, not more serious. Combining this conclusion with the fact that the terms-of-trade shock was less severe in the 1980s

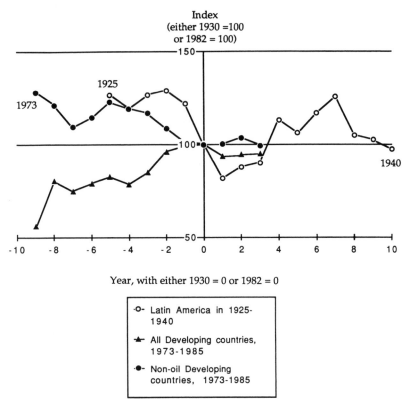

Figure 8.1
Movements in the terms of trade for developing countries, 1925–40 compared with
1973–85. The series on the terms of trade for Latin America, 1925–40, is that cited in
Thorp (1984, p. 331). For similar series, see Maddison (1985, pp. 87, 93). Both series for
1973–85 are from IMF, *International Financial Statistics Yearbook 1987* (pp. 132–33).

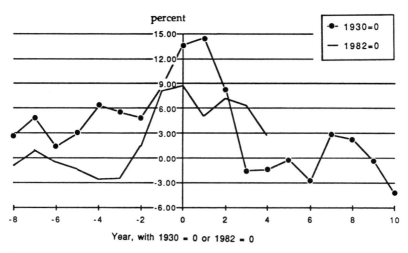

Figure 8.2
Movements in one-year U.S. real interest rates, 1922–40 and 1974–86. For 1922–40, the nominal interest rate is the four- to six-month prime commercial paper (*Historical Statistics,* Series X445). For 1974–86, it is the one-year U.S. bond yield (*Federal Reserve Bulletin*).

means that the world economy shocks were not as extreme for the average debtor in the 1980s as they were in the 1930s.

To add a comparative international dimension to the history of debt crisis, and to address the question "Which countries default, and why?" Fishlow (1985) has usefully distinguished two historical types of debt crisis. In cases of "development default," the lending accelerator and sudden downturn in a developing economy suffice to explain the onset of crisis. The contrasting case is "revenue default," in which fiscal overexpansion and deficits by the debtor government added to its inability (or disincentive) to sustain external debt service when the economy turned sour. Perhaps half of the prewar cases of arrearage on external debt were revenue defaults in significant degree. The proportion was the same, or perhaps greater, in the 1970s and 1980s, when fiscal excess was as strong an international correlate of debt crisis as changes in the terms of trade (Díaz-Alejandro 1984; Sachs 1985). The mixture of proximate causes, then, has not changed fundamentally. Let us turn to other issues more suggestive of recent departures from history.

The Terms of Borrowing

The price of the extra sovereignty of international borrowers has traditionally been an ex-ante interest rate premium over the rates that the top financial centers charge their home governments. The borrower's sovereignty is the lender's risk, and we should expect to see an ex-ante risk premium. The long-run trend in the premia charged to foreign borrowing governments contains at least two surprises, however: developing countries actually borrowed at lower premia after the default waves of the twentieth century than before, and the United States in the 1980s is issuing bonds at higher premia than those on the bank debt of the troubled Third World debtor governments. Table 8.1 and figure 8.3 elaborate.

It is odd to see a long decline in the interest premia contracted on external borrowing by developing-country governments, relative to the rates that the main financial markets charged their home governments. It would have been less puzzling if the decline had been confined to the years before the upswing of bank lending in the 1970s. If we looked only at the first three periods in table 8.1, we could argue that the downturn in the average premium for ten top borrowing countries was only artificial. It was indeed a by-product of increasing selectivity of credit. The revolutionary defaulters—Mexico, Russia and Turkey[2]—had little access to interwar or early postwar credit markets, and their removal left greater weight to low-premium borrowers such as Australia and Canada.

Yet in the upswing of international lending in 1974–81, top borrowers enjoyed lower premia than those demanded before 1914 or in the 1920s. The premia do not look very wide in figure 8.3's comparison of loans to developing countries with the London Interbank Offer Rate (Libor), the traditional base rate for the subset of loans charging variable interest rates. Libor, we should note, is not the best alternative return for judging bank loans to the Third World. Libor is short term, referring to loans maturing in a year or less, whereas the bank loans in question averaged something like eight years to maturity, making any gap between the rate on private bank loans to developing countries and Libor sensitive to changes in the timing of expected inflation (as suggested by figure 8.3 for the inflationary episode 1979–81).[3] Still, table 8.1 and figure 8.3 find the same picture for the 1970s, even when we make the more appropriate comparison to seven-year U.S. bond yields. Thus in the prelude to the crisis that broke in 1982 banks were making loans that suggest less fear of risk than before 1914 or 1930.[4]

The interest rate figures for 1983–86 imply something bizarre. The net premia that private creditors asked of developing-country borrowers not only continued to decline but actually became negative on average, relative to the seven-year U.S. bond yield. The negative premia can mislead yet reveal a basic truth. They can mislead because the fresh loan commitments

Table 8.1
Contracted interest rate premia on governments' borrowings from private foreign creditors, 1850–1986

| Borrowing government | External bonds outstanding in 1850 or issued 1850–1914 | | External bonds issued 1915–45 | | External bonds, held largely by foreign governments, issued 1946–70 | | Fresh public borrowing from private foreign creditors | | | |
| | | | | | | | 1977–81 | | 1983–6 | |
	Premium	Expected loss	Premium	Expected loss	Premium	Expected loss	Premium over 7-year U.S. bonds	Expected loss	Premium over 7-year U.S. bonds	Expected loss
Argentina	2.15%	2.05%	2.05%	1.94%	4.93	4.52	−0.55%	−0.50%	−1.51%	−1.39%
Australia	1.34	1.28	1.16	1.10	0.95	0.90	1.67	1.50	0.66	0.60
Brazil	1.91	1.82	3.34	3.10	—	—	1.87	1.67	0.00	0.59
Canada	1.30	1.24	0.64	0.61	2.23	2.13	2.62	2.33	−0.08	−0.07
Chile	2.42	2.30	3.30	3.06	—	—	−1.32	−1.21	−1.38	−1.26
Egypt	4.07	3.80	—	—	—	—	1.15	1.03	−1.62	1.49
Japan	1.47	1.41	3.24	3.00	2.91	2.73	1.91	1.70	0.46	0.41
Mexico	2.87	2.71	—	—	2.39	2.26	0.53	0.48	−0.73	−0.66
Russia	2.01	1.92	—	—	—	—	2.84	2.52	−1.07	−0.99
Turkey	4.23	3.94	1.00	0.96	0.11	0.11	1.68	1.51	−0.58	−0.52
All 10 nations	2.36	2.24	1.75	1.65	1.38	1.30	1.46	1.31	−0.44	−0.40

Sources: Data on external bonds 1850–70 and data on the 1976–79 premia over Libor are from Lindert and Morton (1989), tables 2 and 5. Libor rates and the yields on U.S. seven-year Treasury bonds are from IMF, *International Financial Statistics*. The 1983–6 yields for developing countries' external debts are the figures on new commitments to private creditors given in World Bank, *World Debt Tables, 1987–8* edition.

Note: Premium = contracted nominal yield to maturity on external borrowing (v_t) at time of issue, generally excluding fees, minus the yield on creditor-country government bonds ($\bar{\rho}$); expected loss = the risk-neutral expected percentage of capital loss implied by the premium = $(v_t - \bar{\rho})/(1 + v_t)$. Readers wishing to inspect the underlying interest rates on the international borrowings (v) and on creditor-country government bonds ($\bar{\rho}$) can calculate them from this table using the formulas $v = $ (premium/expected loss) − 1 and $\bar{\rho} = v$ − premium.

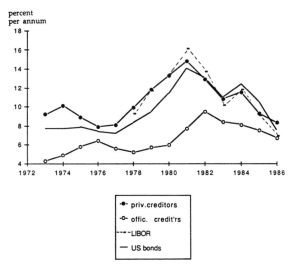

percent
per annum

Figure 8.3
Nominal interest rates on private and official lending to major borrowing countries, compared with Libor and the seven-year U.S. bond yield, 1973–86. Major borrowers consist of Argentina, Brazil, Chile, Egypt, India, Indonesia, Israel, Korea, Mexico, Turkey, Venezuela, and Yugoslavia. The major borrowers series, available for 1973–85, has been extended to 1986, assuming its percentage movements matched those of "highly indebted countries" series in *World Debt Tables*.

to which they refer are not entirely voluntary market loans but conversions and rollovers negotiated with problem debtors. Yet they repeat a truth noted in separate discussions of U.S. deficits and the dollar: the United States has been climbing up a sloped supply curve of foreign credit, paying higher interest-rate differentials over those paid by other industrial-country governments. Yes, this does imply increasing perception of risk in lending to the United States. The risk, however, relates to exchange rates and inflation rather than to default. Increasingly, the buyers of new U.S. long-term bonds have the yen area and the ECU area as their ultimate consumption residence. Given the difficulty of purchasing long-term cover, any given probability of dollar depreciation will look more and more relevant to investors as U.S. dependence on foreign credit grows. The yen rate of return on holding U.S. bills and bonds has already gyrated seriously in the 1980s: the interest premia of about 4.5 percent over government bond rates in Japan have been swamped by a double-digit rate of annual dollar appreciation up to February 1985 followed by a depreciation of around 25 percent a year for 1985–87, the exact percentage depending on dates and currencies. For the first time in centuries, the dominant international debtor is borrowing from foreign investors in its own currency, giving country risk a new look.

The Debt Overhang and Bank Exposure

In the 1970s and 1980s the debt overhang was smaller as a share of world assets but larger as a danger to creditors than ever before.

Across the twentieth century international debt appears to have shrunk as a share of world assets, to judge from the ratio of two inappropriate but helpful measures. As a measure of the relevant international debt, let us take the dollar value of governments' gross external debt to private creditors at three dates: 1913–14, 1929–30 and 1978–79 (Lindert and Morton 1989, table 8.1). As a wealth denominator, let us take the dollar value of U.K. plus U.S. national net worth around the same three dates (Goldsmith 1985, pp. 233, 301). Both measures are somewhat narrow. The numerator fails to include the international debt of private debtors, and the denominator ignores the wealth of countries other than the United Kingdom and the United States. Yet it is worth noting how much the ratio declined: from 5.4 percent on the eve of World War I to 2.7 percent at the onset of the Great Depression to less than 0.8 percent at the end of the 1970s. As a share of either world wealth or the wealth of the top creditor countries, international debt has clearly become less important (at least until America's borrowing binge of the 1980s).

In addition the external debt of governments has become slightly less concentrated among debtor nations, despite our concern over the debt burden of the top borrowers today. The top-ranked 10 percent of debtor nations accounted for a little over half of all external government (and government-guaranteed) debt in 1913–14, about 47 percent of all non-repudiated debt (excluding war debts and reparations) in 1929–30, and less than 45 percent of external public debt in 1978–79 (Lindert and Morton 1989, table 8.1).

If these trends had a policy prediction to offer, it would be that official concern over international crises should have declined—the opposite of the truth.

The meaning of foreign debt for private creditors and their home governments has risen because of the unprecedented exposure of major banks, particularly the top nine American banks, in the 1970s and 1980s. No such concentration of foreign public debt into a few private institutions was evident in the international bond era. The top banks then served as issuers and brokers, more than as holders, of foreign bonds, earning fees as well as interest. The demise of Barings in 1890 does not contradict this point, since Barings's mistake was a decision to make a temporary commitment to guarantee a huge amount of unfloated Argentine debt that they had planned to sell off right after flotation. In the dollar bond boom of the 1920s, survey results show that the same widespread diffusion of bonds to smallholders continued.[5] For all the epidemic of American bank failures in the 1930s, not one was due primarily or even largely to its holdings of depreciating foreign bonds. The contrast with the 1970s and 1980s could hardly be more striking: in 1986 the nine top U.S. money-center banks continued to have over 100 percent of their capital committed in loans to Latin America (Sachs 1987, table 1). The unprecedented exposure of key American banks is an important clue to the policy transformation of the 1980s.

Were Creditor Governments Expected to Intervene?

One would not expect creditor-country governments to make any advanced promise (or threat) of intervention in the event of international repayment difficulties. Any promise to bail out creditors financially would incur moral hazard, and any threat to intervene militarily to insure repayment would be out of order, at least until arrearages had actually arisen. It is therefore not surprising that creditor-country governments have avoided promises and threats about possible repayments crises.

Before World War II officials in creditor countries generally promised to stay on the sidelines. To be sure, in a few cases noted below they actually did intervene after a repayments confrontation. And the age of high imperialism was rich in rumors anticipating official punishment of problem foreign debtors. In the late 1870s, for example, former President Ulysses S. Grant warned the emperor of Japan that the chance to intervene was in fact actively sought by governments even before private lending occurred:

Look at Egypt, Spain, and Turkey ... and consider their pitiable condition .... Some nations like to lend money to poor nations very much. By this means they flaunt their authority and cajole the poor nation. The purpose of lending money is to get political power for themselves. (Takahasi 1969, pp. 185–86, also cited by Wellon 1987, p. 263)

Meiji Japan feared as much, and confined its borrowing to a small 1870s wave and the brief wave of heavy borrowing around the time of the Russo-Japanese War. Scholars have since devoted considerable attention to the ways in which investment might have followed the flag, especially before World War I. A careful reading, however, suggests that active government promotion of overseas bond purchases, possibly implying later emergency aid, was characteristic of French and German policy, but not of British or American policy outside the British Empire itself (Feis 1930, esp. pp. 83–190; Royal Institute of International Affairs 1937, pp. 76–101, 216–20; Davis and Huttenback 1986). Investors had little clear signal that sterling bonds or dollar bonds would be backed by British or American officials, as underlined by the high interest premia they charged (again see table 8.1).

Some have alleged that in the great lending wave of 1974–81 American private banks expected a government bailout if the debtor countries fell into arrears (Sampson 1982, p. 117; Stallings 1987, pp. 140–45). Yet the argument does not withstand scrutiny. The cited statements attributed to bankers were off the record and apparently made after the crisis broke in 1982, when self-interest would advance such a claim even if nobody had really expected help when lending earlier.[6] There is no evidence that such expectations were widespread, or that they were based on any government promises. The testimony of silence on government bailouts supports the risk-premium interpretation of table 8.1's reporting that developing countries generally contracted to pay 1.46 percent over U.S. Treasury bonds in 1977–81.

8.2   The Official Response to Crisis

An international debt crisis breaks when the debtor unilaterally announces that only some new financial concession can prevent arrears. The usual proximate cause of the debtor's announcement of a crisis is a shutdown of access to foreign credit, typically triggered by an economic crisis in the creditor countries or in the debtor country.

In the immediate aftermath of the announcement of crisis, a striking historical contrast appears in the role of creditor-country governments and international institutions. Creditors' ability to get official help followed four distinctive patterns in four eras. In the first, before World War I, the official intervention that was never overtly promised was rarely given. The cases of government intervention were few, but forceful. European creditor powers took over the finances of Tunis in 1869, Egypt in 1880, and Greece in 1898. In the case of Venezuela in 1902, a show of British gunboats sufficed to get debt repayments back on track. The United States used its power in Liberia and the Caribbean, where at different times it exerted varying degrees of administrative control over the finances of Cuba, Santo Domingo, Haiti, Nicaragua, and Panama. Most of the interventions originated before World War I, with little fresh intrusion into debtor countries in the second, interwar, era (Borchard 1951, pp. 286–96; Cleona Lewis 1948, pp. 203–11, Royal Institute of International Affairs 1937, pp. 76–101).

In the third era, from World War II through the 1970s, the international creditors confronted with problem debtor governments were usually governments themselves. In the spirit of the early postwar heyday of foreign aid, crises were often interpreted as forgivable, and debt renegotiations gave varying concessions to the debtor government. At first, until about 1955, the United States led the way, with only moderate conditionality and with concessionary financing, the most extreme form of which was the Marshall Plan flow of outright grants. After 1955 international debt problems were increasingly brought under the aegis of multilateral institutions, in particular the IMF, the World Bank, and the Paris Club. In the 25-year period of 1955 to 1979, about 20 debtor countries were involved in about 52 debt restructurings, the exact number depending on how one counts individual agreements within a series (Bittermann 1973; Hardy 1982; Lindert and Morton 1989, table B1). The write-down costs of such debt restructurings to the creditor nations are sampled in table 8.2. In most cases there were small write-downs that had to be repeated a few years later. In the cases of Ghana, Indonesia, and Turkey, however, creditors acckowledged the loss of about half their contracted investments. The terms of official relending continued to be fairly soft until the end of the 1970s, as shown by the official-creditor interest rate series in figure 8.3. Relative to the prewar and interwar world, the postwar era up through the 1970s was one in which the supply curve of emergency credit shifted out to the right, thanks to the postwar foreign-policy climate and the rise of new multilateral institutions.

The 1980s, however, stand out as the era in which official intervention became global—and, so far, less concessionary. Rising numbers of debt restructurings and a tightening of the terms suggest an outward shift in the demand for, not in the supply of, official intervention. At least 49 debtor countries have signed over a hundred rescheduling agreements in the seven-year period of 1980 to 1986 (Milivojevic 1985; Watson et al. 1986; Dillon and Oliveros 1987; World Bank 1988). Credits from foreign governments and international agencies kept pace with the growth of private loans, though they had declined as a share of all lending back in the 1970s. To interpret the accelerated pace of reschedulings as either a demand shift or a supply shift, we need information on trends in the terms of reschedulings—in the interest rates, grace periods, amortization term and adjustment conditionality. Here we examine only the interest rates charged on new official loans, with the help of figure 8.3 and table 8.3.

Table 8.2
Write-down costs to major creditors of selected multilateral debt reorganizations, as a share of nominal debt outstanding, 1959–74

Debtors	Creditors (%)								
	Canada	France	West Germany	Italy	Japan	The Netherlands	United Kingdom	United States	Weighted average
Argentina									
1962	—	4.3	0.2	0.3	—	3.3	—	0.7	0.6
1965	—	2.2	0.1	(0.1)	2.7	1.1	—	0.3	0.3
Brazil									
1961	—	—	3.4	—	—	—	—	—	3.4
1964	—	3.4	0.3	—	—	—	(0.6)	—	1.7
Chile									
1965	—	28.8	1.5	2.7	—	1.8	2.4	3.2	—
1972	—	1.2	4.1	0.7	—	—	1.3	5.8	4.7
1974	—	1.9	2.4	1.5	—	—	2.5	1.2	1.5
Ghana									
1966–74	—	39.6	41.2	47.8	39.1	43.8	47.2	—	44.7
India									
1968	2.3	4.3	9.5	1.9	5.8	—	7.4	0.8	3.3
1972	0.4	1.3	3.0	—	2.7	—	1.4	0.5	1.4
1973	0.3	1.6	3.0	2.7	3.1	—	1.2	0.5	1.3
1974	—	2.3	3.1	—	3.4	—	1.4	0.7	1.4

Table 8.2 (continued)

	Creditors (%)								
Debtors	Canada	France	West Germany	Italy	Japan	The Netherlands	United Kingdom	United States	Weighted average
Indonesia									
1966–70	—	62.8	43.6	58.7	56.4	66.4	69.3	55.9	56.1
Pakistan									
1972–73	0.5	3.1	4.3	3.1	2.9	—	3.1	0.3	1.6
1974	4.6	21.0	16.5	22.2	24.8	—	11.6	5.2	9.8
Peru									
1968	2.5	2.5	1.6	na	0.2	—	(5.3)	0.7	0.8
1969	(4.2)	(3.0)	(0.3)	0.1	(0.4)	—	(7.3)	(0.5)	(0.7)
Turkey									
1959–65	—	30.4	40.5	56.4	—	—	44.4	64.4	45.6

Source: Hardy (1982), pp. 25–30, 70–72.

Table 8.3
International pattern in lending to debtor nations: regression results for 1985

Independent variables	Dependent variable: Nominal interest rate on new loans from official creditors[a]	Log of PG debts (in millions)	
		Official creditors	Private creditors
Constant	−11.57** (2.62)	1.40* (0.65)	−4.27* (1.72)
Log of absolute nominal PG debt in 1981 ($ millions)	0.81** (0.21)	0.94** (0.05)	1.12** (0.14)
Share of 1981 PG debt held by official creditors	−0.20 (0.62)	0.86** (0.16)	−1.23** (0.41)
Debt service/GNP in 1981	1.49 (3.10)	−0.43 (0.77)	−0.54 (2.03)
Reserves/imports in 1981	4.71 (10.10)	−2.04 (2.51)	−15.52* (6.61)
Log of GDP/capita in 1985 International $/capita	1.63** (0.33)	−0.06 (0.08)	0.35 (0.21)
Money stock growth (log difference, 1985–81)	−0.52 (0.69)	−0.10 (0.17)	−0.37 (0.45)
Defaulted anytime pre-1929 = 1	0.37 (0.85)	0.14 (0.21)	0.77 (0.56)
Defaulted in 1930s = 1	−0.16 (0.81)	−0.26 (0.20)	−0.37 (0.53)
Defaulted anytime 1940–81 = 1	−0.40 (0.74)	−0.15 (0.18)	0.60 (0.48)
Rescheduled debts anytime, 1979–85 = 1 (Predicted[b] value)	−0.60 (1.17)	0.03 (0.29)	−0.98 (0.77)
Years since first rescheduling (= 1986 − this year, back to 1979)	0.14 (0.21)	0.03 0.05	0.05 (0.14)
R^2 (adjusted), standard error of estimate	0.638, 1.60	0.910 0.40	0.830 1.05
Number of countries in sample	51	51	51

Sources: Most data are taken from IMF, *International Financial Statistics*, 1987 yearbook and February 1988 monthly issue. Those on interest rates and debt are from World Bank, *World Debt Tables*, 1987–88 edition. Reschedulings and earlier default histories are from Lindert and Morton (1989), table B.1. PG debt is public and publically guaranteed long-term debt, as defined by the World Bank.

Table 8.3 (continued)

Note: Figures in parentheses are coefficient standard errors. * = significant at 5% level;
** = significant at 1% level. The sample consists of as many developing countries as yielded
plausible data. There were:

Algeria	Ecuador	Kenya	Paraguay
Argentina	Egypt	Korea (South)	Peru
Bangladesh	El Salvador	Malawi	Philippines
Brazil	Fiji	Malaysia	Rwanda
Bolivia	Grenada	Malta	Senegal
Burkina Faso	Greece	Mauritius	Sri Lanka
Burma	Honduras	Mexico	Syrian Arab Republic
Chile	Hungary	Morocco	Thailand
Colombia	India	Niger	Togo
Costa Rica	Indonesia	Nigeria	Trinidad and Tobago
Côte d'Ivoire	Israel	Oman	Tunisia
Cyprus	Jamaica	Pakistan	Turkey
Dominican Republic	Jordan	Panama	

a. No regression is reported for the interest rates asked by private creditors on new loans.
As mentioned in the text, their rates varied less, and showed less pattern, across debtor
countries. In the unreported regressions for the private interest rates, the standard error of
estimate was only 1.17, the adjusted R^2 was only 0.146, and the only significant coefficients
were those for predicted rescheduling (which was positive) and the constant term.
b. This is the value of the rescheduling dummy predicted by the probit equation: Rescheduled
anytime since 1979 (probit form) = 1.465 − 18.60 (growth of GDP/capita, 1977−81) +
22.66 (log of terms of trade 1985−81) + 9.453 (log of terms of trade 1981−77) + 0.1359
(debt/exports ratio in 1981) − 85.69 (reserves/annual merchandise imports)* − 0.05148
(defaulted in the 1930s) + 2.537 (defaulted or rescheduled, 1940−81)*.

Figure 8.3 shows that the 1982 crisis brought a shift in the relative terms
of official lending. In the 1970s official loans had been at lower nominal
rates, and much lower real rates, than the rates being charged by private
creditors to the major borrowing countries. Then in the 1980s, as inflation
was cut, the nominal rate asked by official creditors at first rose and then
fell back, with no net decline by the end of 1986. As a result the (ex-post)
real rate of interest on official loans to troubled borrowers rose faster than
the widely publicized rise of real rates in private markets, so that by
mid-decade the terms on official loans were hard to distinguish from those
on private loans.

The tightening of terms on official credits in the 1980s was not evenly
dealt to all borrowing countries, however. The dozen major borrowers,
accounting for nearly half the world's developing-country debt, paid
higher-than-average rates on official loans, with less gap between the
private-creditor and official-creditor rates. At the other end of the interest-

rate spectrum, low-income African debtors were given fresh official loans at clearly concessionary rates.

Were such superborrowers as Mexico and Brazil charged higher official rates because they were less poor, or because they already owed so much? Or were they charged more for other reasons, such as a prior history of default? Official statements are ambiguous, though they emphasize the debtor's income level as a policy guide. For example, the official communiqué from the Group of Seven's Toronto summit of June 1988 announced plans for substantive relief of African debtors but opposed any such proclamations regarding the superborrowers:

A number of highly indebted middle-income countries continue to have difficulties serving their external debt and generating the investment for sustained growth. The market-oriented, growth-led strategy based on the case-by-case approach remains the only viable approach for overcoming their external debt problems. (IMF *Survey*, June 27, 1988, p. 221)

Again, must they adhere to "market-oriented" rules because they are highly indebted or because they are middle income?

The first two regressions in table 8.3 summarize the multidimensional international patterns in official lending, drawing on the experience of 51 countries in 1985. Let us first note some influences that proved less central as determinants of official foreign lending than one might have expected. The borrower's past repayment record was not a significant influence on the interest rate or the level of official credit,[7] despite a tradition of conjecturing that one of the costs of default is the loss of future creditworthiness. Also insignificant were three other macro trouble variables: debt service as a share of GNP, the adequacy of the country's external reserves, and its money-stock growth between 1981 and 1985.

The debtor country's living standards clearly mattered. Having twice as high an income per capita meant paying an extra 1.13 percent in the official interest rate (while having no significant effect on the amount of official credits). This makes sense. It is not surprising to find that governments and international agencies gave softer loan terms to truly poor nations, demanding higher interest rates of the middle-income NICs. Favoritism for the poorest nations has been characteristic of the entire postwar era. Yet the gap in living standards does not explain why higher interest rates were asked of Brazil and Mexico than of similar-income Algeria or Cyprus, or why Nigeria consistently contracted higher rates of interest than less impoverished Turkey.

Even holding income levels constant, a strong determinant of the terms of official lending is the absolute level of the country's indebtedness back at the end of 1981, on the eve of the crisis. International agencies and financial-center governments have insisted on tougher terms for more heavily indebted countries, other things equal. What is more, this discrimination against large borrowers is new. When the same interest-rate regression was run on pre-1982 experience, using the same variables as in table 8.3 but with 1985 variables replaced by 1981, and 1981 variables replaced by 1977, the only noteworthy difference was that the absolute-debt variable lost all significance. That is, countries with higher absolute debt were charged higher interest rates in 1985, but not in 1981.

The observed pattern is at odds with a number of models of official financial policy. One might have expected behavior to fit some kind of "lender of last resort" model. This overused phrase accommodates many different variants, some of which clearly do not fit here. The variant in which officials bail out the debtors themselves in proportion to the financial crisis does not fit the behavior of the 1980s, even though it was apparently followed in the earlier postwar era. A crisis of overindebtedness (high absolute PG debt and unfavorable values of the macro trouble variables) did not evoke a softer interest rate in 1985. Of the classic lender-of-last-resort models, closer to the mark is Bagehot's rule: in a liquidity or repayments crisis, officials should lend liberally but at a somewhat punitive interest rate. In the many loan conversions worked out with the top-debt countries from 1982 on, official creditors, though not lending liberally, did indeed impose rates higher than those imposed on smaller debtors.

Another natural suspicion is that the international agencies and leading governments, particularly the United States, have given primacy to the goal of rescuing financial-center banks from their biggest absolute exposures, hoping to prevent a more serious default wave than that of the 1930s. Certainly, official statements and actions show a strong preference for working out new loan packages that admit no write-down of private debts. The government of the United States in particular has proposed a variety of plans, most notably the Baker Plan, designed to relend without write-offs. Official American concern has been strong: as Jeffrey Sachs (1987) has rightly stressed, the one thing the Reagan administration has *not* said about the international debt crisis is that it is a matter to be solved by the marketplace without official interference, presumably because a laissez faire stance could lead to extensive write-downs, as in the past.

If the international agencies and American officials were acting just to bail out exposed private creditors, one would expect them to use tax-payers' money to support concessionary official loans to repay private loans fully. Yet, as we have just seen, they did not do so in dealing with heavily indebted or middle-income countries. Their not bailing out existing creditors or debtors with highly concessionary loans admits of several interpretations. One possibility is that rescuing the exposed parties seemed less important to officials than insisting on debtor belt-tightening for its own sake. Another is that they may have feared the moral hazard implicit in bailing out overlenders and overborrowers (Vaubel 1983). Another, the interpretation favored here, is that taxpayer resistance has been too strong to allow large new subscriptions of funds for official concessionary relending. Emphasizing the constraint on access to taxpayers' purses has the merit of fitting the international pattern in official lending since 1982: avoid concessionary loans to large borrowers, where the cost of each percent of interest subsidy is high, yet give less expensive relief to borrowers that are both poor and small (in debt size).

The official lending policy since 1982 contrasts with the behavior of private creditors. Private creditors seem to have been following a credit-rationing model. In (unreported regressions for) both 1981 and 1985 private interest rates were more constant across debtor countries. They also showed little relationship to the independent variables of table 8.3. Such insensitivity of the interest rate is consistent with a model of credit rationing (Stiglitz and Weiss 1981), which predicts that risk-relevant information on the debtor's attributes will affect the quantity of lending, but not the interest rate, for fear of raising default probabilities with higher interest rates. As for the quantities privately lent to developing countries, the final regression equation in table 8.3 finds that the 1985 pattern of private lending was tightly bound to the pre-crisis 1981 pattern, as shown by the first two variables' coefficients. Such a rigidity suggests that whatever determined earlier credit rationing gave proportional credit rations in 1985, probably because the new private lending was dominated by involuntary rollovers.[8]

8.3   The Returns to Private Creditors

The unprecedented foreign debt exposure of financial-center banks in the 1980s demands a closer look at the prospects for their recouping their investments. Lending to sovereign borrowers is a special kind of gamble. The limit to prudent lending without collateral is clearly defined in theory (Lindert 1986; Lindert and Morton 1989) but cannot be easily forecast in practice.

Over a century of international debt history can help educate expectations about the chances of private creditors' recovering their investments. A companion study has measured private returns on foreign government bonds and on private bonds backed by government guarantee in ten debtor countries since 1850. Table 8.4 summarizes the results about realized real rates of return, which can be compared with the (ex-ante) contracted nominal rates in table 8.1.

The long bond era yielded many faithful repayments and a few large defaults. The underlying defaults were indeed spectacular. In the 1910s revolutions in Mexico, Russia, and Turkey imposed large capital losses on foreign investors, as did the widespread defaults of the 1930s. Yet it is important to juxtapose the unspectacular with the spectacular. As Sidney Homer has reminded us (1963, p. 202), "history tends to overemphasize newsworthy defaults and leaves in obscurity periodic debt repayments between nations." Even a total default on an outstanding balance after a decade can leave the creditors well compensated, relative to other investments, if they received a high interest premium on the risky investment over that decade. Table 8.4 underlines the point with its mixture of results. In the heyday of international bond lending before World War I, investors lending to ten top borrowing nations received a positive real return, one slightly below the return on the alternative of lending to their home governments (Britain and the United States). Most debtors repaid faithfully (some, as noted earlier, because the creditor government intervened). The overall rate of return was positive, though it fell slightly below the rate on lending to Britain or to the United States. Somewhat surprisingly, the net return to interwar lending proved more positive, despite the famous crisis of the 1930s. True, many countries defaulted in the 1930s, but others repaid the high ex-ante premium interest rates throughout. When the prewar and interwar experiences are combined with the smaller postwar bond activity, it turns out that the ten debtor governments repaid an average real premium of about 0.42 percent, once the many repayments at premium interest rates are mixed in with the less frequent, usually large, defaults.

Have the private lenders who enthusiastically bought developing-country debt since 1973 done as well? To what extent have they been rescued by the official policy regime of the 1980s? The jury is still out, of course. Yet we must not overlook the history that has already unfolded. Some repayment has already occurred in the 1980s. To judge the extent of repayment, and what it means for the range of possible rates of return, let us first consider figure 8.4's time series for the real net flows between private creditors and the 97 debtor countries on which we have data. Resources continued to flow toward the 97 debtors throughout the 1970s, and since 1980 have flowed back toward private creditors because interest payments have exceeded the net flow of lending (new loans minus principal repayments). At first, from 1981 to 1984, the net transfer back to private creditors was about the same rising percentage of debt outstanding

Table 8.4
Realized real returns on bond lending to ten foreign governments, 1850–1983

Borrowing nation	Real rates of return (%)			(Real value lent (L_0) (in millions of 1913 $)
	v	$\bar{\rho}$	$v - \bar{\rho}$	
A. 695 bonds issued, 1850–1914 (or outstanding in 1850)				
Argentina	3.52	1.81	1.71	928.1
Brazil	2.27	1.38	0.89	841.8
Chile	2.79	1.31	1.48	249.7
Mexico[a]	−0.74	1.98	−2.72	475.7
Total	2.21	1.65	0.57	2,495.0
Australia	3.02	2.01	1.01	1,525.2
Canada	4.77	3.50	1.27	65.7
Egypt	6.41	3.49	2.92	367.9
Japan	1.85	0.60	1.25	914.9
Russia[b]	1.31	2.94	−1.63	3,340.9
Turkey	1.61	3.17	−1.56	695.4
Total	2.09	2.48	−0.39	6,910.0
Total for all ten	2.12	2.26	−0.14	9,405.0
B. 534 bonds issued 1915–45				
Argentina	3.34	1.39	1.95	928.0
Brazil	4.31	3.61	0.70	436.7
Chile	0.54	2.44	−1.90	251.6
Mexico	0	0	0	0
Total	3.17	2.15	1.01	1,616.3
Australia	4.18	2.97	1.21	2,165.1
Canada	3.41	2.76	0.65	379.1
Egypt[c]	4.41	5.41	−0.73	40.9
Japan	5.89	3.62	2.26	340.2
Russia	0	0	0	0
Turkey[d]	−3.16	−2.27	−0.88	47.2
Total	4.16	2.97	1.20	2,972.5
Total for all ten	3.81	2.68	1.13	4,588.8
C. 323 bonds issued after 1945				
Argentina	5.51	0.81	4.70	87.3
Brazil	0	0	0	0
Chile	0	0	0	0
Mexico	2.67	0.35	2.31	89.1
Total	4.08	0.58	3.50	176.4.

Table 8.4 (continued)

Borrowing nation	Real rates of return (%)			(Real value lent (L_0) (in millions of 1913 $)
	v	$\bar{\rho}$	$v - \bar{\rho}$	
Australia	0.81	0.09	0.72	1,183,3
Canada	0.47	−1.78	2.25	524.3
Egypt	0	0	0	0
Japan	2.32	0.06	2.25	91.4
Russia	0	0	0	0
Turkey	1.21	1.55	−0.34	176.5
Total	0.83	−0.28	1.10	1,975.5
Total for all ten	1.09	−0.21	1.30	2,151.9

Source: Lindert and Morton (1989), table III.
Notes: Algebraic symbols are defined in table 8.1, except that real rates replace nominal. Rates of return v and $\bar{\rho}$ now contain subtractions for the ex-post rate of consumer-price inflation in the lending country, and every flow is deflated by a lending-country consumer price index. Variations in the real rates of return on the alternative investments on U.K. or U.S. bonds (variations in $\bar{\rho}$) stem from differences in the dates of issue of different loans, some on the eve of deflation and some on the eve of inflation. The measurement algorithm is so designed that deflation or inflation cannot reverse the sign of the key differential ($v - \bar{\rho}$), as shown in Lindert and Morton (1989), app. A.
a. As in table 8.1, two unsuccessful Mexican conversion loans from the 1915−45 period have been shifted in the pre-1914 period.
b. Two dollar loans to czarist Russia in 1916 have been shifted to the pre-1914 period.
c. Three loans unsuccessfully aimed at settling Egypt's Ottoman debt.
d. Three bonds issued by Turkey in 1933−35, just before commodity prices rebounded from their trough. Hence the negative $\bar{\rho}$.

as it was in 1929−32, early in the interwar debt crisis. Then in 1985 and 1986 annual net transfers to creditors rose far beyond the tendency to repay in the interwar years. Creditors have been partly repaid in the 1980s; yet they have received only a small fraction of the original values lent, leaving most debt still outstanding.

Table 8.5 gives sharper quantitative focus to the partial returns of the 1980s. With each passing year since the crisis struck in 1982, the bottom safety net has been raised for private creditors. That is, the worst rate of return they would have suffered from complete default (v_0) has become less disastrous, from − 100 percent at the end of 1982 to − 17.5 percent at the end of 1986 (far right column in table 8.5). At the same time the best rate of return the creditors could reap if they are fully repaid (v_f) has also been rising because the cooling of inflation in the 1980s has raised real interest rates of all sorts. In other words, both the worst and the best possible rates of real gross return for private creditors have been improving with each passing year.

Table 8.5
Private real rates of return and possible default losses on public external debt of developing countries, 1973–86, under various assumptions about repayments in the 1980s

Outstanding debts paid or defaulted at end of year[a]	If all debts are fully repaid			Default variations		
				Percent capital loss to make returns match		Complete default: internal rate v_0
	Internal rate of return (v_f)	Real rate of return on U.S. bonds ($\bar{\rho}$)[b]	Spread ($v_f - \bar{\rho}$)	U.S. bonds ($v = \bar{\rho}$)	"History" ($v = \bar{\rho} + 0.42$)	
1982	−1.80%	−1.93%	0.13%	0.7%	−1.9%	−100.0%
1983	−0.05	0.34	−0.39	−3.3	−6.5	−53.4
1984	1.14	0.76	0.38	3.0	−0.6	−33.7
1985	2.05	1.76	0.29	3.1	−1.3	−23.5
1986	2.61	2.37	0.24	3.4	−1.7	−17.5

Note: The data refer to all public and publically guaranteed external debt for 97 Third World nations in World Bank, *World Debt Tables*, 1988–89 edition, deflated by the U.S. consumer price index. The given year is when the debts were assumed to have been completely settled, with the indicated degrees of default. Rates of return were defined in table 8.4. All estimates refer to rates earned by private creditors, with initial loan fees apparently netted out of the amounts lent. For additional notes, see appendix A.

a. Debt outstanding at end of stated year is assumed to have been repaid in full.

b. $\bar{\rho}$ is the average of real rates of return on seven-year U.S. Treasury bonds (ρ_t) held, and rolled over, from year t to end of stated year as an alternative to the net transfers to the developing country in year t. $\bar{\rho}$ was calculated from the ρ_t's for 1973–1981 only, leaving alone the ρ_t's unaveraged for the net-repayment years from 1982 on, as explained in the notes to table 8.6.

The amount of default at the end of the final year that would bring v down to match $\bar{\rho}$ equals the end-of-1982 value gained by capitalizing, at the ρ_t real rates, all actual flows between the private foreign creditors and the debtor country. The same procedure is repeated to calculate how much default would make the ex-post returns match a premium earned by earlier generations of international investors. Lindert and Morton (1989), table III, found that premium to be on the order of 0.42% per annum.

Yet creditors have not been gaining *net* ground, in the sense of getting higher premia over alternative investments. Loans to developing countries were rendered less liquid by the debt crisis. Creditors have become locked into rescheduling loans instead of being repaid and investing in increasingly competitive U.S. bonds. As table 8.5 shows, U.S. bonds have risen in real return as fast as have loans to the Third World. As a result, the maximum possible spread ($v_f - \bar{\rho}$) has stayed low, slightly below the historical average of 0.42 percent a year suggested by experience in the bond era. Although their worst-case safety net (v_0) has been raised, private creditors are no closer to guaranteeing a competitive return (with $v = \rho + 0.42$ percent) than they were in 1982, despite net resource inflows.

8.4 Who Has Been Repaying?

Why don't the hard-pressed debtors of the 1980s just default? Why do they go on repaying? If the crisis is truly severe, and there is little prospect of a problem debtor's receiving a fresh inflow of net lending, why not suspend outpayments? Why not follow the lead of Peru in 1985, or of Brazil in February 1987? This is the crucial set of questions about debtor-country behavior in the 1980s.

In fact, most debtor countries have not been repaying significantly since 1982. The global net transfers of resources from 97 developing-country debtors to creditors has been small as a share of debt outstanding. Nearly half the repayments received by private creditors have come on loans to just three "repayer" countries close to the United States. In three other countries, net repayments to private creditors have come from new official lending, not from debtors' sacrifices.

These findings emerge from a careful handling of the best available data. The best data for an international study of debt transfers are the World Bank's widely-used *World Debt Tables*. They provide better detail on debt-related flows than any other official international source (for a comparison, see World Bank et al. 1988). But they can mislead. For all the professional effort put into their refinement, the figures in the *World Debt Tables* are based on inconsistent loan coverage. Especially fragile are the estimates of nonguaranteed private debt and short-term debt. Figure 8.4 and table 8.6 handle the available data, with a procedure described at length in the notes to table 8.6 and in appendixes A and B. The most reliable results are those relating to long-term public and publically guaranteed (PG) debt.

To judge tentatively from figure 8.4 and table 8.6, most debtor nations have not been repaying much—making sizable net resource out transfers —in the 1980s. Most of them have participated in a three-party stalemate,

(billions of
1980 dollars)

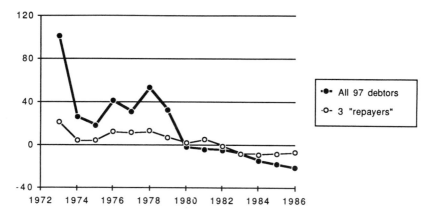

Figure 8.4
Net real transfers from all creditors to 97 debtor nations on PG debt, end of 1973–86.
The three repayers are Ecuador, Mexico, and Venezuela. Figures for 1973 are the loan
stocks outstanding at the end of that year. Sources: World Bank, *World Debt Tables,*
1988–89, and table 8.6.

in which official agencies, private creditors, and the debtor countries agree,
after repeated struggles and much uncertainty, to reschedule in a way that
postpones large net resource flows. Figure 8.4 hints as much by showing
that nearly half of the net repayments to private creditors in the 1980s is
accounted for by just three "repayer" countries—Ecuador, Mexico, and
Venezuela. The other 92 countries have repaid less to private creditors in
the 1980s, even though figure 8.4 shows they had borrowed much more in
the 1970s.[9]

Table 8.6 develops this point, using two kinds of summary statistics. The
kind of measure bearing most directly on the resources already transferred
from debtors to creditors is shown in the two right-hand columns, which
give the percentage repaid so far. Given the transfers already made, these
right-hand columns show that two variants on the percentages of losses
that creditors could sustain at the end of 1986 while still breaking even.
The greater the previous transfers from debtors, the greater this "losable"
share of the remaining debt. The second kind of summary statistic gives the
returns creditors would reap if repayment turned out to be perfect after
1986. This second measure appears in the left three columns. Let us survey
the results in table 8.6 part by part, beginning with the experience of
private long-term creditors in panel A.

Table 8.6
Realized real rates of return for creditors on lending to selected developing countries, 1973–86

Debtor	Internal rate of return with full repayment v_f	Average return on U.S. Treasury bonds $\bar{\rho}$	Differential $(v_f - \bar{\rho})$	PG debt outstanding to private creditors, 12/86 ($ billions)	Repaid so far: outstanding debt that could be defaulted 12/86	
					Match U.S. bonds	Match "history"
A. Private creditors only, PG loans, and their ancestors						
Ten top developing-country borrowers[a]						
Algeria	1.45%	0.67%	0.78%	16.0	28.8%	21.0%
Argentina	2.88	1.98	0.90	33.8	12.8	7.7
Brazil	2.94	2.08	0.86	63.9	11.5	6.4
Chile	2.93	1.67	1.26	11.5	10.7	6.2
Korea	3.10	2.30	0.80	18.3	9.8	3.8
Mexico	4.57	2.54	2.03	64.2	28.0	23.1
Nigeria	3.47	3.82	−0.35	13.8	−7.8	−11.7
Peru	0.92	1.73	−0.81	5.9	−17.5	−21.1
Turkey	2.62	2.35	0.27	9.2	9.0	4.1
Venezuela	3.65	1.64	2.01	24.3	37.7	31.0
Total	3.25	2.06	1.19	196.2	17.2	11.9
Additional cases						
Africa south of the Sahara[b]	0.35	2.36	−2.01	25.0	−23.9	−29.7
Bolivia	0.25	1.80	−1.55	1.3	−23.6	−28.6
Dominican Republic	4.22	1.06	3.16	0.8	74.5	67.3

Ecuador	5.30	2.60	2.70	5.6	36.9	32.8
Egypt[c]	1.50	2.25	-0.76	5.8	-11.5	-15.7
Jamaica	3.15	2.08	1.07	0.5	32.5	18.9
Philippines	1.39	2.41	-1.02	12.0	-13.2	-17.2
All developing-country debtors	2.61	2.37	0.24	435.8	3.4	-1.7

B. All creditors, PG loans, and their ancestors

Ten top developing-country borrowers[a]

Algeria	0.87%	1.32%	-0.45%	16.1	8.2%	-0.9%
Argentina	2.32	1.96	0.36	38.8	6.6	1.0
Brazil	2.32	2.14	0.18	84.3	3.0	-2.4
Chile	0.88	1.84	-0.96	14.6	-16.2	-23.4
Korea	1.63	2.39	-0.76	29.3	-9.4	-15.1
Mexico	4.10	2.54	1.54	76.0	20.8	15.7
Nigeria	2.50	3.28	-0.78	20.6	-13.2	-17.3
Peru	-0.44	1.80	-2.24	11.0	-31.3	-36.7
Turkey	-0.50	2.57	-3.07	24.3	-35.6	-42.1
Venezuela	3.30	1.67	1.63	25.2	33.7	27.5
Total	2.26	2.17	0.09	255.7	3.1	-2.6

Additional cases

Africa south of the Sahara[b]	-1.79	2.52	-4.31	85.7	-55.5	-61.7
Bolivia	-1.50	2.10	-3.60	4.1	-59.1	-66.9
Dominican Republic	0.25	2.72	-2.47	2.7	-31.0	-37.1
Ecuador	3.52	2.74	0.71	8.2	15.1	10.8

Table 8.6 (continued)

Debtor	Internal rate of return with full repayment v_f	Average return on U.S. Treasury bonds $\bar\rho$	Differential $(v_f - \bar\rho)$	PG debt outstanding to private creditors, 12/86 ($ billions)	Repaid so far: outstanding debt that could be defaulted 12/86 Match U.S. bonds	Match "history"
Egypt[c]	−2.82	2.44	−5.28	32.1	−81.2	−90.1
Jamaica	1.50	2.80	−1.30	3.1	−20.2	−25.9
Philippines	0.83	2.62	−1.79	20.4	−21.5	−26.1
All developing-country debtors	0.21	2.44	−2.23	800.3	−28.3	−34.2
C. All creditors, all long-term loans, and ancestors						
Brazil	2.68	2.06	0.62	99.0	16.9	6.1
Mexico	4.09	2.62	1.44	91.1	24.3	18.7
All 97 debtors	0.54	2.33	−1.79	893.9	−25.4	−32.3

Source: All data from World Bank, *World Debt Tables, 1988–89 edition*, and from unpublished World Bank data, with adjustments as noted.

a. The top ten developing-country borrowers ranked by debt outstanding at the end of 1979 (Lindert and Morton 1989, table 1).

b. There was variation in the set of countries covered by the data for Africa south of the Sahara. For 1974 and 1976 data it consisted of 36 countries. For 1973 and 1977–79 data it consisted of 41 countries. For 1975 and 1980–86 data 43 countries were covered. The variation made little difference in dollar value because the joining or exiting countries were very small as borrowers. Nonetheless, the variation called for an adjustment. Incoming or departing countries were treated like reclassified loans.

c. The peculiarity of the Egyptian results stems primarily from the fact that Egypt borrowed mainly in the 1980s, and at interest rates generally below the seven-year yield on U.S. Treasury bonds. But the peculiarity of the Egyptian case may have been slightly exaggerated by the data given in *World Debt Tables*. Egypt is the one country for which the interest rates implied by the *Tables* ran a percent or two below those on her fresh borrowings from private creditors, suggesting some degree of mismeasurement.

For each country, the calculations began with the PG (long-term public and publicly guaranteed) debt to private foreign creditors. All nominal stocks of debt outstanding and disbursed, and all flows of new disbursed credits, interest payments, and repayments of principal were converted into 1980 dollars using the U.S. consumer price index.

For additional notes, see appendix A.

Private Creditors, PG Debt Only

We begin with the question: On which countries' guaranteed loans are private creditors being repaid? For six debtor countries in table 8.6, the transfers up through 1986 were already sufficient to have given private creditors a noticeable cushion against subsequent default. The six are Algeria, Dominican Republic, Ecuador, Jamaica, Mexico, and Venezuela. The extreme case is the Dominican Republic, which could have defaulted on 69.1 percent of her PG debts to private foreign debtors at the end of 1986 and still have left them as high a return as if they had lent to the United States all along. It is ironic that Mexico also stands out as a genuine repayer, given the fame of her rescue in 1982. The fact remains that private loans to Mexico, like those to the other five countries,[10] have been repaid in significant part during the crisis. In this respect the private loans to Mexico contrast sharply with those to Brazil, whose debt has always been of similar size but who has kept from paying out much resources until 1985–86, and then suspended payments in February 1987.[11]

The left-hand columns show that four of these six countries (all but Algeria and Jamaica) are also countries that were charged exceptionally high interest premia (trusted less?) from the start. More precisely, they are countries whose interest premia will prove largest in real terms if all real debt values as of December 1986 are paid off. Their private foreign creditors are being rewarded both by higher interest premia and by more prompt repayment.

All Creditors, PG debt

More central is the related question: Which debtor countries are actually repaying their foreign creditors, both private and public? The list dwindles. Loans from official creditors have partially replaced private loans since 1982, so that the net transfers of resources from debtor countries are less than the limited repayments received by private creditors. Table 8.6 reveals the replacement, in the contrast between the A and B panels. The "repaid so far" statistics are more negative when all creditors are viewed together. Negative values here mean that the creditors would have to receive more than 100 percent of the real outstanding debt to make competitive rates of return, because they lent at concessional interest rates. The shift to more concessional official loans in the 1980s has been more prominent vis-à-vis smaller and poorer borrowers. The estimates in table 8.6 thus fit the global pattern shown earlier in this chapter: the largest borrowers received less concessional help than smaller and poorer borrowers in the 1970s and 1980s. The official help was enough to keep Algeria, the Dominican Republic, and Jamaica, the smallest of the "repayer" nations from actually repaying—that is, even though their debts to private creditors have been paid off in large part, the repaying has been done by the new official loans, not by transfers from the Algeria, Dominican Republic or Jamaica. That leaves Ecuador, Mexico, and Venezuela—three oil-exporting large borrowers—as the countries actually sacrificing resources to repay large shares of their foreign debts. For the other 94 debtor countries, those shares "repaid so far" are small or negative.

All Creditors, All Long-Term Debt
The same question—Who is repaying?—should also be addressed with data on all types of debt, not just the PG debt. As explained earlier, this is difficult because of the unreliability of the data on nonguaranteed and short-term debts. Panel C of table 8.6 dares to bring nonguaranteed long-term debt into the picture only for two relatively well-documented nations and for the 97-nation aggregate. Again, as with the more reliable measures of panels A and B, Mexico seems to have repaid more faithfully, and been charged higher interest rates, than Brazil. It also seems that the 97 debtor nations as a group have not been repaying.

A current puzzle thus becomes less puzzling. The question of why debtor nations gave large amounts resources back to creditors in the crisis of the 1980s needs to be confronted only for a handful of countries— perhaps only three countries.

Further, the three main repayers have some things in common: proximity to the United States, and oil exports. Ecuador, Mexico, and Venezuela may be under stronger pressure than Brazil or Argentina to repay American creditors in order to avoid unfavorable effects on their trade. This trade-linkage hypothesis is one of four possible explanations for their actions. A second is that they may genuinely believe, against the general verdict of history, that faithful repayment will soon bring a fresh inflow of voluntary private lending. A third is that they may believe that continuing to repay will earn them concessionary official loans. A fourth is that debtor-country officials and powerful private groups may have domestic reasons for wanting to repay: belt-tightening austerity may bring its own rewards in a domestic fight against advocates of runaway spending (see the similar hypothesis advanced by Fishlow in chapter 4). These explanations are not mutually exclusive, and each demands future research. However, only the first—the trade-linkage hypothesis stressing ties to the United States—offers a systematic explanation of why only this handful of countries has endured significant out-transfers of resources to creditors.

8.5   The Uncertain Recovery of Debtors in the 1980s Round

With so much institutional innovation in the postwar era, an essential task is to judge whether the recovery of debtor countries, particularly those who have negotiated reschedulings with third-party official intervention, has been more satisfactory than in recoveries before the 1980s.

The long sweep of history gives a range of outcomes so wide as to force caution. The recoveries after revolutionary "debt crises," such as the Mexican, Turkish, and Russian revolutions, should not be weighed here because of the impossibility of separating any influence of debt nonsettlements from other forces. In the prewar cases of peaceful write-down of debts (e.g., Argentina in the 1890s, Mexico 1885–86, and Brazil 1914), the recoveries were satisfactory enough to add a positive note about the recovery prospects when debtors and creditors negotiated write-downs bilaterally. Perhaps the write-downs aided the recoveries, but it is hard to be certain.

The recovery experience of the 1930s contrasts with that of the 1980s in some surprising ways. For the industrial creditor nations, of course, recovery was far slower in the 1930s than in the 1980s. Among debtor nations, however, the difference between the two eras was not as great, as table 8.7 and figure 8.5 suggest. Though we are accustomed to thinking of the 1930s as an era that was particularly harsh on developing countries exporting primary products, their production recovered more quickly than did that of the main industrial countries, especially the United States, Canada, and Germany.[12] In fact, table 8.7 and figure 8.5 suggest that six Latin American nations that suspended payments on their debts recovered faster after 1932 than those that repaid faithfully, and especially faster than the industrial creditor nations. There is, of course, an immediate rebuttal to the suggestion that default helped clear the way for recovery: other things were not necessarily equal. Other differences between these sets of countries might explain the differences in recovery. In particular, their monetary, fiscal, and exchange-rate policies differed. Yet default may have played a constructive role here. Defaulting countries like Brazil may have found it easier to promote industrialization and recovery because their taxpayers were less burdened with external debt service.

The basic growth pattern of the 1980s presents a striking contrast to that of the 1930s. The industrial, and creditor, countries were no longer the most afflicted ones, as figure 8.6 suggests. On the contrary, they switched from growing slightly slower than developing countries, on average, in the 1970s to being just as fast in the 1980s, despite the acceleration of growth in a few newly industrializing countries. The real growth crisis of the 1980s has been in Latin America, as in figure 8.6, and in Africa. In general, the growth crisis grips the regions most heavily involved in debt reschedulings. What is the causation behind the correlation? Are debtor coutries enmeshed in the rescheduling process because they are in poor health for other reasons, or is the process itself an impediment to recovery? Without a deeper study, blaming the debt-rescheduling policies for slow debtor growth might be as bad a mistake as blaming doctors for the fact that people around them are in poor health. Still, the raw correlations fail to show that those debtor countries participating in the rescheduling and adjustment process are visibly healthier.

A simpler look at the rescheduling process itself supports the cautious suspicion that the negotiations over relending and rescheduling in the 1980s have impeded recovery, instead of promoting it. The institutions were designed to solve temporary liquidity crises, and to be self-erasing by allowing the debtor to re-enter private financial markets. Two key signs of their success should therefore be (1) the revival of private lending and (2) the extinguishing of official participation in multilateral loan packages. Yet neither has occurred.

Aggregate signs of revival in private lending have been unimpressive, both for highly indebted developing countries and for all developing debtor countries. The stocks of short-term credits and private non-guaranteed credits have fallen since 1982. Many of these have been converted into the residual category of what can be called PG debt, namely, public and publically guaranteed long-term debt. Within that category, however, loan disbursements minus retirements have been dropping since 1982, both for official creditors and (especially) for private creditors. The stock of PG debt has grown slowly, with the help of conversion of previously short-term or nonguaranteed debt. In the process the ratio of private-creditor to official-creditor debt has not risen.

Official commitment to special loan-restructuring packages has not decreased. In fact, the rescheduling process has conformed to the addiction model in most cases: going through the process once is a strong positive predictor of the likelihood of going through it again within one year, two years, three years, and beyond. Multilateral debt-restructuring institutions have not shown the self-extinction required by the liquidity-crisis model. Of the 49 or more countries rescheduling in 1979–82, only four (I believe) have not rescheduled in 1983–86: Malawi, Pakistan, Turkey, and Uganda. Of this group Turkey has been singled out as a success story, a country with impressive growth, declining dependence on official aid, and growing

Table 8.7
Real GDP per capita in selected countries, 1925–39

Year	"Repayer" Argentina	Default '31 Brazil	Default '37 Costa Rica	Default '31 Chile	Default '32 Colombia	No loans Mexico	Default '32 Guatemala	Repayer Honduras
1925	90.0	82.4	106.0	74.5	81.0	97.1	87.7	87.4
1926	91.8	85.0	114.7	65.0	86.9	107.2	87.1	86.8
1927	95.5	92.7	102.4	68.1	93.6	100	91.6	93.5
1928	98.9	101.0	105.8	93.5	98.9	101.4	91.8	102.9
1929	100.0	100.0	100.0	100.0	100.0	100.0	100.0	100.0
1930	93.2	96.0	103.2	84.7	97.1	94.7	101.9	104.0
1931	84.9	91.2	100.1	65.9	94.1	96.0	93.0	105.2
1932	80.6	93.1	89.5	64.0	97.8	80.8	79.8	92.1
1933	82.9	99.5	104.1	73.4	101.3	91.7	79.0	84.9
1934	87.8	106.5	90.2	82.5	105.5	94.6	87.2	81.7
1935	90.7	107.0	95.3	83.1	105.9	101.1	98.5	76.8
1936	90.0	117.8	100.2	85.4	108.9	107.3	132.5	76.4
1937	95.4	120.5	114.1	91.2	108.3	111.5	127.1	71.6
1938	95.4	123.0	118.3	90.7	112.7	111.3	128.5	74.7
1939	94.6	122.1	114.2	91.9	120.1	119.4	161.2	81.1

Table 8.7 (continued)

Year	Repayer Nicaragua	Default'32 El Salvador	Repayer Australia	Repayer Canada	Repayer Japan	Creditor France	Creditor United Kingdom	Creditor United States
1925	86.0	89.2	111.7	85.0	95.4	86.7	95.0	92.6
1926	73.2	103.4	105.1	89.1	94.7	89.8	90.8	96.8
1927	73.2	88.7	105.3	94.1	96.4	86.3	96.7	95.4
1928	90.3	102.1	102.4	100.5	101.1	91.0	97.9	94.7
1929	100.0	100.0	100.0	100.0	100.0	100.0	100.0	100.0
1930	79.8	100.8	98.8	91.7	99.5	98.2	99.5	89.2
1931	73.5	89.0	87.6	74.0	91.1	93.6	93.9	81.6
1932	64.6	78.3	87.5	59.5	98.1	87.0	93.1	69.1
1933	80.1	88.7	91.2	54.0	100.7	87.5	94.5	67.2
1934	71.4	90.4	92.9	60.6	110.0	85.7	100.5	73.0
1935	70.9	97.6	93.3	65.1	110.9	82.0	104.0	79.7
1936	55.5	94.5	96.0	69.5	113.6	81.2	106.7	90.1
1937	58.8	102.4	98.6	77.8	140.0	84.0	110.2	94.3
1938	59.5	94.0	103.2	77.4	143.3	83.2	112.9	88.9
1939	80.1	107.7	97.8	81.8	143.0	89.1	115.8	95.7

Sources: Real GDP figures for the Latin American nations are from Thorp (1984, pp. 308, 334). Latin American population figures are interpolations of the 1920, 1930, and 1940 CELADE estimates given in Wilkie and Perkal (1985, p. 79). Figures for other countries are from the various *Historical Statistics* volumes complied by Brian R. Mitchell.

Note: Argentina is classified as a "repayer" in the sense that her external federal debt was repaid, but some state and local bonds were defaulted in the early 1930s. Mexico floated no external bonds in this period, owing to the nonresolution of the arrears on her prerevolutionary debts.

(1929=100)

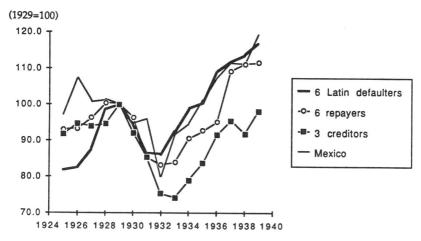

Figure 8.5
Real GDP per capita in selected countries, 1925–39. Sources: For Latin American nations, Thorp (1984, pp. 308–34). Latin American population figures are interpolations of the 1920, 1930, and 1940 CELADE estimates given in Wilkie and Perkal (1985, p. 79). For other countries, *Historical Statistics* (various years).

(1980 = 100)

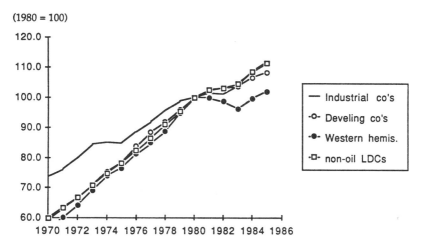

Figure 8.6
Real GDP in selected groups of countries, 1970–85.

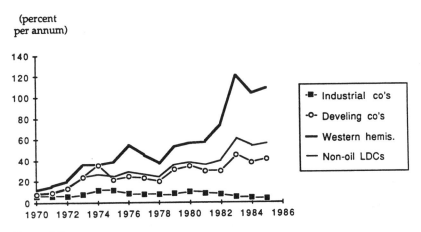

Figure 8.7
Inflation in selected groups of countries, 1970–85.

access to world capital markets across the 1980s (Dervis and Petri 1987, esp. pp. 248–49). Both the Turkish growth success and its relationship to the IMF-linked stabilization measures of 1978–82 are genuine (see also Okyar 1983). Yet the graduation of Turkey—and of Malawi and Pakistan —from rescheduling commends the concessionary policy of the earlier postwar era, not the tight-terms rollovers of the 1980s. All of these countries received a high share of their credit on concessionary official terms, like earlier postwar (e.g., Turkish) write-down packages. If there is a success story here, it does not apply to the arrangements that have been repeatedly negotiated with the major borrowers.

For all the evidence that recovery has been at least as slow among rescheduling countries, one could still argue that any negative effect on growth in the period is a short-run investment in austerity that has a long-run payoff in stability and growth. Yet here, too, the signs are disturbing. The short-run adjustment should take the form of a rise in the share of national product devoted to capital formation and a drop in price inflation. Neither has happened. On the contrary, debtor countries' investment shares are slightly depressed relative to their own past levels and relative to trends in industrial countries (IMF, *International Financial Statistics*, and Sachs 1985). The war against inflation is going most poorly in countries whose debt settlements call for special "adjustment." As figure 8.7 makes clear, countries of the Western Hemisphere— in particular, where the debt negotiations have called most insistently for price stabilization— have worsening inflation relative both to other countries and to their own pre-1982 experience. Hindsight is likely to conclude that the 1980s were an era in which the growth tables were turned against the debtor countries. We need to know the extent to which the new policy solutions have contributed to the problem.

8.6   Conclusion

What is different about the 1980s is a global official intervention, one shaped at least in part by an unprecedented exposure of a few major lending banks to country risk. The new intervention has sharply differentiated the treatment of major debtors and middle-income debtors from the treatment of smaller and low-income debtors. The former are held to near-market terms of repayment, while the latter have received concessionary treatment reminiscent of the response of major industrial-country governments and the international agencies to debt crises from the 1950s to the 1970s. Both types of debtor have been enmeshed in a protracted rescheduling process, with no clear end in sight.

The new policy regime has not yet succeeded in ensuring private creditors the historical-average interest premium on risky foreign lending. Although debt service in the 1980s has been sufficient to cut the worst possible losses, a new inconvenience has limited creditors' chances of earning truly high premia. By being locked into rollovers of developing-country debt, the creditors have not been free to shift to U.S. bonds, on which the real interest rates have been rising faster than the rates negotiated on rollovers of developing-country debt.

The prospect for creditors' returns have been further limited by the fact that, for all the negotiations, most debtor countries have not been making true transfers of resources back to creditors. Out of 97 debtor countries, about half the true transfers to creditors have come from only three "re-payer" nations close to the United States—Ecuador, Mexico, and Venezuela. The others have been making nearly all their debt service payments from the loan rollovers themselves. There is little reason to wonder why, as many observers have wondered, debtors have decided to repay in the 1980s. Most have not.

The new institutions have failed to make any clear contribution to recovery in the debtor countries. Debtors engaged in negotiations with their creditors and official third parties have grown slightly more slowly than debtors who stayed out of such negotiations. It could still be, of course, that the negotiations have helped foster recovery and yet have had their curative effect hidden by the worse condition of the countries who found it necessary to enter negotiations in the first place. Nevertheless, a variety of indirect clues fail to find the curative effect. Where the new policies have been most in force, the debtors have shown a slightly lower investment share, accelerating inflation, and slightly slower growth.

From the debtors' viewpoint, as well as from the private creditors', there is reason to question whether the current policy of "muddling through" is anything more than muddling.

Appendix A: Additional Notes to Tables 8.5 and 8.6 and Figure 8.4

Notes to Table 8.5

The v_f were calculated using the end-of-1973 disbursed debt outstanding as the initial flow to the borrowing country. For the purpose of calculating v_f, the debt outstanding at the end of the stated year was assumed to be repaid in full.

The $\bar{\rho}$ is the average of the real rates of return on seven-year U.S. Treasury bonds (ρ_t) held, and rolled over, from year t to the end of the stated year, as an alternative to the net transfers to the developing country in year t. The average $\bar{\rho}$ thus corresponds to its formula in Lindert and Morton (1989, app. A), except that discounting is forward to the end of a final year rather than backward to an initial loan date. More precisely, $\bar{\rho}$ was calculated from the ρ_t's for 1973–81 only, leaving alone the ρ_t's unaveraged for the net repayment years from 1982 on, as explained in the notes to table 8.6.

Notes to Table 8.6 and Figure 8.4

Dealing only with data on the PG loans themselves would give a biased picture of the returns to lending. Each year's change in debt outstanding (ΔD_t) should equal the difference between fresh loan disbursements (L_t) and repayments of principal (R_t). It does not, because of (1) the "reincarnation" (reclassification) of loans into or out of the PG class due to reschedulings and consolidations, (2) write-offs, and (3) exchange rate adjustments on loans in nondollar currencies (World Bank 1988, pp. 109–13, and telephone conversations with World Bank staff). Of these, the first discrepancy seems to be the largest. Comparison of aggregates makes it clear that the difference between (ΔD_t) and ($L_t - R_t$) for PG loans is large and positive after 1982 for many countries because short-term loans and nonguaranteed loans have been reincarnated as PG loans. (In 1978–81, by contrast, there was the reverse tendency to re-issue maturing long-term loans as short-term loans.) A correct overall perspective on lending experience since 1973 requires including the history of non-PG loans. The direct route would be to measure all flows and stocks for all loans. Yet data are lacking on non-PG loans before 1980.

I have therefore inferred the histories of the short-term and nonguaranteed loans across the 1970s that were the direct ancestors of the PG loans into which they were reincarnated. Starting backwards from 1986, the discrepancy $(\Delta D - L + R)_t$ become the flow of "repayments" of the previous non-PG loans. The discrepancy stabilizes around zero sometime in the period 1976–80, the year varying from country to country. For earlier years, I infer the growth of these ancestor loans by assuming that it was proportional to the growth of PG loans from the end of 1973 to the pivot date between 1976 and 1980. The interest payments on the ancestor loans can be fairly assumed to flow at the same interest rates as on PG loans in the 1970s. The interest rates on nonguaranteed long-term ancestor loans should have been slightly higher than those on PG loans, but the interest rates on short-term loans would have been somewhat lower than those on PG loans for loans before interest rate "backwardation" set in during the second oil shock (1979–81). On the whole, the interest rate assumption seems to fit indirect evidence about overall premia over Libor.

The PG loans and their non-PG ancestors are then combined into an overall country history for 1973–86, setting the stage for summary measures of rates of return.

All long-term loans consist of both publically guaranteed and nonguaranteed loans. Their ancestors would be only short-term loans later converted into long-term loans. Calculations for all long-term loans were attempted only for Mexico, Brazil, and a group of 97 countries because such calculations (1) require unpublished data from the World Bank and (2) include the shaky figures on private nonguaranteed debt.

The *internal rate of return* (v) is the rate that makes the entire history of net real flows from creditor to debtor discount out to a zero present value. (For the algebraic formula, see Lindert and Morton 1989, app. A.) The variant v_f is the internal rate based on the assumption that the entire debt outstanding at the end of 1986 (latest data) was fully repaid.

The *alternative rate of return* ($\bar{\rho}$) is the average of the real rates of return on seven-year U.S. Treasury bonds (ρ_t) held, and rolled over, from year t to the end of 1986. Each ρ_t applies to the net transfers in year t so that it is a hypothetical alternative net investment in U.S. bonds in a year in which there was a net transfer toward the debtor with which lending to the U.S. government is to be compared. Correspondingly, for years of net transfer back from the debtor to the creditor, ρ_t serves as a real rate of return foregone on those alternative U.S. bonds no longer held from t to the end of 1986. The rate $\bar{\rho}$ is thus a net-transfer-weighted average (equal to its formula in Lindert and Morton 1989, app. A, except that discounting is forward to the end of 1986 instead of backward to an initial loan date).

The amount of default at the end of 1986 that would bring the internal rate of return (v) down to the alternative rate of return ($\bar{\rho}$) equals the end-of-1986 value gained by capitalizing, at the ρ_t real rates, all actual flows between the private foreign creditors and the debtor country. This value gained by the end of 1986 is the amount of default that would bring v down to equal the rate $\bar{\rho}$ on lending to the U.S. government. The same procedure is repeated to calculate how much default would make the ex-post returns match a premium earned by earlier generations of international investors. The Lindert-Morton study found that premium (over loans to the United States or Britain) to be on the order of 0.42 percent per annum.

In calculating $\bar{\rho}$, however, an amendment of the preceding formula was necessary. Some countries, such as Mexico, made heavy net transfers back to the private creditors in the 1980s. For these countries, the procedure for $\bar{\rho}$, strictly followed, shows the real rate of return up through 1986 on holdings of U.S. bonds that accumulated during the 1970s but were massively negative in the 1980s. Such a calculation of $\bar{\rho}$ would give the correct answer to a question readers would not be very interested in. More interest would attach to the question: What average rate of return on U.S. bonds acquired in 1973–81, before the crisis, would have yielded the same present value when their flows, compounded at that rate, combined with the flows of 1982–86 and the end-of-1986 stock to give the same net present value as that derived using the separate ρ_t for all years? This is the question addressed by the calculations for all countries. In the Lindert-Morton algebra, $\bar{\rho}$ is the rate such that

$$\left(\frac{L}{p}\right)_{1973} (1 + \bar{\rho})^{13} + \Sigma_{t=1974}^{1981} \left(\frac{L-S}{p}\right)_t \cdot (1 + \bar{\rho})^{1986.5-t}$$

$$+ \Sigma_{t=1982}^{1986} \left(\frac{L-S}{p}\right)_t \cdot (1 + \rho_t)^{1986.5-t}$$

$$= \left(\frac{L}{p}\right)_{1973} (1 + \rho_{1973})^{13} + \Sigma_{t=1974}^{1986} \left(\frac{L-S}{p}\right)_t \cdot (1 + \rho_t)^{1986.5-t},$$

where

$L =$ gross loan outflow,

$S =$ debt service,

$p =$ U.S. consumer price index.

Appendix B: A Warning about Inferring Transfers from *World Debt Tables*

As noted in the text, the best available data on developing-country debt misrepresent resource flows between debtors and creditors. This appendix identifies some difficulties with the World Bank's *World Debt Tables* that may distort our view of net transfers between developing-country debtors and their creditors in the 1970s and, especially, the 1980s.

The World Bank's Debtor Reporting System, set up in 1951, has the design one would hope for in a large professional data service. Loan reports are comprehensively gathered. Confidentiality is promised and, presumably, honored. The reporting system has built-in cross-checks, which eliminate some errors. The Bank initiates follow-up investigations of seeming discrepancies. It also cross-checks the plausibility of its figures against debt statistics and balance-of-payments statistics gathered by other international organizations and by debtor and creditor countries. The data show more detail on flows than any other source (World Bank et al. 1988).

Yet the data can mislead as indicators of either debt stocks or flows between debtors and creditors. The World Bank has said as much regarding the stocks of debt outstanding. The Bank gives its sternest warnings about short-term debt and nonguaranteed private long-term debt, preferring to emphasize its figures on public and publically guaranteed long-term debt (called PG debt in this chapter). It has recently added a more general caution: "As the example of private non-guaranteed debt indicates, considerable additional work is needed in order to arrive at reliable and comprehensive figures on total external debt" (World Bank et al. 1988, p. 106). The caution, however, is presented only as a prelude to a longer discussion of the Bank's techniques for data refinement, leaving the impression of a problem already well handled. A sterner warning is in order.

The magnitudes of possible distortion become clearer when one compares the flow data with change-of-stock data. Aside from changes in market loan valuation, it should be the case that $L - R = \Delta D$, where L is the inflow of new loans, R is the repayment of principal, and ΔD is the year's change in the stock of debt outstanding. Unfortunately, the discrepancies between the two seem greater than changes in market valuation alone could explain, as illustrated by the differences in implied net transfers to Brazil in the 1980s:

	On PG debt to private creditors		On PG debt to all creditors		All long-term debt to all creditors	
Year	$L - R - I$ vs. $\Delta D - I$		$L - R - I$ vs. $\Delta D - I$		$L - R - I$ vs. $\Delta L - I$	
1980	−0.1	0.1	0.1	0.3	−1.8	−1.1
1981	0.5	−0.6	0.9	−0.3	0.7	0.1
1982	−0.1	−0.7	0.4	−0.4	−1.5	−0.5
1983	0.0	2.3	0.7	3.3	−3.3	−0.9
1984	1.5	4.1	2.0	5.7	−2.1	1.4
1985	−5.1	4.0	−5.4	−1.9	−7.8	−5.7
1986	−5.4	0.9	−5.5	4.6	−7.7	0.6

Note: In billions of current U.S. $; + = net flow to Brazil.

The mismatches of signs and magnitudes worsen around 1983, and again in 1986 (and remained wide in 1987, not shown here). Note that in all cases from 1983 on, the inward transfers $\Delta D - I$ exceeded the published $L - R - I$ transfers, implying a consistent bias in one of the series.

To interpret the large deviations of $L - R$ from ΔD, one needs to understand the World Bank's accounting decisions on the following issues (see World Bank et al. 1988, pp. 111–13):

1. Treatment of debt reorganization: (a) write-offs, (b) "involuntary" refinancing, (c) other refinancing and rescheduling, and (d) consolidation of short-term debt into long-term debt.

2. Method of currency conversion.

3. Treatment of arrears.

Two of these decisions—those on (1b) refinancing and (1d) consolidation of short-term debt into long-term debt—seriously bias the measurement of net transfer flows, in the direction of overstating the outflows from debtors to creditors in the 1980s. Two others—(2) and (3)—introduce additional likely errors, though without a clear systematic bias.

To start on the least problematic front, the Bank correctly adjusts for (1a) write-offs and (1c) reschedulings, to judge from its official description of procedures. Write-offs (debt forgivenesses) are deducted from the stock of outstanding debt, but they do not affect the net flow of resources at the time of write-off. Restructurings also seem to have been handled correctly. The stocks and flows contracted under the old loans are removed from all data, starting from the date of restructuring, and all restructured stocks and flows are followed thereafter.

Unsystematic errors can arise from (2) the method of currency conversion and (3) the treatment of arrears. The Bank uses different IMF exchange rates for stocks versus flows. The debt stocks are converted at year-end exchange rates, while the flows are converted at year-average exchange rates. Ratios of flows to start-of-year stocks could be distorted. Whether the sign of a year's net transfers could be reversed remains to be seen. That could happen only if the inflows of fresh loans were denominated in different currencies from the outflows of debt service, probably not a serious problem in practice. In correspondence (November 1, 1988) World Bank officials have suggested that exchange-rate adjustments may have had a large effect on the 1986 and 1987 data.

As for arrears, any distortions are again likely to be small. Interest in arrears is correctly excluded from long-term debt outstanding. Principal in arrears is included but not separately identified, leading to overstatement of the recoverable debt outstanding. The treatment of arrears does not, in any case, misstate net transfer flows.

Serious biases center on (1b) "involuntary" refinancing and (1d) consolidation of short-term debt into long-term debt. Regarding refinancing loans, the World Bank's reporting policy draws a line ill-suited to the present purpose of judging resource flows between debtors and creditors:

... refinancing may ... take place in circumstances where the country does not have free access to capital markets. In such circumstances refinancing is an alternative to rescheduling, undertaken by agreement between debtor and creditor to avoid imminent default, and is treated as an 'involuntary' refinancing by the World Bank. The Bank does not consider that genuine flows have taken place and the [Debtor Reporting System does not record commitment, disbursement and repayment transactions. The distinction between "voluntary" and "involuntary" refinancings is not always easily defined .... (World Bank et al. 1988, p. 112)

Thus in the 1980s, when refinancing became frequent (Watson 1986; Dillon and Oliveros 1987; *World Debt Tables 1987–88*, vol. 1, pp. xxxvi–xlii), a large share of gross new lending has been omitted from the data. Just how great a share depends on how much of the refinancing was officially defined as "involuntary." Yet the data will go on reporting debt service paid on the old loans (by the unreported new ones), and may even report debt service on the new involuntary loans. There is a bias whichever way the Bank treats debt service on refinanced loans, especially if it follows the second path. The arbitrary elimination of some lending as involuntary overstates what debtor countries are giving up each year in net out-transfers.

The same undercounting of inflows into debtor countries arises regarding the consolidation of short-term debt into long-term debt. Such consolidations were performed on a massive scale between 1982 and 1985. Here again, the Bank draws an arbitrary line:

A new debt is created that reflects the debt consolidation, but there are no entries for lenders' commitments and disbursements, as such entries are reserved as far as possible to represent the flow of new financial resources to developing countries. (World Bank et al. 1988, p. 113)

If it were just a matter of shifting the same debt from the short-term to the long-term category, no problem would arise regarding total (short-term plus long-term) resource flows. Unfortunately, the subsequent debt service on the new long-term loans starts weighing into the flow data for long-term debt (and is not reported for short-term debt). That is, the data show us the debt service outpayments on long-term loans *that were never recorded as initial inflows*. This oddity in the system of data reporting helps explain why net resource outflows from debtor countries seemed to grow between 1982 and 1986, since the published figures relate only to long-term debt.

In fact the failure to count conversions from short-term debt as a disbursement inflow into the debtor country might account for *all* of the level of net long-term transfers from developing countries reported by the World Bank since the crisis broke. For 1983–86, the Bank reports a net out-transfer of $57.4 billion on long-term public and private debt (*World Debt Tables 1988–89*, vol. 1, p. xii). Yet for the same four years, the composition of debt changed markedly. Although the stock of long-term debt outstanding rose greatly (by $331 billion), the stock of short-term debt dropped $49.7 billion (First Supplement, June 1988, p. 2). Failure to count the $49.7 billion in new long-term debt (minus a bit of fresh interest payments within the same years) as an inflow more than accounts for all the transfer outflow on long-term debt announced by the Bank.[13] Even this adjustment takes account of only the bias (1d) relating to consolidation of short-term debt. The bias (1b) relating to refinancing must also be added in.

The data in *World Debt Tables* thus may give a biased view, overstating the net out-transfer of resources from the debtor countries since 1982. The reporting procedures should be re-examined to minimize such bias. In the meantime I have developed a way of approximating the possible bias in flow accounting. I interpret the differential $\Delta D - (L - R)$ as a measure of new long-term loans that were consolidated from previous short-term loans, as in (1d) above. One could simply view them as brand new long-term loans and produce reasonable histories of recent lending and repayment experience. A better approximation of the overall debtor-creditor exchange, however, is to include as part of each history the experience with the assumed previous short-term "ancestor" loans. The ancestor loans are observed only "at death," that is, when they are converted into long-term loans in the amounts $\Delta D_t - (L - R)_t$ for each conversion year t within the 1980s. To recreate the "births" and "lifetimes" of the ancestor loans, I assumed that their stock accumulated in fixed proportion to the stock of PG debt from 1973 to a year around 1980 when they began being converted to long term, and that they paid the same average interest rates each year as were paid on the PG debt. The interest-rate assumption probably overstates short-term interest rates for 1974–78 but understates them during the yield-curve reversal (backwardation) of 1979–81, leaving little likely error in judging the whole experience. This is the procedure followed, and explained more briefly, in table 8.6 and appendix A. It will be approximately correct if I am right in attributing most of the discrepancies $\Delta D - (L - R)$ to "involuntary" lending and conversions of short-term debt to long-term debt. It is liable to greater error to the extent that exchange-rate movements and other factors explain these discrepancies.

Notes

The author thanks the Institute of Governmental Affairs, University of California, Davis, and the National Science Foundation (Grant SES-8606737) for financial support. He is also grateful to Wendy Eudey, Kara Hayes, Stephanie Luce, Rob McClelland, Peter Morton, and especially to Maite Cabeza-Gutes for research assistance, and participants in the conference for this volume and the Stanford economic history workshop for comments. The errors are his alone.

1. This chapter can only emphasize certain aspects of so broad a topic. As will become evident, it emphasizes external long-term government debts and those long-term private debts backed by government guarantee. For the postwar period, the focus will be on external debt of developing countries, leaving aside the heavy borrowings by Canada, Norway, New Zealand, and other developed countries.

2. The apparently low premia at which Turkey seemed to be borrowing between 1915 and 1970 are artificial. The low premium shown in table 8.1 for 1915–45 was negotiated on a small volume of loans converting previous debt, and that for 1946–70 was the result of concessional lending by the United States and other governments.

3. Libor might seem more appropriate on the grounds that bank loans to developing countries are often variable-interest-rate loans tied to Libor. But variable-rate loans have never accounted for half of the debt outstanding. And even on variable-rate loans, the schedule of principal repayments remains fixed, again recommending comparison with long-term alternative loans (to creditor-country governments).

4. A great likelihood of default is often perceived right before the crisis breaks, of course. For an illustration from nineteenth-century Egypt, see Feder and Just (1984). The figures in table 8.1 and figure 8.3 reflect the more sanguine views of investors at the time the loans were originally made.

The "expected loss" figures bear that exact meaning only when investors are completely risk neutral and perceive zero net amenity to the asset in all other respects. If investors are risk averse, the premium in a risky asset can reflect the degree of their (marginal) risk aversion rather than just the expected value of a capital loss.

5. Morrow 1927. The author is indebted to Barry Eichengreen for this reference. See also the U.S. bank evidence in Eichengreen and Portes (1987, pp. 23–24).

6. In addition two of Stallings's citations do not deliver the evidence ascribed to them. Gisselquist (1981, p. 142) did not say that bankers in the 1970s inferred government guarantee, as Stallings implies. Citing nobody, Gisselquist said only that officials in the Nixon administration "announced the graduation of middle-income developing countries from aid to commercial credit, arguing that aid should be reserved for the poorest. On a country-by-country basis bankers were invited to replace shrinking U.S. aid flows with bank loans." Similarly, Stallings's citation of Darity fails to show that official aid was expected. In the cited passage, Darity (1985, pp. 43–46) only conjectured that bailouts would invite moral hazard if they were actually given.

More pertinent is Gisselquist's (1981, pp. 216–17) citation of 1980 testimony by economist William Cline that banks were expecting a "bailout" even then, before the crisis broke. But this too is little more than a third-party rumor.

7. The default history variables are insignificant not only separately but also jointly. In each equation it is impossible to reject the stronger null hypothesis that the default variables for pre-1929, the 1930s, and 1940–81 are all equal to zero.

8. A curious side-pattern is the negative significance of the (reserves/imports) variable, for which a positive sign was expected. The same negative influence showed up in an unreported regression for private credits in 1981. The present conjecture is that a debtor's holding onto larger reserves is seen by private creditors as a sign that the debtor is more prepared to ride out a nonrepayments crisis, raising suspicions of willingness to enter into arrears.

9. Among the other 91 countries, there are many who have been making net transfers by servicing concessionary loans. Africa south of the Sahara is a leading example. These transfers are, of course, a resource loss relative to being excused from repayment, but they are de-emphasized in the text because they flow out at a slower percentage rate, thanks to the easier terms of the loans to these countries.

10. Of all countries entering into debt-rescheduling negotiations, it may well be that the six "repayers" identified here are the only ones who have repaid so consistently that the "repaid so far" percentages in the right two columns of table 8.6 exceed, say, 20 percent for private creditors or 10 percent for all creditors on PG debt. What other countries might have approached this repaying status? In recent years the most likely candidate is Romania, who seems to having been making transfers to all creditors since the start of continuous data in 1980. The same behavior is not shown by others, except that Grenada's debts to private creditors have been largely repaid, thanks to new bilateral credits from the U.S. government.

Another point, one that has been implied by omission in the text, should be noted. Debtor countries that have not become problem debtors, such as Korea, have also not endured much resource outflow in the 1980s, in their case because they have received fresh voluntary credits.

11. The difference between Mexican repayments and Brazilian rollovers could stem from the fact that Mexico contracted higher interest rates on the average (higher i on her debt outstanding, D), or from the fact that she received less of a surplus of new loan inflows (L) over repayments of principal (R). What proportions of the overall differences between Mexican experience and Brazilian experience are due to the difference in interest rates? To find out, let us ask two accounting questions. (1) When we ask "How closely would Mexican experience have resembled Brazilian experience if Mexico had her true L's, R's, and D's but Brazil's interest rates?" the answer is "Very closely." That is, differences in interest rates would seem to account for all of the difference between the two national experiences. (2) When we ask "How closely would Mexican experience have resembled Brazilian experience if Mexico had her true interest rates but Brazil's L's, R's, and D's?" the answer is "Not very closely." So say these comparisons of the counterfactual cases with the actual ones from panel A in table 8.6:

	v_f	$\bar{\rho}$	$v_f - \bar{\rho}$	$v = \bar{\rho}$	$v = \bar{\rho} + 0.42$
				Default % that allows:	
Actual Mexico	4.57	2.54	2.03	28.0	23.1
Mexico's L, R, D, Brazil's i	3.07	2.58	0.49	7.9	2.6
Mexico's i, Brazil's L, R, D	4.43	2.00	2.43	31.6	26.8
Actual Brazil	2.94	2.08	0.86	11.5	6.4

Apparently, it was Mexico's interest-rate history that made for a much greater repayment burden.

12. The contrasts in recoveries of real GDP per capita slightly overstate the contrasts in real purchasing power per capita for the 1930s. The terms of trade swung against the debtor countries, as shown in figure 8.1. The worsening of the terms of trade, weighted by the share of imports in national expenditure, would yield relatively less recovery in real purchasing power for the debtor nations. Most of figure 8.5's contrasts would remain, however.

13. Note that the World Bank's net transfer measure relates to long-term debt alone. One might ask: What would net transfers have been like if they were measured for all external debts, all maturities? Might the mistake about (1d) cancel out if we tried to estimate the net transfers on both short- and long-term debt? Shouldn't the $49.7 billion converted from short-term debt be counted as a repayment outflow, thus leaving us with an overall net transfer like the one the Bank reported for long-term debt alone?

The tentative answer is twofold: (1) nobody really knows what is happening to all short-term debts, and (2) I doubt that they have been repaid as much as the Bank estimates. On the great uncertainty surrounding short-term debt and capital flight, again see World Bank et al. (1988, p. 107). It appears that the Bank is better able to track a certain subset of short-term debts that get captured in BIS and other data. The Bank started reporting estimates of the short-term debt outstanding only at the end of 1980, just before the reported stock started a 30% drop from the end of 1982 to the end of 1986. I believe that the estimates of short-term debts are better at recording those later consolidated into long-term debts than the possibly growing short-term debts that were not consolidated under official supervision, and thus under-recorded. The situation appears, then, to be this: the available measures relate to long-term debt, on which there is reason to doubt significant transfers from most debtors after 1982, and nobody knows about transfers relating to all external debts on all maturities.

References

Bittermann, Henry J. 1973. *The Refunding of International Debt*. Durham, N.C.: Duke University Press.

Borchard, Edwin. 1951. *State Insolvency and Foreign Bondholders: General Principles*. Vol. 1. New Haven: Yale University Press.

Dervis, Kemal, and Peter A. Petri. The Macroeconomics of Successful Development: What Are the Lessons? In Stanley Fischer (ed.), *NBER Macroeconomics Annual 1987*. Cambridge: MIT Press, pp. 211–62.

Davis, Lance, and Robert Huttenback. 1986. *Mammon and Empire*. Cambridge: Cambridge University Press.

Díaz-Alejandro, Carlos F. 1984. Latin American Debt: I Don't Think We Are in Kansas Anymore. *Brookings Papers in Economic Activity* 2.

Dillon, K. Burke, and Oliveros, Gumersindo. 1987. *Recent Experience with Multilateral Official Debt Rescheduling*. Washington: IMF, February.

Eichengreen, Barry. 1989. "Til Debt Do Us Part: The U.S. Capital Market and Foreign Lending, 1920–1955." In Jeffrey D. Sachs (ed.), *Developing Country Debt and Economic Performance: The International Financial System*. University of Chicago Press for the National Bureau of Economic Research. (Condensed in Sachs, ed., *Developing Country Debt and the World Economy*, same publisher.)

Eichengreen, Barry, and Portes, Richard. 1986. Debt and Default in the 1930s: Causes and Consequences. *European Economic Review* June.

Eichengreen, Barry, and Portes, Richard. 1987. The Anatomy of Financial Crises. In Richard Portes and Alexander K. Swoboda (eds.), *Threats to International Financial Stability*. Cambridge: Cambridge University Press.

Feder, Gershon, and Just, Richard E. 1984. Debt Crisis in an Increasingly Pessimistic International Market: The Case of Egyptian Credit, 1862–1876. *Economic Journal* 94, 2 (June): 340–56.

Feis, Herbert. 1930. *Europe, The World's Banker, 1870–1914*. New Haven: Yale University Press.

Fishlow, Albert. 1985. Lessons from the Past: Capital Markets during the Nineteenth Century and the Interwar Period. *International Organization* 39, 3 (Summer): 383–439.

Fishlow, Albert. 1987. Lessons of the 1890s for the 1980s. Department of Economics, University of California, Berkeley. Working Paper 8724. January.

Gisselquist, David. 1981. *The Political Economics of International Bank Lending.* New York: Praeger.

Goldsmith, Raymond F. 1985. *Comparative National Balance Sheets: A Study of Twenty Countries, 1688–1978.* Chicago: University of Chicago Press.

Lewis, Cleona. 1948. *The United States and Foreign Investment Problems.* Washington: Brookings Institution.

Lindert, Peter H. 1986. Relending to Sovereign Debtors. Institute of Governmental Affairs, University of California, Davis. Working Paper. September.

Lindert, Peter H., and Peter J. Morton. 1989. How Sovereign Debt Has Worked. In Jeffrey D. Sachs (ed.), *Developing Country Debt and Economic Performance: The International Financial System.* University of Chicago Press for the National Bureau of Economic Research. (Condensed in Sachs, ed., *Developing Country Debt and the World Economy,* same publisher.)

Maddison, Angus. 1985. *Two Crises: Latin America and Asia, 1929–38 and 1973–83.* Paris: OECD.

Milivojevic, Marko. 1985. The Debt Rescheduling Process. London: Frances Pinter.

Morrow, Dwight. 1927. Who Buys Foreign Bonds? *Foreign Affairs* 5, 2 (January): 219–32.

Okyar, Osman. 1983. "Turkey and the IMF: A Review of Relations, 1978–82." In John H. Williamson (ed.), IMF Conditionality. (Washington D.C.: Institute for International Economics), pp. 533–62.

Royal Institute for International Affairs. 1937. *The Problem of International Investment.* Oxford: Oxford University Press.

Sachs, Jeffrey D. 1985. External Debt and Macroeconomic Performance in Latin America and East Asia. *Brookings Papers in Economic Analysis* 2: 523–74.

Sachs, Jeffrey D. 1987. International Policy Coordination: The Case of the Developing Country Debt Crisis. National Bureau of Economic Research. Working Paper No. 2287. June.

Sampson, Anthony. 1982. *The Money Lenders.* New York: Viking Press.

Stallings, Barbara. 1987. *Banker to the Third World: U.S. Portfolio Investment in Latin America, 1900–1986.* Berkeley: University of California Press.

Stiglitz, Joseph E., and Andrew Weiss. 1981. Credit Rationing in Markets with Imperfect Information. *American Economic Review* 71, 3 (June): 393–410.

Takahashi, Kamekichi. 1969. *The Rise and Development of Japan's Modern Economy.* Tokyo: Jiji Press.

Thorp, Rosemary (ed.). 1984. *Latin America in the 1930s: The Role of the Periphery in World Crisis.* London: Macmillan.

Vaubel, Roland. 1983. The Moral Hazard of IMF Lending. *World Economy* 6: 291–303.

Watson, Maxwell, Russell Kincaid, Caroline Atkinson, Eliot Kalter, and David Folkerts-Landau. 1986. *International Capital Markets: Developments and Prospects.* Washington: International Monetary Fund. December.

Wellons, Philip. 1987. *Passing the Buck: Banks, Governments and Third World Debt.* Boston: Harvard Business School Press.

Wilkie, James W. and Adam Perkal (eds.). 1985. *Statistical Abstract of Latin America.* Vol. 24. Los Angeles: UCLA Latin American Center Publications.

Williamson, John (ed.). 1985. *IMF Conditionality.* Washington: Institute for International Economics.

World Bank. 1985. *World Development Report 1985.* New York, Oxford University Press.

World Bank. 1980, 1984, 1988. *World Debt Tables, 1980, 1983–84 and 1987–88* editions. Washington: The World Bank.

World Bank, International Monetary Fund, Bank for International Settlements, and Organization for Economic Cooperation and Development. 1988. *External Debt: Definition, Statistical Coverage and Methodology.* Paris.

Index